Design Research in Education

Design Research in Education is a practical guide containing all the information required to begin a design research project. Providing an accessible background to the methodological approaches used in design research as well as addressing all the potential issues that early career researchers will encounter, the book uniquely helps the early career researcher to gain a full overview of design research and the practical skills needed to get their project off the ground. Based on extensive experience, the book also contains multiple examples of design research from both undergraduate and postgraduate students, to demonstrate possible projects to the reader.

With easy to follow chapters and accessible question and response sections, *Design Research in Education* contains practical advice on a wide range of topics related to design research projects including:

- The theory of design research, what it entails, and when it is suitable
- The formulation of research questions
- How to structure a research project
- The quality of research and the methodological issues of validity and reliability
- How to write up your research
- The supervision of design research.

Through its theoretical grounding and practical advice, *Design Research in Education* is the ideal introduction into the field of design based research and is essential reading for bachelor's, master's, and PhD students new to the field, as well as to supervisors overseeing projects that use design research.

Arthur Bakker is a Fellow at the University of Bremen, Germany, and an Associate Professor at Utrecht University, the Netherlands.

Design Research in Education

A Practical Guide for Early Career Researchers

Arthur Bakker

Routledge
Taylor & Francis Group

LONDON AND NEW YORK

First published 2018
by Routledge
2 Park Square, Milton Park, Abingdon, Oxon OX14 4RN

and by Routledge
711 Third Avenue, New York, NY 10017

Routledge is an imprint of the Taylor & Francis Group, an informa business

© 2019 Arthur Bakker

British Library Cataloguing-in-Publication Data
A catalogue record for this book is available from the British Library

Library of Congress Cataloging-in-Publication Data
A catalog record has been requested for this book

ISBN: 9781138574472 (hbk)
ISBN: 9781138574489 (pbk)
ISBN: 9780203701010 (ebk)

Typeset in Bembo
by Apex CoVantage, LLC

I dedicate this book to my wife Jantien Smit, with whom I can share so many facets of life.

Contents

Tables

Figures

Preface

The purpose of this book is to introduce early career researchers, including master's and PhD students as well as postdocs, to the methodological approach of design research. I also hope it will be useful to supervisors who have experience in educational research but not necessarily with design research. The term *design research* is used for a family of approaches including educational design research, design based research, design experiments, formative experiments, design experimentation, design studies, development research, or developmental research – terms that are explained in Chapter 2. These approaches have in common that the design of educational materials or environments is an integral part of the research in search of solving an educational problem or to help learners achieve particular goals. The main reason for intertwining design and research is to close the widely experienced gap between the practice and theory of education. There have often been, and still are, calls for more educational design that is based on insights from research, and for research that is about the potential of new technology or how to achieve educational goals of current or future societies.

One reason for writing this book was that there seemed to be so little I could recommend to my master's and PhD students or even postdocs. Many of them considered key publications in this field unsuitable as introductions to design research. These publications have mostly been written to inform or convince established researchers who already have considerable experience with educational research. I therefore saw the need to write for an audience who does not have that level of experience but wants to know about design research. When writing I have kept students in mind who have little background in research methodology in education, and who do not speak English as their first language. Chapter 8 is about supervision of design research.

Part II offers examples of design research from a range of disciplines within education and ends with a wish list for the future (Chapter 22). For Chapter 9 I asked my colleague and friend Dor Abrahamson to write about his design based research course. There are not that many courses on design research in education, so sharing experiences from such courses is important to me: If the learning sciences community wants design research to be used by a broader range and a new generation of educational researchers (Collins, Joseph, & Bielaczyc, 2004), then we learning scientists need to ensure that design research is also teachable and learnable:

> If design research is to become accepted as a serious scholarly endeavor, the learning-sciences community needs to take responsibility for creating standards that make design experiments recognizable and accessible to other researchers.
>
> (p. 16)

Compared to other research approaches, educational design research is relatively new (Anderson & Shattuck, 2012). This is probably why it is not discussed in most books on research methodology (Denscombe, 2010). For example, Creswell (2007) distinguishes five qualitative approaches, but these do not include design research. An exception is the American Educational Research Association's *Handbook on Complementary Methods in Education Research* (Schoenfeld, 2006). Yet design research is worth knowing about, especially for students who will become teachers, teacher educators, or researchers in education: Design research is claimed to have the potential to bridge the gap between educational practice and theory, because it aims both to develop theories about domain-specific learning and the means that are designed to support that learning. Design research thus produces both useful products (e.g., educational materials) and accompanying scientific insights into how these products can be used in education (McKenney & Reeves, 2012; Reinking & Bradley, 2008; Van den Akker, Gravemeijer, McKenney, & Nieveen, 2006; Brown, 1992). It is also said to be suitable for addressing complex educational problems that should be dealt with in a holistic way (Plomp & Nieveen, 2010).

Research approaches are normative practices that scholars adopt to find answers to specific types of questions to which the answer is not yet known. They are not strict procedures to be followed blindly. Each research project requires creativity. This does not mean that anything goes or that scientific method should be anarchistic (cf. Feyerabend, 1975/1993). The great advantage of scientific investigation being informed by research methodology is two-fold:

- It creates a context of discovery (Reichenbach, 1938): Following a particular approach gives you a way to start your scientific project and offers a strategy to proceed with finding answers in a systematic manner. The approach has been used by many others, so there is experience with the types of answers found, ways to avoid bias, making conclusions reliable and so forth.
- It provides a context of justification: By following an approach that has been successful in the experience of others, and reporting in a similar way, it becomes easier for the readers of your work to have a sense of what you have done and why you have done so. It is impossible to justify each and every step of your research but referring to the main steps in a particular approach, such as design research, makes your procedure more transparent.

The advice given in this book should be seen as a normative description of current research practices, with an occasional idea for improvement. The structure I suggest for studies within a design research project in Chapters 4 and 6 is a starting point, not something to adhere to. If you do not know where to start, begin with these suggestions. Any research approach should fit the purpose of the study. Design research is certainly not the only or the best solution to any educational question. If it turns out you need to adjust or use a different approach, feel free to be creative while keeping methodological norms in mind. Study other people's research to see how they approached a similar problem and find your own solutions. Designing and researching are both creative processes, and design research is doubly creative. I hope you enjoy both learning about and performing it!

My mission with the book

Many colleagues in the educational sciences consider design research to be among the most challenging research approaches. They often discourage their students from doing it because their perception is that there is no time for multiple iterations, that a big team is needed to do design research, or that its goals of giving evidence-based advice is too ambitious. So many times, I have seen students and educational researchers start with a question on how to improve education, and end up with a descriptive study that may be informative, but does not match their initial interest. The methodological challenges that come with interventionist research often make scholars cautious and hesitant to design the intervention they want to do.

It was refreshing to interview some scholars who emphasize that design research is like most other qualitative or mixed-methods research approaches, by no means more difficult, or that it is actually a very "safe" approach because you always learn something interesting. With large quantitative studies there is always the risk, after all the hard work of finding enough participants, of seeing no significant differences or negligible effect sizes, and not knowing to what this disappointing finding could be attributed.

The mission of this book is to present design research as an approach that can be taught and learned. Admittedly, it may be more of an adventure than taking an approach that has been around for much longer. As Bronkhorst and De Kleijn (2016) wrote, it was rewarding for them as early career researchers to engage in design research because it made them think about many deeper issues that had remained undiscussed if they had just used well-known procedures. The book is an attempt to "didacticize" design research as well as a plea to colleagues to join forces in making it doable. It is also for students and teacher-researchers who are not necessarily part of a big research team.

Structure of the book

Part I is about the theory and practice of design research. What design research entails and when it is suitable is the topic of Chapter 1. Chapter 2 then goes deeper by sketching design research's multiple historical roots. A first inter-mezzo is a hypothetical dialogue between two research approaches, randomized controlled trials and design research. The idea of summarizing the key ideas in this form is inspired by Plato's and Lakatos's dialogues. As Lakatos (1976) writes, these are distilled rational constructions of the discussion in the field, but hope-fully in an accessible form. Chapter 3 is about design principles, conjecture maps, and hypothetical learning trajectories. Again, an intermezzo summarizes in dialogic form the differences and similarities between two different ways of doing research. Research questions and delineating studies within the larger project are topics of Chapter 4. Chapter 5 subsequently addresses the quality of research, and hence methodological issues of validity and reliability. In Chap-ter 6 I present my recent ideas on argumentative grammars for design research as an attempt to clarify what design research can and cannot claim. Writing up your research is the subject of Chapter 7, and in Chapter 8 I address the supervision of design research as it comes with specific challenges, from selec-tion or admission of candidates to assisting with publication. You will find some guidelines and several Question and Response (Q&R) boxes, which are drawn from questions that were asked during the workshops I did on design research.

Part II provides multiple examples of design research. After Chapter 9 on Abrahamson's course on design research, one bachelor's (undergraduate) and several master's (graduate) students from his course present the two-pagers they wrote for this course on their design project. Then two full papers show what these students managed to do within the time frame of this course. I include these because I often hear colleagues say that a design research project may be too difficult for students to conduct within one semester. The papers demon-strate that a small design research project is possible, and that design research can be taught and learned. Please note that their texts were left as closely as possible to the original versions.

Then Part II continues with cases from PhD students in various stages of their research. The first is from two first-year students who combine a teacher education program with a PhD program (Werner, Düerkop). The next case comes from a PhD student (Konrad) who is nearly ready and reflects on the changing role of the teacher involved in her research. Last, I reflect with Smit on the role of hypothetical learning trajectories in her research, and the strug-gles she had with publishing particular parts of her work. I think such concrete examples can be helpful because early career researchers are likely to encounter many practical, methodological, and theoretical issues that are slightly different from the challenges that students using other research approaches may face. After all, design research, and especially learning to conduct and to supervise it, are relatively new practices.

References

Anderson, T., & Shattuck, J. (2012). Design based research: A decade of progress in education research? *Educational Researcher, 41*(1), 16–25.

Bronkhorst, L. H., & de Kleijn, R. A. (2016). Challenges and learning outcomes of educational design research for PhD students. *Frontline Learning Research, 4*(3), 75–91.

Brown, A. L. (1992). Design experiments: Theoretical and methodological challenges in creating complex interventions in classroom settings. *Journal of the Learning Sciences, 2*(2), 141–178.

Collins, A., Joseph, D., & Bielaczyc, K. (2004). Design research: Theoretical and methodological issues. *Journal of the Learning Sciences, 13*(1), 15–42.

Creswell, J. W. (2007). *Qualitative inquiry and research design: Choosing among five approaches* (2nd ed.). Thousand Oaks, CA: Sage.

Denscombe, M. (2010). *The good research guide*. Maidenhead, UK: Open University Press.

Feyerabend, P. (1975/1993). *Against method* (3rd ed.). London: Verso.

Lakatos, I. (1976). *Proofs and refutations: The logic of mathematical discovery*. Cambridge, MA: Cambridge University Press.

McKenney, S., & Reeves, T. C. (2012). *Conducting educational design research*. London, UK: Routledge.

Plomp, T., & Nieveen, N. (2010). *An introduction to educational design research*. Enschede, the Netherlands: SLO.

Reichenbach, H. (1938). *Experience and prediction: An analysis of the foundations and the structure of knowledge*. Chicago, IL: University of Chicago Press.

Reinking, D., & Bradley, B. A. (2008). *On formative and design experiments: Approaches to language and literacy research*. New York, NY: Teachers College Press.

Schoenfeld, A. H. (2006). Design experiments. In J. L. Green, G. Camilli, & P. B. Elmore (Eds.), *Handbook of complementary methods in education research* (pp. 193–206). London, UK: Routledge.

Van den Akker, J., Gravemeijer, K. P. E., McKenney, S., & Nieveen, N. (2006). *Educational design research*. London: Routledge.

Acknowledgments

The idea for this book arose at a workshop on design research that I gave at the University of Bremen (Germany) in December 2015. During the second day I realized there is so much more for PhD students to learn about design research, and I suggested to Prof. Angelika Bikner-Ahsbahs I should perhaps write a book. I had other plans for writing, but the decision for composing this book on design research was somehow taken outside myself. It just felt timely. I asked if Bremen welcomed visiting professors, which apparently was not the route to go, but Prof. Bikner-Ahshahs talked to Prof. Sabine Doff, who managed to allocate internationalization money to make the writing possible. This money is part of the funding allocated to the Creative Unit *Fachbezogene Bildungsprozesse in Transformation* (subject-specific formation processes) at the University of Bremen. This interdisciplinary research group is funded by the German Research Foundation (DFG) within the program of the German *Excellence Initiative* (line: "Institutional Strategies," 2015–2017). I acknowledge the University of Bremen for honoring with me the title of Fellow to make this work possible.

Thanks also to the PhD students present at the workshops in Bremen (2015–2017), in particular Katharina Düerkop, Valentina Hahn, Marlon Schneider, Malte Ternieten, Nathalie Werner, and Eric Wolpers, who do a dual promotion trajectory (to become teacher and PhD as part of the same program) and Mareike Best, Ute Konrad, Larena Schäfer, Dominique Panzer, and Christina Inthoff, who were nearing the end of their PhD projects in the Creative Unit program.

I also learned a lot from the students I have supervised in the Netherlands, and the many colleagues that I talked to about design research and methodology in general. My colleague and friend Sanne Akkerman, though not a design researcher, has had a major impact on what I learned about methodology and theory development. I also owe much to the many experts in design research and related approaches that I interviewed as preparation to this book: Dor Abrahamson, Brenda Bannan, Paul Cobb, Mike Cole, Allan Collins, Jere Confrey, Andy diSessa, Koeno Gravemeijer, Chris Hoadley, Celia Hoyles, Yael Kali, Anthony Kelly, Rich Lehrer, Susan McKenney, Nienke Nieveen, Richard

Noss, Kevin O'Neill, Bill Penuel, Tjeerd Plomp, Tom Reeves, David Reinking, Andee Rubin, Ken Ruthven, Bill Sandoval, Leona Schauble, Adri Treffers, Jan van den Akker, Qiyun Wang, and Rupert Wegerif. Many of their ideas have influenced my thinking about design research, and in clear cases I refer to personal communication with a particular scholar.

The assistance by Antigoni Karnesioti (transcription) and Rutmer Ebbes (general valuable help with the book) is much appreciated, just like the many sessions with Jo Liu and Costas Nikandros on the videos and blog we made about the topic (https://designresearcheducation.wordpress.com). Nathalie Kuijpers assisted greatly in getting the manuscript ready for submission. Apart from people already mentioned, numerous colleagues have given feedback on versions of the chapters here. With the risk of forgetting some of them, I acknowledge: Dor Abrahamson, Harrie Eijkelhof, Jo Nelissen, Andy diSessa, Nathalie van der Wal, Judith Korhorn, Floor Kamphorst, Winnifred Wijnker, Yael Kali, Anne-Marie van Soelen, Tessa Vossen, Jan van den Akker, Tjeerd Plomp, Sanne Akkerman, and Koeno Gravemeijer.

I am very grateful for the opportunity to write this book. The fact that PhD students have anxiously awaited new chapters has been encouraging. At the same time it has been a humbling experience; there are so many thoughtful scholars from whom I have learned so much. I hope this book helps to bring the best of their ideas together for a next generation of educational researchers in the continued endeavor to make design research a mature methodological framework.

With thanks to Springer for permission to include materials from Bakker, A., & Van Eerde, H. A. A. (2015), An introduction to design based research with an example from statistics education. In A. Bikner-Ahsbahs, C. Knipping, N. Presmeg (Eds.), *Approaches to qualitative research in Mathematics education* (pp. 429–466), on which parts of Chapter 1 are based.

Contributors

Dor Abrahamson holds a Diploma in music performance (cello, Jerusalem Academy of Music and Dance), an MA in cognitive psychology (Tel Aviv University), and a PhD in the learning sciences (Northwestern University, 2004). Following a postdoctoral fellowship at the Center for Connected Learning and Computer-Based Modeling (Uri Wilensky, Director), Abrahamson took a faculty position in the Graduate School of Education, University of California at Berkeley, where since 2005 he has directed the Embodied Design Research Laboratory. dor@berkeley.edu

Arthur Bakker studied mathematics (University of Amsterdam), received a teaching degree in mathematics, and taught mathematics at secondary school. In 2004 he finished his PhD project on design research in statistics education at Utrecht University. At the Institute of Education (now part of the University College London) he studied and designed for techno-mathematical literacies in the workplace. Back at Utrecht University he is now Associate Professor. As a Fellow at the University of Bremen he got the opportunity to write this book on design research in education. A.Bakker4@uu.nl

Nadir Bilici (BA) studied neurobiology and education at the University of California, Berkeley. After graduation, he developed health and fitness iPhone/Android apps before starting medical school at the University of Pennsylvania. He aims to pursue a career at the intersection of technology and medicine. nadirbilici@berkeley.edu

Kiera Chase's work provides professional learning opportunities for teachers and leaders toward transforming teaching and leading practices in schools across the US. In her dissertation she explores both theoretical and practical aspects of discovery-based learning including the articulation of a didactical and pedagogical approach termed Reverse Scaffolding. Kiera.Chase@gmail.com

Katharina Düerkop (MEd) studied German, music, and mathematics to become a primary school teacher. With the dual promotion scholarship at the University of Bremen, she can currently combine her teacher training with a PhD program. Her dissertation project, conducted in her own school, focuses on how to use narrative video games to promote literary learning. k.dueerkop@uni-bremen.de

Emily Huang (MD, MAEd) is a surgeon and surgical educator. While completing her residency in general surgery at the University of California San Francisco (UCSF), she obtained a master's degree in education from the University of California Berkeley, and honed her pedagogical skills at the UCSF Surgical Skills Center. Her work on operative developmental trajectories during this time has fostered ongoing investigation into methods for making intraoperative interactions between surgical teachers and learners more meaningful. milyehuang@gmail.com

Ute Konrad studied music, German, and mathematics didactics to become a teacher in secondary education. After her teacher training, she worked in a comprehensive school. Currently she is a research assistant at the Hanover University of Music, Drama and Media and conducts her dissertation project as part of the Creative Unit: Fachbezogene Bildungsprozesse in Transformation project at Bremen University. In her project she combines her research interests "practical music lessons with instruments" and "negotiations of meanings as part of cultural learning processes" in a design based research study. Ute.Konrad@hmtm-hannover.de

Kathryn Lanouette is a PhD candidate at University of California Berkeley's Graduate School of Education. In her dissertation, she is engaging in design based research to advance our understanding of how elementary children create, share, and contest explanations about the surrounding schoolyard soil ecosystem. She is particularly interested in the ways in which children use varied data representations and their daily experiences to reason about complex ecological relationships. kathryn.lanouette@berkeley.edu

M. Lisette Lopez, MA, is a Chancellor's Fellow and doctoral student in language, literacy, and culture at UC Berkeley's Graduate School of Education. Her research on dialogic classroom discourse, teacher learning, disciplinary literacy, and argumentation build on her experience as a classroom teacher in East Oakland, CA, and as a curriculum developer for a disciplinary literacy science curriculum created by the Learning Design Group at the Lawrence Hall of Science. mlisettelopez@berkeley.edu

Leah Rosenbaum is a PhD student in the Graduate School of Education at the University of California at Berkeley. Drawing on theories that highlight the role of sensori-motor activity in cognitive development, Leah creates and evaluates interactive environments designed to foster mathematics learning. Her recent design research projects include an embodied, collaborative geometry game. leahr@berkeley.edu

Rebecca Shareff is a PhD student at UC Berkeley, with a background in cognitive science and environmental education. She studies teaching and learning in outdoor agricultural spaces, including school gardens, and the benefits of integrating hands-on farming practices with virtual interactive environments. rlshareff@berkeley.edu

Jantien Smit studied Dutch language and literature at the University of Amsterdam, the Netherlands, and worked for a newspaper and for a training and advice company as a trainer in written communication. She then enrolled in a teacher training program while working as a primary school teacher at a Montessori School in Amsterdam, and later in London. Her PhD project, at Utrecht University, was design research on scaffolding language for mathematical learning (2013). For the last years she has been associate lecturer at Saxion University of Applied Sciences, where she supervised a PhD student on writing research in higher education. Smit currently works at SLO, the Dutch Center for Curriculum Development. j.smit@slo.nl

Anna Weltman is a PhD student in the Graduate School of Education at the University of California, Berkeley. Her research is on teacher learning in mathematics education, particularly through interactions with colleagues and students around new lessons and technologies. She is also the author of two mathematical art activity books for kids, *This is Not a Math Book* and *This is Not Another Math Book*. aweltman@berkeley.edu

Nathalie Werner (MEd) studied art and English at the University of Bremen, Hobart and William Smith Colleges in New York, and La Trobe University in Melbourne to become a secondary school teacher. Since 2016 she has been a dual promotion scholarship holder in art education at the University of Bremen, combining her teacher training with a PhD thesis. Her dissertation project focuses on students' change of perspective through aesthetic research-based learning with tablet computers. Nathalie.Werner@hotmail.de

Part I

Theory and practice

Part I provides a theoretical background of design research and practical advice on how to conduct it, with Chapter 1 looking into what design research entails. Chapter 2 sketches design research's multiple historical roots. A first intermezzo is a hypothetical dialogue between two research approaches, randomized controlled trials and design research. Chapter 3 is about design principles, conjecture maps, and hypothetical learning trajectories, followed by another dialogic intermezzo summarizing the differences and similarities between working with design principles or hypothetical learning trajectories. Research questions that are typical of design research are discussed in Chapter 4. Chapter 5 looks at the quality of research in terms of validity and reliability. Chapter 6 contains my recent ideas on argumentative grammars for design research to clarify what design research can and cannot claim. Writing up your research is the topic of Chapter 7, and Chapter 8 addresses the supervision of design research. Many chapters contain Question and Response (Q&R) textboxes, which are drawn from questions that were asked during the workshops I gave on design research.

Chapter 1

What is design research in education?[1]

Summary

This chapter is an introduction to design research. After a very brief characterization, it compares design research with related research approaches such as experiments, action research, and lesson studies. The chapter ends with a list of five characteristics of design research.

Design research in a nutshell

Most educational research describes or evaluates education as it currently *is*. Some educational research analyzes education as it *was*. Design research, however, is about education as it *could be* or even as it *should be*. Perhaps you say, like Martin Luther King Jr., "I have a dream," and try to contribute to, say, more equitable education. Design research is the science fiction, or rather science faction, among the research approaches.

Typically, design researchers want to solve a problem; they see the potential of new technology for teaching and learning, or argue for the need to help learners prepare for skills increasingly needed in the future. The type of learning they envision cannot yet be observed in naturalistic settings; hence new settings have to be engineered in which the intended learning processes can be researched and improved. The focus of design research on what is possible rather than actual fits Vygotsky's (1987) view on teaching: "*The teacher must orient his work not on yesterday's development in the child but on tomorrow's*" (p. 211; emphasis in the original).

Design research in education is research in which the design of new educational materials (e.g., computer tools, learning activities, or a professional development program) is a crucial part of the research. McKenney and Reeves

(2012) characterize educational design research as a blend of "scientific investigation with systematic development and implementation of solutions to educational problems" (title page). Plomp (2010) defined educational design research

> as the systematic study of designing, developing and evaluating educational interventions, – such as programs, teaching-learning strategies and materials, products and systems – as solutions to such problems, which also aims at advancing our knowledge about the characteristics of these interventions and the processes to design and develop them.
>
> (p. 9)

The adjective *educational* in front of design research helps to distinguish it from design research in human-computer interaction, industrial engineering, architecture, and similar disciplines. However, in the context of educational research most people leave out the adjective, and so do I if I do not expect confusion with other disciplines.

In design research, design and research are intertwined: The design is research based and the research is design based. The design of learning environments is further interwoven with the testing or developing of theory. The theoretical basis and outcomes distinguish design research from studies that aim to design educational materials through iterative cycles of testing and improving prototypes.

Design research has been proposed as a potential solution to a variety of problems that have persisted throughout the history of education. One problem is that the development of new educational approaches is often not based on the knowledge base available from research, and thus does not benefit from the most recent insights. Researchers saw how the quality of design could be improved by basing design on research. Another problem is that most research provided little insight that practitioners could benefit from. A common concern is that knowledge based on research carried out in laboratory situations was of little use for the reality in schools, because messy educational settings are so different from laboratory situations in which conditions can be controlled. Chapter 2 further summarizes the history of the various ways in which scholars tried to resolve such problems and how these solutions led to variations of design research in the specific contexts in which these scholars operated.

Due to its diverse history in various countries *design research* is known under various names. Other terms for similar approaches are:

- developmental or development research (Freudenthal, 1988; Gravemeijer, 1994; Lijnse, 1995; Romberg, 1973; Van den Akker, 1999)
- design experiments or design experimentation (Brown, 1992; Cobb, Confrey, diSessa, Lehrer, & Schauble, 2003; Collins, 1990, 1992)
- design based research is the name used by Hoadley (2002) and the Design Based Research Collective (2003); see the special issue in *Educational Researcher* (2003)

- educational design research (McKenney & Reeves, 2012; Plomp & Nieveen, 2013; Van den Akker, Gravemeijer, McKenney, & Nieveen, 2006)
- formative experiments (Reinking & Bradley, 2008).

Related but slightly different approaches are design based implementation research (Penuel, Fishman, Cheng, & Sabelli, 2011) and formative interventions (Engeström, 2011). Chapter 2 addresses the history of these terms as well as subtle differences between these approaches.

A key characteristic of design research is that educational ideas for student or teacher learning are formulated in the design, but can be adjusted during the empirical testing of these ideas – for example if a design idea does not quite work as anticipated. In most other interventionist research approaches, design and testing are cleanly separated. Elaboration of this and other characteristics follows later in this chapter.

Textbox 1.1

Question: Design of new instructional materials is a key part of my research. Does this mean I do design research?

Response: It depends. If you use your research to improve your design according to scientific standards, and use your design to conduct scientific research, then you do design research. However, if you design in an intuitive way without basing it on research or if you do not operate in the spirit of the characteristics at the end of this chapter, then I would not call it design research. I should stress, however, that design research is an evolving genre of research approaches without strict boundaries.

What is design?

It is worth spending a few words on what design researchers mean by design. You may initially think of how buildings are designed by architects, or the design of your mobile phone, clothes, or furniture. Most people will probably think of the design of objects, but one can also design working procedures, for example in factories. In a management context, Argyris (1996) defined designs as "specifications of actions to be taken (often specified in a sequence) to achieve the intended consequences" (p. 396). In the context of design based school improvement, Mintrop (2016) characterized design as follows:

An intervention design consists of a sequence of activities that together or in combination intervene in existing knowledge, beliefs, dispositions, or routines in order to prompt new learning that leads to new practices.

(p. 133)

The word design stems from the Latin *designare*, which means "to mark out." In dictionaries you will find many definitions such as "to make or draw plans for something, for example clothes or buildings" (Cambridge Dictionary, n.d.).

So the term design is also used for more abstract or process-like entities. In education, not only educational materials such as computer tools, tasks, or learning environments are designed, but one can also design how students or teachers are expected to communicate – for example by means of suggesting ground rules for communication (Mercer, Wegerif, & Dawes, 1999). As Mintrop (2016) wrote with John Hall:

> The purpose of design development is to discover an ensemble of tools, materials, tasks, organizational structures, and any other activities that are apt to set in motion a process of learning that improves on a focal problem of practice. This ensemble is the intervention, the final product of a given design development effort.
>
> (p. 219)

Textbox 1.2

Question: What is the difference between teaching methods, learning environments, learning ecologies, etc.?

Response: There are indeed many terms for somewhat similar things that can be designed. The different terms typically emphasize different aspects, from micro- to macro-scales. For example, psychological studies often focus on tasks and learning activities with an interest in what happens within students. Tasks are the thing you ask a student to do. The term learning activity is ambiguous: It is both used for tasks and for the activity that learners engage in when they do particular tasks. Domain-specific pedagogy, or didactics, is interested in learning trajectories from some starting point to particular learning goals; then terms such as instructional sequence, teaching-learning strategy, unit, module, or teaching methods are used. When people write "learning environment" or "learning ecology" they want to emphasize that learning and teaching take place in a social and cultural setting that is intricately connected with what happens (or does not happen).

Methodology or method?

Is design research a methodology? I would say no. Methodology is the science of methods. "Method" here refers to the systematic way of doing things. The suffix "-logy" makes the study of what comes in front of it scientific: Psychology studies the psyche and sociology studies social phenomena. "Method" prescribes the "how"; "-logy" explains the "why."

To clarify what design research is, it is useful to make a distinction between methodology, research approach, and research methods. Particular common approaches to doing research are called research approaches or strategies (Denscombe, 2014). Confusingly, many people also call these methodologies. Then within research approaches or strategies (e.g., observation, survey), researchers use particular methods or techniques (e.g., video-recording, eye tracking, interview, questionnaire). "Method" typically refers to how you collect (and then analyze) your data (see Table 1.1).

Design research experts I interviewed agree that design research is neither methodology nor method. It is something in between. Design research is an approach in the sense that it can be compared with action research or experiment. However, it is also more general than particular strategies such as survey, case study, or experiment in the sense that within design research these strategies can be used. This is the reason that some experts prefer to call design research a methodological framework rather than a strategy. It is a genre of flexibly using existing research approaches for the purpose of gaining design based insights and research-based designs. For example, it is possible that within a design study (a design research project) you first use a survey to do a problem or needs analysis, do a case study of a teacher using your design, and use evaluation to identify learning effects. Design researchers typically need to learn about several research approaches, in particular survey, case study, and experiment. If you do not yet know about these, it would be wise to get acquainted with them. References to some well-known books on these approaches are provided in the Appendix.

It is perhaps unsatisfactory to anyone new to methodology that there are no clear-cut categories in which methods and approaches neatly fall – in particular that design research is more general than most research approaches. However, this is inevitable in the humanities and social sciences: Whenever we make categories, we also create boundary cases (Bowker & Star, 2000). Moreover,

Table 1.1 Methodological terminology

Term	Meaning	Examples
Methodology	The science of methods	
Methodological framework	A set of approaches with family resemblances	Design research
Research approaches/ strategies (sometimes called methodologies)	A way of conducting research	Action research, experiment, case study, survey
Research methods/ techniques	A way of collecting or analyzing data	Video-recording, eye-tracking, interview, questionnaire

scholars are creative in that they use whatever is useful. For example, it is not uncommon to use surveys or case studies within other research approaches such as action research or ethnography.

As Phillips (2006) argues, design research can be seen as a family of approaches with resemblances. This argument is inspired by Wittgenstein's observation that it is hard to define a game. Games have similarities but there is no single set of characteristics that makes something a game. Phillips writes:

> I do not regard it as productive to spend much time trying to come up with a simple account that ends all controversy about "what design experiments really are" — there is no right answer. There *is no one thing that they are like.*
>
> (p. 93, emphasis in original)

It is by comparing approaches with neighboring frameworks, approaches, and methods that it becomes clearer what design research is. This is what I aim to do in the following sections. In the last section I summarize how Cobb and colleagues (2003) define cross-cutting characteristics of design research.

Advisory nature of design research

To further characterize design research it is helpful to classify research functions in general (cf. Plomp, 2010):

- To describe (e.g., What conceptions of sampling do Grade 7 students have?)
- To compare (e.g., Does instructional strategy A lead to better test scores than instructional strategy B?)
- To evaluate (e.g., How well do German students pronounce Danish?)
- To explain (e.g., Why do so few students choose a bachelor's degree in mathematics or science?)
- To predict (e.g., What will students learn from using a particular software package?)
- To design/develop (e.g., What is a teaching strategy that may help students improve their band playing skills?)
- To advise (e.g., How can primary school students be supported to learn narration through games?).

Many research approaches such as surveys, correlational studies, and case studies typically have descriptive functions. Experiments often have a comparative function, even though they should in Cook's (2002) view "be designed to *explain* the consequences of interventions and not just to describe them" (p. 181, emphasis in original). Design research includes a design or development function but this is not enough to be research. It also has an *advisory* function (or aim), namely to give theoretical insights into how particular ways of teaching and learning can be promoted. The type of theory developed can be of a predictive nature: Under conditions X using educational approach Y, students are likely to learn Z (Van den Akker et al., 2006).

Research projects usually have one overall function or aim, but several stages of the project can have other aims. For example, if the main aim of a research project is to advise how a particular topic (e.g., sampling) could be taught, the project most likely has parts in which phenomena are described or evaluated (e.g., students' prior knowledge, current teaching practices). It will also have a part in which an innovative learning environment has to be designed and evaluated before empirically grounded advice can be given. This implies that research projects are layered. Design research projects (also called design studies) have an overall predictive or advisory aim, but often include research stages or substudies with a descriptive, comparative, or evaluative aim.

Textbox 1.3

Question: My research aim is to design an educational module that helps students learn X. Is that OK?

Response: Not really. The aim of research is to add to the scientific knowledge about a particular topic, so I recommend rephrasing your aim as follows: "The aim of this research is to add to the knowledge base about how students can be supported to learn ..." or something along these lines. Of course, as part of this overall aim, you will need to design a learning ecology that intends to help students learn X, and to evaluate to what extent you are successful. But a module in itself without accompanying knowledge about how and how well it works is not a scientific contribution.

A similar response holds for research aims such as: "to improve educational situation Y," for example the teaching and learning about relativity. Here the same critique holds: Make sure you do not just improve something, but also provide insight into how this could be and was done.

Textbox 1.4

Question: My research question is: How can an effective instructional sequence with learning goal X be designed? Is that a suitable question within design research?

Response: Not really, because you ask about the process of designing rather than about the insight how learners can be supported to learn X. So taken literally, your question belongs to another discipline, say the sociology of design, or a design science, that is interested in design processes and practices. I admit this is a subtle formulation issue, but it is an important one. If you keep your current question and give an answer in the form of the product, you do not really answer your question. This would make your report incoherent and potentially ambiguous to the reader.

Open and interventionist nature of design research

Another way to characterize design research is to contrast it with other approaches on the following two dimensions: naturalistic vs. interventionist and open vs. closed. Naturalistic studies analyze how learning takes place without interference by a researcher. Examples of naturalistic research approaches are ethnography and surveys. As the term suggests, interventionist studies intervene in what naturally happens: Researchers deliberately manipulate a condition or teach according to particular theoretical ideas (e.g., inquiry-based or problem-based learning). Such studies are necessary if the type of learning that researchers want to investigate is not present in naturalistic settings. Examples of interventionist approaches are experimental research, action research, and design research.

Research approaches can also be more open or closed. The term *open* here refers to little control of the situation or data whereas *closed* refers to a high degree of control or a limited number of options (e.g., multiple choice questions). For example, surveys using questionnaires with closed questions or responses on a Likert scale are more closed than surveys using semi-structured interviews. Likewise, an experiment comparing two conditions is more closed than a design research project in which the educational materials or ways of teaching are emergent and adjustable. Different research approaches can thus be positioned in a two-by-two table as in Table 1.2. Design research thus shares an interventionist nature (and some other characteristics) with experiments and action research.

Table 1.2 Naturalistic vs. interventionist and open vs. closed research approaches

	Naturalistic	Interventionist
Closed	Survey: questionnaires with closed questions	Experiment (randomized controlled trial)
Open	Survey: interviews with open questions	Action research
	Ethnography	Design research

We therefore continue by comparing design research with experiments and with action research. The first comparison is important because in my experience many early career researchers approach design research with an experimental mind-set. The comparison with action research is important because when social scientists hear about design research they sometimes think it is a form of action research, which however is different (Anderson & Shattuck, 2012).

Comparison of design research and randomized controlled trials

A randomized controlled trial (RCT) is sometimes referred to as a "true" experiment. This research approach was originally named randomized field trials (RFT) because of its origin in agriculture (Fisher, 1925). In the 1920s this innovative strategy was used to test scientifically whether particular agricultural treatments were beneficial for crops. By randomly allotting patches of land to an experimental treatment or control condition it became possible to draw rigorous conclusions about the effects of the new treatment.

Turning to education, assume we want to know whether a new teaching strategy for a specific topic in a particular grade is better than the traditionally used one. To investigate this question one could randomly assign students to the experimental (new teaching strategy) or control condition (e.g., the regular or traditional strategy), measure performances on pre- and posttests, and use statistical methods to test the null hypothesis that there is no significant difference between the two conditions. The researchers' hope is that this hypothesis can be rejected so that the new type of intervention (informed by a particular theory) proves to be better. The underlying rationale is: If we know what works, then we can implement this method and have better learning results (see Figure 1.1).

This so-called experimental approach of randomized controlled trials (Creswell, 2005) is sometimes considered the gold standard of research (Slavin, 2002). It has a clear logic and is mostly seen as a convincing way to make causal and general claims about what works. It is based on a research approach that has proven extremely helpful in the natural sciences that studies the causal laws of nature.

However, its limitations for education are discussed extensively in the literature (Biesta, 2007; Engeström, 2011; Olson, 2004). Here I mention three related arguments. First, humans only follow causal natural laws to some extent, so it is not self-evident that the rigorous methods used for studying natural objects apply to humans. Second, if we know what works, we still do not know why and when it works. Even if the new strategy is implemented, it might not work as expected because teachers use it in less than optimal ways.

An example can clarify this assertion. When doing research in an American school, I heard teachers complain about their managers' decision that every teacher had to start every lesson with a warm-up activity (e.g., a puzzle). Apparently, it had been proven by means of an RCT that student scores were

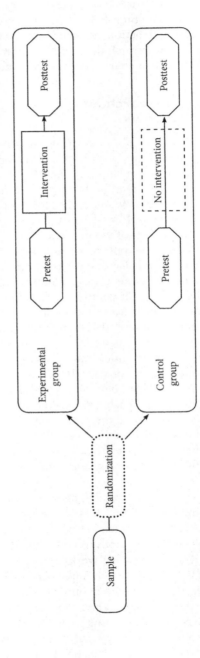

Figure 1.1 A pre-posttest experimental design (randomized controlled trial)

significantly higher in the experimental condition in which lessons started with a warm-up activity. The negative effect in teaching practice, however, was that teachers ran out of good ideas for warm-up activities, and that these often had nothing to do with the topic of the lesson. Effectively, teachers therefore lost five minutes of every lesson. Better insight into how and why warm-up activities work under particular conditions could have improved the situation, but the comparative nature of RCT had not provided this information because only the variable of starting the lesson with or without a warm-up activity had been manipulated.

A third argument for why RCT should not be the dominant research approach (as it now is in some countries) is that a new teaching strategy has to be designed before it can be tested. A Boeing airplane cannot be compared with an Airbus without a long tradition of engineering and producing such airplanes. In many cases, considerable research is needed to design innovative approaches. In such formative stages, RCTs have only limited value. Design research emerged as a way to address this need of developing new strategies that could solve long-standing or complex problems in education (see Chapter 2).

Two discussion points in the comparison of design research and RCT are the issues of generalization and causality. The use of random samples in RCT allows generalization to populations, but in most educational research random samples cannot be used. In response to this point, researchers have argued that theory development is not just about populations, but rather about propensities and processes (Frick, 1998). Hence rather than generalizing from a random sample to a population (statistical generalization), many (mainly qualitative) research approaches aim for generalization to a theory, model, or concept by presenting findings as particular cases of a more general model or concept; this is called theoretical or analytic generalization (Yin, 2009). Examples are given in other chapters.

RCT and design research are compared here as different research approaches (see Table 1.3). However, it is possible to do an RCT at the end of a design research project (design study).

Table 1.3 Comparison of experimental versus design research

Experiment (RCT)	Design research
Testing theory	Developing and testing theory simultaneously
Comparison of existing teaching methods by means of experimental and control groups	Design of an innovative learning environment
Proof of what works	Insight into how and why something works
Research interest is isolated by manipulating variables separately	Ecological approach
Statistical generalization	Analytic or theoretical generalization, transferability to other situations

Textbox 1.5

Question: What is the fundamental difference between design research versus a series of experiments in which a design is improved and insight is gained in various factors?

Response: Some researchers indeed do series of experiments in a spirit that is similar to what design researchers do. They design something and after each experiment they gain new insights on the basis of which they improve their design. Kanselaar (1993) already noticed this continuity between the two approaches. Kelly (personal communication, 2 December, 2017) also pointed out that when designing MOOCs (massive online open courses) with thousands of students, one can do many experiments while designing (see also Intermezzo 1). In such a design and research context, the difference disappears (see also Chapter 6). However, in most cases, design researchers put more emphasis on studying learning in an ecologically valid way, and they typically pay attention more explicitly to what is designed, whereas most researchers who do series of experiments tend to report the knowledge gained from the experiments. The design process and knowledge then remain more implicit.

Textbox 1.6

Question: What is the difference between design research and research design?

Response: The term "research design" is used within methodology for the structure of the research that ensures that in the end one can draw particular types of conclusions. For example, starting with a random sample from a population is one step potentially described as part of a research design. This would allow generalization of conclusions to the population from which the sample was drawn. Another important feature of the experimental research design in Figure 1.1 is randomization of participants to the experiment or control condition. This allows the research to assume that any differences between results in the two groups are due to the treatment or intervention (and not to the samples). The decision to work with experimental and control groups is also part of the research design. So in this phrase, "design" refers to the structure of the research procedures.

However, in educational design research, the term design typically refers to what is designed to promote learning or solve an educational problem (module, unit, tools, classroom culture, organizational infrastructure). So indeed, research design and design research refer to very different things, and use the term design for different things being designed: the structure of the research versus the educational materials.

Comparison of design research with action research

Action research, in education typically done by teachers, focuses on solving a practical problem and aims to produce practical guidelines (Bradbury, 2015; Denscombe, 2014). Like action research, design research is interventionist and open, involves a reflective and often cyclic process, and aims to bridge theory and practice (Opie & Sikes, 2004). In both approaches the teacher can also be the researcher. In action research, the researcher is not the observer (Anderson & Shattuck, 2012), whereas in design research s/he can but need not be the observer. Furthermore, in design research, design is a crucial part of the research, whereas in action research the focus is on action and change, which can but need not involve the design of a new learning environment. Design research also more explicitly aims for instructional theories than does action research. These points are summarized in Table 1.4. Inevitably, the boundaries between the two approaches can be fuzzy. For example, Silverman (2015) writes about "designerly ways for action research."

Table 1.4 Commonalities and differences between design research and action research

	Design research	Action research
Commonalities	Open, interventionist, researcher can be participant, reflective cyclic process	
Differences	Researcher can be observer	Researcher can only be participant
	Design is necessary	Design is possible
	Focus on instructional theory and improved design	Focus on action and improvement of a situation

Comparison with lesson studies

Design research shares some features with the approach of lesson studies (see Table 1.5). In lesson studies, teachers collaboratively design lessons that they test in their classrooms (Fernandez & Yoshida, 2004; Hart, Alston, & Murata, 2011).

Table 1.5 Differences between lesson studies and design research

Feature	Lesson study	Design research
Main aim	Professional development of teachers and teams	Design and research
Drive	Education driven	Research driven
Unit	One lesson	Can be series of lessons, course, tool, environment ...
Role of theory	Only input	Input and output
Iterative	Yes	Yes, though not always (see Cobb et al., 2003)
Concern	Optimization	Innovation
Sharing	Lessons, local	Publications, design
Prior predictions/plans	Anticipations	Hypothetical learning trajectories, scenarios, conjecture maps, design principles

In many cases, researchers are involved to guide this process or help in the co-design. While one teacher conducts the lesson, the other teachers observe. When the teachers are satisfied, the lessons can be taught by other teachers too. In this way, schools can improve their education step by step and contribute to the professional development of their teachers.

With this last point, it becomes clear what an essential difference is between design research and lesson studies: The primary purpose of lesson studies is originally and typically professional development of teachers rather than research adding to the scientific knowledge base. Oftentimes, success is not shared outside the school. The role of the researcher is often to facilitate this development and perhaps assist with the design of lessons. However, note that lesson study is increasingly used also for research purposes, illustrating how different approaches can cross-fertilize over time.

Formative interventions and design based implementation research

Some versions of design research originally seemed to strive for a rather high degree of control of variables (Collins, 1990, 1992). From a cultural-historical activity theoretical (CHAT) perspective, Engeström (2011) criticized such closed forms of design research (he refers to Collins, Joseph, & Bielaczyc, 2004) as unsuitable for most situations where outcomes of interacting practices are not predefined. Rather, as soon as researchers co-design with teachers or other stakeholders in education (workplace trainers, school leaders, district leaders) then goals become negotiable targets. They are shaped in the process of working together. In such more open-ended situations, Engeström proposes to do formative interventions rather than controlled versions of design research. However, when I interviewed Collins about this (Collins, personal communication, 28 June 2017) he wondered what distinctions Engeström sees that he did not see himself, because he does not want to fix variables or educational goals upfront.

For a long time, design researchers and CHAT-informed scholars had little dialogue. This situation has fortunately changed. For example, in the CHAT journal *Mind, Culture, and Activity*, Penuel (2014) eloquently argued for the need of such dialogue. With colleagues (Penuel et al., 2011), he proposed a hybrid form of design research and formative intervention, which he calls design based implementation research (DBIR). As Fishman and Penuel (in press) write, most research treats sustainability as something thought about after the research, and often left to others to care about. DBIR can be characterized by its core principles:

1 A focus on persistent problems of practice from multiple stakeholders' perspectives;
2 A commitment to iterative, collaborative design;
3 A concern with developing theory and knowledge related to both classroom learning and implementation through systematic inquiry; and
4 A concern with developing capacity for sustaining change in systems (Penuel et al., 2011).

One striking difference with most types of design research is that DBIR involves stakeholders rather than trying ideas out before scaling up. Another is the involvement of policy to ensure sustained change in practice.

In a special issue in the *Journal of the Learning Sciences*, guest-edited by Penuel, Cole, and O'Neill (2016), the CHAT theorists and American learning sciences communities were brought into dialogue. The guest editors wanted to show the similarities between design research and cultural-historical research inspired by Russian psychologists (e.g., Vygotsky, Luria, Leontiev, Davydov) and the Finnish third-generation activity theorists (e.g., Engeström). Thus the different communities seem to have gradually come to understand each other's perspectives better.

Five characteristics of design research

So far I have characterized design research in terms of its predictive and advisory function, its engineering nature and differences from other research methods. To end this chapter, I summarize five key characteristics of design research as identified by Cobb et al. (2003); see also Confrey and Maloney (2015). The five criteria do not necessarily all have to be fulfilled. As pointed out by Phillips

(2006), they are like family characteristics that often but not always need to go together:

1   The first characteristic is that its purpose is *to develop theories about learning and the means that are designed to support that learning.*

2   The second characteristic of design research is its *interventionist* nature. In many research approaches, changing and understanding a situation are separated. However, in design research these are intertwined in line with the following idea: If you want to change something you have to understand it, and if you want to understand something you have to change it (Bakker, 2004).

3   The third characteristic is that design research has *prospective and reflective components* that need not be separated by a trial or so-called teaching experiment (Steffe & Thompson, 2000). In implementing hypothesized learning (the prospective part) the researchers confront conjectures with actual learning that they observe (reflective part). Reflection can be done after each lesson, even if the teaching experiment is longer than one lesson. Such reflective analysis can lead to changes to the original plan for the next lesson. Kanselaar (1993) argued that any good educational research has prospective and reflective components. As explained before, however, what distinguishes design research from other experimental approaches is that in design research these components are not separated into the formulation of hypotheses before and after the implementation of a design (e.g., in a teaching experiment).

4   The fourth characteristic is the *cyclic* nature of design research: Invention and revision form an iterative process. Multiple conjectures on learning are sometimes refuted and alternative conjectures can be generated and tested. The cycles typically consist of the following phases: preparation and design phase, teaching experiment, and retrospective analysis. The results of such a retrospective analysis mostly feed a new cycle. Other types of educational research ideally also build upon prior experiments and researchers iteratively improve materials and theoretical ideas in between experiments, but in design research changes can take place during a teaching experiment or series of teaching experiments. Another difference is the perspective on variation. Where experimentally oriented researchers mostly try to control or plan variation, design researchers welcome unexpected variation to see how robust their ideas and designs are (irrespective of the question to what extent control is really possible in naturalistic settings).

5   The fifth characteristic of design research is that the *theory* under development *has to do real work.* As Lewin (1951) wrote: "There is nothing so practical as a good theory" (p. 169). Theory generated from design research is typically humble in the sense that it is developed for a specific domain, for instance within history education. Yet it must be general enough to be applicable in different contexts such as classrooms in other schools in other countries. In such cases one can speak of transferability.

Textbox 1.7

Question: Why is most design research conducted in science, technology, engineering, and mathematics (STEM) domains? Is there anything in particular that makes design research particularly suited for these domains but perhaps less so for other domains, for example the more specific learning goals?

Response: I do not think so. I think that the main reason for the focus on STEM is that this is where the bulk of the research money is spent. Perhaps the problems are experienced most in subjects that remain a stumbling block for many students. Given the shortage of STEM expertise in the labor market, society cares much about the quality of science and mathematics education.

However, I do not see any reason why design research could not be used in language, music, art, physical education, or any type of education where something can be designed to improve the teaching and learning of that subject. The examples in the second part of this book are a testament to this idea.

Some people indeed assume that STEM learning goals are clearer than in some other domains, but this need not be the case. Also in STEM education research, researchers try to promote affective variables and are interested in elusive processes and skills such as modeling, insight into the nature of science, aesthetic experience, collaborative learning, and twenty-first century skills.

Note

1 Parts of this chapter are based on Bakker and Van Eerde (2015), with permission of Van Eerde and of the publisher.

References

Anderson, T., & Shattuck, J. (2012). Design based research: A decade of progress in education research? *Educational Researcher, 41*(1), 16–25.

Argyris, C. (1996). Actionable knowledge: Design causality in the service of consequential theory. *The Journal of Applied Behavioral Science, 32*(4), 390–406.

Bakker, A. (2004). *Design research in statistics education: On symbolizing and computer tools.* Utrecht: CD-β Press.

Bakker, A., & Van Eerde, H. A. A. (2015). An introduction to design based research with an example from statistics education. In A. Bikner-Ahsbahs, C. Knipping, & N. Presmeg (Eds.), *Approaches to qualitative research in mathematics education* (pp. 429–466). New York, NY: Springer.

Biesta, G. J. J. (2007). Why "what works" won't work: Evidence-based practice and the democratic deficit in educational research. *Educational Theory, 57*(1), 1–22.

Bowker, G. C., & Star, S. L. (2000). *Sorting things out: Classification and its consequences*. Cambridge, MA: MIT press.

Bradbury, H. (Ed.) (2015). *The Sage handbook of action research* (3rd ed.). Thousand Oaks, CA: Sage.

Brown, A. L. (1992). Design experiments: Theoretical and methodological challenges in creating complex interventions in classroom settings. *Journal of the Learning Sciences, 2*(2), 141–178.

Cambridge Dictionary. (n.d.). Design. Retrieved from https://dictionary.cambridge.org/dictionary/english/design

Cobb, P., Confrey, J., diSessa, A., Lehrer, R., & Schauble, L. (2003). Design experiments in educational research. *Educational Researcher, 32*(1), 9–13.

Collins, A. (1990). *Toward a design science of education. Technical report*. New York, NY: Center for Technology in Education.

Collins, A. (1992). Toward a design science of education. In E. Scanlon & T. O'Shea (Eds.), *New directions in educational technology* (pp. 15–22). New York, NY: Springer.

Collins, A., Joseph, D., & Bielaczyc, K. (2004). Design research: Theoretical and methodological issues. *Journal of the Learning Sciences, 13*(1), 15–42.

Confrey, J., & Maloney, A. (2015). A design study of a curriculum and diagnostic assessment system for a learning trajectory on equipartitioning. *ZDM Mathematics Education, 47*(6), 919–932. doi:10.1007/s11858–015–0699-y

Cook, T. D. (2002). Randomized experiments in educational policy research: A critical examination of the reasons the educational evaluation community has offered for not doing them. *Educational Evaluation and Policy Analysis, 24*(3), 175–199.

Creswell, J. W. (2005). *Educational research: Planning, conducting, and evaluating quantitative and qualitative research* (2nd ed.). Upper Saddle River, NJ: Pearson Education.

Denscombe, M. (2014). *The good research guide: For small-scale social research projects*. New York, NY: McGraw-Hill Education.

Design Based Research Collective. (2003). Design based research: An emerging paradigm for educational inquiry. *Educational Researcher, 32*(1), 5–8.

Engeström, Y. (2011). From design experiments to formative interventions. *Theory & Psychology, 21*(5), 598–628.

Fernandez, C., & Yoshida, M. (2004). *Lesson study: A Japanese approach to improving mathematics teaching and learning*. Mahwah, NJ: Erlbaum.

Fisher, R. A. (1925). *Statistical methods for research workers*. Edinburgh: Oliver & Boyd.

Fishman, B. J., & Penuel, W. R. (in press). Design based implementation research. In F. Fischer, C. Hmelo-Silver, P. Reimann, & S. R. Goldman (Eds.), *International handbook of the learning sciences*. New York, NY: Routledge.

Freudenthal, H. (1988). Ontwikkelingsonderzoek [Developmental research]. In K. P. E. Gravemeijer & K. Koster (Eds.), *Onderzoek, ontwikkeling en ontwikkelingsonderzoek [Research, development and developmental research]* (pp. 49–54). Utrecht, the Netherlands: OW&OC.

Frick, R. W. (1998). Interpreting statistical testing: Process and propensity, not population and random sampling. *Behavior Research Methods, Instruments, & Computers, 30*(3), 527–535.

Gravemeijer, K. P. E. (1994). Educational development and developmental research in mathematics education. *Journal for Research in Mathematics Education, 25*(5), 443–471.

Hart, L. C., Alston, A., & Murata, A. (2011). *Lesson study research and practice in mathematics education*. New York, NY: Springer.

Hoadley, C. P. (2002). Creating context: Design based research in creating and understanding CSCL. *Paper Presented at the Proceedings of the Conference on Computer Support for Collaborative Learning: Foundations for a CSCL Community*. Boulder, CO.

Kanselaar, G. (1993). Ontwikkelingsonderzoek bezien vanuit de rol van de advocaat van de duivel [Design research: Taking the position of the devil's advocate]. In R. de Jong & M. Wijers (Eds.), *Ontwikkelingsonderzoek, theorie en praktijk* (pp. 63–66). Utrecht: NVORWO.

Lewin, K. (1951). *Field theory in social science: Selected theoretical papers.* Ed. D. Cartwright. New York: Harper & Row.

Lijnse, P. L. (1995). "Developmental research" as a way to an empirically based "didactical structure" of science. *Science Education, 79*(2), 189–199.

McKenney, S., & Reeves, T. C. (2012). *Conducting educational design research.* London: Routledge.

Mercer, N., Wegerif, R., & Dawes, L. (1999). Children's talk and the development of reasoning in the classroom. *British Educational Research Journal, 25*(1), 95–111.

Mintrop, R. (2016). *Design based school improvement: A practical guide for education leaders.* Cambridge, MA: Harvard Education Press.

Olson, D. R. (2004). The triumph of hope over experience in the search for "what works": A response to Slavin. *Educational Researcher, 33*(1), 24–26.

Opie, C., & Sikes, P. J. (2004). *Doing educational research.* London: Sage.

Penuel, W. R. (2014). Emerging forms of formative intervention research in education. *Mind, Culture, and Activity, 21*(2), 97–117.

Penuel, W. R., Cole, M., & O'Neill, D. K. (2016). Introduction to the special issue. *Journal of the Learning Sciences, 25,* 487–496. doi:10.1080/10508406.2016.1215753

Penuel, W. R., Fishman, B. J., Cheng, B. H., & Sabelli, N. (2011). Organizing research and development at the intersection of learning, implementation, and design. *Educational Researcher, 40*(4), 331–337.

Phillips, D. (2006). Assessing the quality of design research proposals. In J. Van den Akker, K. P. E. Gravemeijer, S. McKenney, & N. Nieveen (Eds.), *Educational design research* (pp. 93–99). London, UK: Routledge.

Plomp, T. (2010). Educational design research: An introduction. In T. Plomp & N. M. Nieveen (Eds.), *An introduction to educational design research* (pp. 9–35). Enschede, the Netherlands: SLO.

Plomp, T., & Nieveen, N. (2013). *Educational design research: Introduction and illustrative cases.* Enschede: SLO.

Reinking, D., & Bradley, B. A. (2008). *On formative and design experiments: Approaches to language and literacy research.* New York, NY: Teachers College Press.

Romberg, T. A. (1973). *Development research: Overview of how development-based research works in practice.* Madison, WI: Wisconsin Research and Development Center for Cognitive Learning.

Silverman, H. (2015). Designerly ways for action research. In H. Bradbury (Ed.), *The Sage handbook of action research* (3rd ed., pp. 716–723). Thousand Oaks, CA: Sage.

Slavin, R. E. (2002). Evidence-based education policies: Transforming educational practice and research. *Educational Researcher, 31*(7), 15–21.

Steffe, L. P., & Thompson, P. W. (2000). Teaching experiment methodology: Underlying principles and essential elements. In R. Lesh & A. E. Kelly (Eds.), *Handbook of research design in mathematics and science education* (pp. 267–306). Hillsdale, NJ: Erlbaum.

Van den Akker, J. (1999). Principles and methods of development research. In J. van den Akker, R. M. Branch, K. Gustafson, N. Nieveen, & T. Plomp (Eds.), *Design approaches and tools in education and training* (pp. 1–14). Dordrecht, the Netherlands: Springer.

Van den Akker, J., Gravemeijer, K. P. E., McKenney, S., & Nieveen, N. (2006). *Educational design research*. London, UK: Routledge.

Vygotsky, L. S. (1987). Thinking and speech. In R. Rieber, & A. Carton (Vol. Eds.), L. S. Vygotsky, *Collected works*. Vol. 1. (pp. 39–285). New York, NY: Plenum (N. Minick, Trans.)

Yin, R. (2009). *Case study research: Design and methods*. Thousand Oaks, CA: Sage.

Chapter 2

History of design research in education

Summary

Whereas Chapter 1 characterizes design research, the current chapter unravels its historical roots. While summarizing the history of design research I point to issues of terminology and the connotations that come with the terms development, developmental, and design based research, design experiment, etc. I focus on the history in the United States and the Netherlands, where design research has been discussed most extensively, but also point to influences from Russian psychology.

Design research has multiple historical origins. Those in the US and the Netherlands are the most apparent, as is evident from the American and Dutch authors contributing to books on educational design research (McKenney & Reeves, 2012; Van den Akker, Gravemeijer, McKenney, & Nieveen, 2006) and historical context provided in other publications (Penuel, 2014; Prediger, Gravemeijer, & Confrey, 2015). Cobb, Jackson, and Dunlap (2017) wrote:

> In some countries, including the United States, design research emerged as researchers with backgrounds in cognitive psychology attempted to overcome perceived limitations of experiments that compared treatment and control groups (hence the name "design experiment"). In other countries, including the Netherlands, the methodology emerged in the context of developing and improving curriculum materials (hence the name "developmental research").

(p. 208)

One important influence in the early days of design research has been Herb Simon's (1967, 1996) argument that education research is fundamentally a design science (Glaser, 1976; Collins, 1990; O'Neill, 2012):

> Design, so construed, is the core of all professional training; it is the principal mark that distinguishes the professions from the sciences. Schools of engineering, as well as schools of architecture, business, education, law, and medicine, are all centrally concerned with the process of design.
>
> (Simon, 1996, p. 111)

Already in the 1970s, Romberg (1973) used the term *development research* for research accompanying the development of curriculum. Design research and related approaches such as formative experiments (Reinking & Bradley, 2008) also have roots in Russia, France, Germany, Finland, and other countries. Discussions on the relation between research and design in education, especially mathematics education, mainly took place in Western Europe in the 1980s and 1990s, particularly in the Netherlands (Freudenthal, 1988; Goffree, 1979), France (Artigue, 2014, 2015), and Germany (Wittmann, 1992). Penuel (2014) points to the history of Russian psychology via Vygotsky and Davydov to Engeström's *development work research* and his *change laboratories* in Finland as well as the Scandinavian approach to participatory design.

After initial optimism about and development in the field of educational research in the 1960s, in the 1970s there were also critical voices about its value and limitations (Glaser, 1976). A long-standing dominance in educational psychology of empiricist, neopositivist emphases on quantitative studies was increasingly being criticized (De Landsheere, 1985; Van Parreren, 1962). Over a long stretch of decades, different camps within educational psychology do not seem to have come closer (Cronbach, 1975; Flis & Van Eck, in press). Educational researchers often found no significant differences (Russell, 1999) or found research difficult to replicate,[1] which makes a lot of experimental research uninformative. Educational policy-makers wanted educational research that would help improve education, and educational psychologists became more interested in disciplines that studied phenomena more holistically, such as anthropology (cf. Lave, 1988), but also disciplines that were concerned with change, such as engineering and technology design (Collins, 1990). I start with an historical account in the US, with influences from multiple sources, and then pay special attention to the Dutch history, because it is much less accessible, yet interesting to an international audience due to due to the different reasons that drove design research in the Netherlands. In both historical threads, the influence of Russian and Soviet educational psychology is visible.

Emergence of design research in the US

In his presidential address to the American Psychological Association in 1899, Dewey (1900) talked about the importance of *linking sciences*. Engineering is an intermediate science between physics and practical work; and scientific medicine between natural science and the physician. From his talk, the need for a linking science between psychology and educational practice was clear, a science that Glaser (1976) proposed to call the psychology of instruction.

In her summary of the evolution of design experiments and design studies in the US, Confrey (2006) does indeed mention John Dewey for his pragmatist view on inquiry. Scientific claims, for him, must be useful in different situations. Also Lev Vygotsky's ideas, once they were known in the US, had a major impact on how people came to appreciate the importance of the sociocultural environment in which individuals develop. The influence of Russian psychology has led to a strong emphasis on learning ecologies (Bronfenbrenner, 1979) rather than the individualistic views on learning that were then current. Third, Confrey points to the influence by Jean Piaget's clinical methods in which interviewers both experimented and observed when children were solving problems. In line with emerging constructivist and sociocultural theories, Piagetian clinical interviews (Ginsburg, 1997) grew into teaching experiments in the 1980s. Teaching experiments (Thompson, 1979) are similar to clinical interviews but more oriented to teaching children something new. The interviewer tries to teach adaptively while observing. It is a form of experimentation in which insights into productive ways of teaching are identified (Cobb & Steffe, 1983; Steffe, 1991).

Confrey (2006) notes that although most people trace design experiments back to Collins (1992) and Brown (1992), the approach was foreshadowed by teaching experiments and similar approaches in which new technologies were designed and tested out in classrooms (Papert, 1980; Pea, 1987). With reference to Simon's (1967) *The sciences of the artificial*, Collins (1990) coined the term *design experiment*. He wanted to experiment with new technology in authentic classrooms. He also saw the need to measure learning outcomes beyond the narrow measures that were commonly used in research, such as recall. Coming from artificial intelligence and computer science, what he had in mind was an approach of trying things and refining them, as is common in engineering design. In my interview with Collins (personal communication, June 28, 2017), he said, "while I invented the term [design experiment] I only really affected one person, happening to be Ann Brown, and so she made it famous."

Brown's (1992) article in *The Journal of the Learning Sciences* has indeed become a classic, with at the moment of writing this chapter about 4,600 citations. In the editorial for the special issue in which her article appeared, Schoenfeld (1992) explains how Brown, Saxe, and he himself all had different routes to design experimentation. He semi-jokingly wrote that Brown, a famous reading expert with a background in experimental psychology, "made the mistake of getting interested in education" (Schoenfeld, 1992, p. 137). "The laboratory methods and models in which she received her academic upbringing are, alas, of little direct use in explaining things that she now wishes to explain" (pp. 137–138). More generally, he argued that learning scientists needed new approaches to understanding learning and promoting education in ecologically valid ways.

Brown (1992) started her article with a personal history beginning with her background in laboratory settings, focusing on memory and training, with the advantage of having control over particular variables. However, she experienced several limitations. One was that the work mostly had no educational relevance. She summarized ten years of work in two statements: "*Training worked*" (to use simple strategies) and "*Training didn't work*" (no evidence of retention or transfer) (p. 145, emphasis in original). Gradually, the field moved on to acknowledge the social context of learning, whether in everyday life, school, or the workplace. Theoretical insights into this issue of context asked for nontrivial methodological innovations. Brown (1992) stated, "These changes in learning theory led me down the slippery slope to educational theory and practice" (p. 148). Ideas about reciprocal teaching, distributed expertise, and communities of learners nudged her and her colleagues to create communities of learners in which new ideas could be enacted and tested – the conditions for doing design experiments.

Not everyone adopted this terminology. For example, Mike Cole was concerned, like Ann Brown and many other colleagues with whom he worked closely, about the ecological validity of psychological experiments. In his research he tried to set up a curriculum for handicapped children, but he found that available research was of little help. In after-school clubs, Cole and colleagues (2006) gave children tasks, but what was going on in the classrooms was so complex that they felt they lacked the research methods to understand what was typically conceptualized in terms of transfer, generalization, or context.[2] It was only much later that he engaged in drawing connections between the cultural–historical framework in which he worked and the language used by design researchers (Cole & Packer, 2016; Nicolopoulou & Cole, 2009). I give this example of Cole's research because there had been fertile ground for new approaches to interventionist research for a long time, even among educational researchers who did not adopt the terminology of design experiment, design study, or design experimentation.

Reinking and Bradley (2008) compared the history of design experiments and the related approach of formative experiments with the convergence of many streams into a river. The aforementioned lack of ecological validity with most experimental research in laboratory situations (Jacob, 1992) was one of the important streams. Another stream was the wish to create the future: Descriptive studies "tell us little about what *could* be" (Jacob, 1992, p. 321, emphasis in original). Educational researchers increasingly became concerned about "Change as the Goal of Educational Research," the title used by Moll and Diaz (1987). It is worth noting that their article was published in an anthropology journal; first because of the awareness that educational researchers may need more of the approaches taken by ethnographers, and second because anthropologists typically observed rather than tried to change the situations they studied. Moll and Diaz wrote that they analyzed problems in education for a long time, "But we did not stop there" (p. 300). They were after educational change.

Also worth mentioning is that they wrote the terms "intervention" (p. 303) and "ethnographic experiment" (p. 309) in inverted commas, probably to avoid disapproving readers who have different images of interventions and experiments. Collins and colleagues (2004) later characterized design experiments as combining ethnographic and quantitative analysis (p. 16).

This brief history of the US context would not be complete without explicit reference to the influence of Russian or Soviet psychology. Many scholars such as Brown, Campione, Cole, and Palincsar were acquainted with, for instance, Vygotsky's writing that then became better known in the US. They knew about the kind of *formative, transformative,* or *transforming experiments* that were common in Russian psychology in which researchers tried to create educational situations and change education. Bronfenbrenner (1979, p. 40) characterized a transforming experiment as an "experiment that radically restructures the environment, producing a new configuration that activates previously unrealized behavioral potentials of the subject." A famous example is the school in Moscow that was based on Davydov's ideas on learning. To the American Urie Bronfenbrenner (1979), the Russian developmental psychologist Leontiev once said (see also Cole, 2016):

> It seems to me that American researchers are constantly seeking to explain how the child came to be what he is; we in the U.S.S.R. are striving to discover not how the child came to be what he is, but how he can become what he not yet is.
>
> (Bronfenbrenner, 1979, p. 40)

Comparisons between Soviet and American approaches to education and educational research happened more frequently. For example, Easley (1977) noted the following differences:

> The curriculum as it is, and long has been, conceived by teachers, parents, students, and administrators is accepted as the starting point of research. Improvements are sought within it, not by replacing of it. . . . The USSR may be the last major country preserving a close relation between the academicians and the school practitioners.
>
> (p. 26)

> Soviet investigators, unlike European and American mathematics educators, have accepted the traditional goals and practices of teachers as given and not attempted to replace them, except to provide clear, practical solutions to problems identified by teachers themselves.
>
> (p. 36)

Clearly, several American educational scholars appreciated aspects of Soviet approaches to education and educational psychology, in particular the smaller gap between research and practice. This was not so surprising in a time when the social pressure for useful scientific knowledge was increasing (Glaser, 1976).

Terminology: design experiment, design based research, design research

The fact that a renowned psychologist such as Ann Brown, trained in experimental studies, made the transition to design experiments, seems to have facilitated the reception of this methodological approach. Using the term *experiment* also made it still sound scientific. Yet not everyone was so pleased with this term, and today it is used much less than other terms.

One disadvantage of the term *design experiment* can be explained by reference to a critical paper by Paas (2005) titled "Design Experiment: Neither a Design Nor an Experiment." The confusion to which his pun refers is two-fold. First, in many educational research communities the term *design* is reserved for research design (e.g., comparing an experimental with a control group), whereas the term in *design research* refers to the design of educational interventions (Sandoval, 2004). Second, many researchers in the social sciences reserve the term *experiment* for "true" experiments or RCTs, even though other types of experimentation can be distinguished (Reinking & Bradley, 2004; Schön, 1987). In design experiments, hypotheses certainly play an important role, but they are not fixed and tested once. Instead they may be emergent, tentative, multiple, and temporary.

It is therefore not surprising that the term design experiment is used less and less today. In line with the Design Based Research Collective (2003), many use the term *design based research*, proposed by Hoadley (2002), because this suggests that it is predominantly research (hence leading to a knowledge claim) in the context of a design process. In my interview with Hoadley (personal communication, November 9, 2017), he explained that the term design experiment also had a "Google problem," or in those days rather a "Yahoo problem," because searchers would find a lot of information about research design and experiments, but not about design experiments. One candidate, *design studies*, was favored by Marcia Linn, Jere Confrey, and several other scholars, but there was already a journal titled *Design Studies*, outside education, which aims to understand design processes in various disciplines and thus has a different focus.

The term design based research has become quite popular. In their review study, Anderson and Shattuck (2012) even confined their search to articles that use this exact phrase of design based research. Scholars such as Abrahamson (2009) prefer the term design based research for research that is possible thanks to new learning ecologies facilitated by new designs. For example, embodied learning of proportion can be investigated now because of a long history of designs (pulleys, Wii controls, Kinect, iPad apps) in which students interact with two hands with pulleys or features on a computer screen. In many of these studies, he and his colleagues explore some theoretically interesting phenomenon without paying explicit attention to the exact features of the design or the improvement of the apps. The word *based* in *design based research* then indeed emphasizes the relative importance of research compared to design.

Confrey (personal communication, July 29, 2016) wonders why the suffix "-based" is needed, and prefers the terms design research or design studies. The latter term is also used by Cobb (e.g., Cobb, Jackson, & Dunlap, 2014), although he has also used other terms over time: design research (Cobb, 2001) and design experiments (Cobb, Confrey, diSessa, Lehrer, & Schauble, 2003). McKenney and Reeves (2012) prefer the term *educational design research*. The adjective "educational" helps to distinguish it from a discipline called *design research* with a focus on architecture and related fields but not education (cf. Laurel, 2003).

In this book I have opted for the term *design research* for the general methodological framework. Where confusion with design research outside education may arise, I add the words "in education" or "educational." I propose to use the term *research-based design* for design that is informed by research, and *design based research* for research that is possible due to the existence of a new design. I see design research as a combination or alternation of the two (see Chapter 1). I use the term *design research project* for larger units such as a PhD project, and follow Cobb et al. (2017) in using the term *design study* for specific investigations using design research.

Developmental research at Utrecht University, the Netherlands

Because the Dutch context is far less known than that of the US (Confrey, 2006; Reinking & Bradley, 2004, 2008), I elaborate here on how design research emerged in the Netherlands, in particular at what is now called the Freudenthal Institute at Utrecht University. The Dutch history points to reasons for design research other than ecological validity, which was one of the primary motives found in the American history of design research.

As a reaction to the formalistic, mechanistic, and top-down ways in which mathematics was often taught until the 1960s, a group of mathematics educators around Hans Freudenthal had ideas about how to improve mathematics education to be more useful (Freudenthal, 1968; La Bastide-van Gemert, 2015). They were critical of both the existing curriculum and of available research that could inform the development of mathematics education in the Netherlands (Freudenthal, 1977). Their ideals were to make mathematics accessible for all, to engage students in doing mathematics rather than teaching mechanistic rules. In Gravemeijer's (1998) words "the core principle is that mathematics can and should be learned on one's own authority and through one's own mental activities" (p. 277). One of the ideals was guided reinvention – an active process in which students create understanding of mathematics under the guidance of the teacher and instructional materials (Freudenthal, 1991; Streefland, 1991; Treffers, 1987; Van den Brink & Streefland, 1979). In 1971, Freudenthal became the director of an institute (Instituut voor de Ontwikkeling van het Wiskunde Onderwijs, or IOWO) that aimed to develop mathematics education in this direction for both primary and secondary education.

To realize their ideals the group had to design educational materials, and so they did – based on whatever theoretical and practical insights were available. The conventional research approaches were considered far too slow to be of use. Design ideas were typically tested out in classrooms and revised based on observations. It is in this way that the domain-specific theory of Realistic Mathematics Education (RME) developed with its design heuristics and concretely worked out examples of its principles in various mathematical domains (Gravemeijer, 1994; Streefland, 1991; Van den Heuvel-Panhuizen, 1996).

Freudenthal used the term *developmental research (ontwikkelingsonderzoek* in Dutch) for this type of joint development and research (Freudenthal, 1988). The core idea of developmental research was that development of learning environments and the development of theory were intertwined. Freudenthal was very critical of existing research in education: Most of it was not informative, and the route from research to development and dissemination was too slow (Gravemeijer & Terwel, 2000). He therefore preferred to take an approach in which design and research go hand in hand. As Goffree (1979) put it:

> Developmental research in education as presented here, shows the characteristics of both developmental and fundamental research, which means aiming at new knowledge that can be put into service in continued development. It also means that the need for fundamental research is nurtured in the developmental process. The underlying problematic is to be understood both in their [sic] context of instruction itself and the development of instruction.
>
> (p. 347)

The focus of Freudenthal and his colleagues was on designing according to their principles. In 1973 he wrote "We of the IOWO regard ourselves as engineers" and "we are making something – something that requires a scientific background, but that is itself not a science" (cited in Freudenthal, 1987, p. 13). He emphasized one difference, though: engineers can base their work on solid theory from physics, where educational designers cannot.

Theory development was very local (domain- or topic-specific), and methodological issues were not a primary concern. However, some developmental researchers had a background in educational research, and felt the need to underpin and defend their new ways of working. One of them was Gravemeijer, who published extensively on the topic of developmental or design research later on, also from a philosophy of science standpoint (Gravemeijer, 1988, 1998; Gravemeijer & Cobb, 2006).

Several conferences on developmental research took place (e.g., 1986 and 1993). From the reports of these conferences (De Jong & Wijers, 1993;

Gravemeijer & Koster, 1988;Van Die & Knip, 1986) it is evident that the same issues kept reappearing as reasons for doing this engineering type of research and design:

1   Available research on mathematics learning was descriptive and focused on the testing of theoretical hypotheses that were of little relevance to educational practice (e.g.,Van Die & Knip, 1986, p. 58). Adjectives such as "sterile" and "incoherent" were used as characteristics of research typically carried out in the area of mathematics education.
2   Goffree (1986) argued that the then current theories on learning mathematics were simplistic and one-dimensional, and led to one-dimensional teaching and learning.
3   By contrast developmental research was called "fruitful" and "constructive," and "attentive to current educational practices."Typical questions were about how some ideal could be achieved; for example, "how can a problem-solving attitude be promoted?"

However, what was also evident was the difficulty of getting such research funded as the approach was mostly considered unscientific. One of the key points of critique was (and still is) that design researchers update their conjectures and adjust their designs while experimenting. Clearly there was high demand for scrutiny of its scientific value and methodological approach.

The debates at the 1993 conference went a step further. A wide range of developmental researchers, educational researchers, and designers were brought together. The aforementioned arguments about developmental research were reiterated, but also complemented with new ones. For example, most educational researchers (not doing design research) argued that no separate methodology with its own criteria was needed.The available research approaches could be used for whatever purposes the design researchers had: case study, ethnography, survey, etc. (Koster, 1993).The criteria for validity and reliability used in qualitative research also apply to developmental research (Kanselaar, 1993; see also Chapter 5). Moreover, the talk about a paradigm shift was in their view an exaggeration (Elbers, 1993).Verschaffel (1993) pointed to parallel trends in the US and cited a then recent special issue in the *Journal of the Learning Sciences* (Brown, 1992; Schoenfeld, 1992) – already mentioned earlier in this chapter. In 2003 an expert meeting took place with many American guests. It was funded by the Netherlands Organisation for Scientific Research (NWO) and formed the basis for the book edited byVan den Akker et al. (2006).

So far I have concentrated on the emergence of development research as an approach to designing new educational materials to improve mathematics education. However, I would like to point to political forces too. First, the institute that Freudenthal directed (IOWO) once had a fight in the 1970s against the trend of specialization by function rather than content.Where the IOWO wanted to keep curriculum design, research, teacher education, and assessment together for mathematics, the national trend was to institutionalize these functions separately, but for all school subjects, and create another type of coherence (across subjects). With a recently established national curriculum institute (Stichting Leerplanontwikkeling, or SLO) and a national center for assessment (Centraal Instituut voor Toetsontwikkeling, or CITO), and with universities covering research and teacher education, policy-makers saw no need for a separate institute that tried to keep everything around mathematics education together. As I understand it from Treffers (personal communication, October 11, 2017), the choice for the term *developmental research* was connected with arguments for keeping an institute like IOWO within Utrecht University: to develop mathematics education coherently with attention to teaching practice, informed by and informing research. The term *developmental* links to Freudenthal's (1991) emphasis on educational development (in contrast to linear approaches such as research-development-dissemination), and the term *research* is distinctive for investigations at a university as opposed to national expertise centers.

The term was not uncontested (Treffers, personal communication, October 11, 2017). In 1979 Treffers wrote a summary about research relevant to the IOWO's work (Treffers, 1979). When the IOWO staff had a meeting about it, different terms were discussed. One was *constructive research* in which something new was made (as opposed to *constaterend onderzoek*, Dutch for observational research). *Frontline research* was also suggested (*grensverleggend* in Dutch, literary *boundary pushing*). Another term was *formative* research, in line with the aforementioned Soviet tradition (cf. Penuel, 2014). Davydov had been in Utrecht, and several staff members had met him and knew about the school with which he worked. The Dutch educational psychologist Carel van Parreren, influential on several educational scientists, knew the Soviet traditions very well (Van Parreren & Carpay, 1972; Van Parreren, 1962, 1988), but unfortunately hardly wrote anything in English. A third term discussed was *ontwerponderzoek* (literally design research), in line with the *ontwerpschool* (design school) that Treffers and other colleagues worked with to test out their new didactical ideas.

This brief history shows that ecological validity was not the main concern for the staff at Utrecht University. Their focus was to design a modern mathematics curriculum that embodied a particular view (philosophy rather than a theory – Freudenthal, 1988) on what it means to do mathematics as a human being. Traditional research methods were considered inappropriate (too slow, too narrow, sterile, descriptive rather than prescriptive). An approach closer to engineering was needed. In Freudenthal's (1976) words: "Engineering needs background research and can produce research as fall out" (p. 189). By "fall out" he meant something like a byproduct: "chopping wood produces chips, and the practical work of engineers may eventually also yield scientific residues (Freudenthal, 1987, p. 13).

Hence, the emphasis was on educational development driven by a background philosophy, with theory development as a byproduct. In retrospect one could call this research-based design. Over time more and more research took place that can be characterized as design research.

Development and design research at the University of Twente

At another Dutch university, the University of Twente, a slightly different term, *development research (ontwikkelingsonderzoek* in Dutch), was used (Van den Akker, 1988), but its focus was less on testing specific learning theories, and more on proving a research base for curriculum development (in many domains). The history of this group is worth telling because it shows again different reasons to move into a similar direction as scholars from Utrecht or the US. As Plomp and Van den Akker told me during my interviews, traditionally curriculum development was rather intuitive. They were convinced that research could in principle support decision making during curriculum development, but often the information from available research was "too narrow to be meaningful, too superficial to be instrumental, too artificial to be relevant, and, on top of that, too late to be of any use" (Van den Akker, 1999, p. 2).

Moreover, there was an interesting institutional force that set a particular type of research into motion: The University of Twente was founded as a technological university with a distinct engineering spirit. In that context, its Faculty of Education tried to educate so-called educational engineers or designers. Their educational program was not only rooted in the social sciences (pedagogy, psychology, sociology), but also strongly in the engineering sciences.

In line with Simon's (1967) idea, education was considered a design science. Given this context, scholars such as Tjeerd Plomp and Jan van den Akker, and their PhD students Nienke Nieveen and Susan McKenney, thought deeply about what it means to take an engineering perspective on educational science. The scholars from Twente had connections with colleagues from the US such as Tom Reeves, who was (like his former supervisor Don Ely) also interested in educational technology – a topic that was upcoming due to its rapidly growing possibilities (Plomp, Feteris, Pieters, & Tomic, 1992; Jan van den Akker & Plomp, 1993). The orientation was mainly research-based design: the design of high-quality educational interventions in a research-based, systematic way.

One disadvantage of the terms *development* and *developmental* is their connotations of developmental psychology and research on children's development of concepts (cf. Bronfenbrenner, 1979). This might be one reason the term is hardly used anymore, also not by the Twente curriculum scholars. Another reason, mentioned by Van den Akker (personal communication, September 7, 2016) is that in deliberation with his American colleague Decker Walker he agreed that *design* sounds more appealing and trendy than *development* given the upcoming trend of design thinking in many professional domains and academic disciplines (also think of the popularity of Danish design and Dutch design). The Twente approach to design research has been well documented in various publications in subsequent years (McKenney & Reeves, 2012; Plomp & Nieveen, 2010; Van den Akker et al., 2006) and applied in dozens of doctoral dissertations, for example in the second part of Plomp and Nieveen (2013) with 51 illustrative cases of educational design research.

Notes

1 https://en.wikipedia.org/wiki/Replication_crisis
2 lchcautobio.ucsd.edu

References

Abrahamson, D. (2009). Embodied design: Constructing means for constructing meaning. *Educational Studies in Mathematics, 70*(1), 27–47.

Anderson, T., & Shattuck, J. (2012). Design based research: A decade of progress in education research? *Educational Researcher, 41*(1), 16–25.

Artigue, M. (2014). Didactic engineering in mathematics education. In S. Lerman (Ed.), *Encyclopedia of mathematics education* (pp. 159–162). Dordrecht, the Netherlands: Springer.

Artigue, M. (2015). Perspectives on design research: The case of didactical engineering. In A. Bikner-Ahsbahs, C. Knipping, & N. Presmeg (Eds.), *Approaches to qualitative research in mathematics education* (pp. 467–496): Springer.

Bronfenbrenner, U. (1979). *The ecology of human development: Experiments by design and nature.* Cambridge, MA: Harvard University Press.

Brown, A. (1992). Design experiments: Theoretical and methodological challenges in creating complex interventions in classroom settings. *Journal of the Learning Sciences, 2*(2), 141–178.

Cobb, P. (2001). Supporting the improvement of learning and teaching in social and institutional context. In S. M. Carver & D. Klahr (Eds.), *Cognition and instruction: Twenty-five years of progress* (pp. 455–478). Mahwah, NJ: Lawrence Erlbaum.

Cobb, P., Confrey, J., diSessa, A., Lehrer, R., & Schauble, L. (2003). Design experiments in educational research. *Educational Researcher, 32*(1), 9–13.

Cobb, P., Jackson, K., & Dunlap, C. (2014). Design research: An analysis and critique. In L. D. English & D. Kirshner (Eds.), *Handbook of international research in mathematics education* (pp. 481–503). New York, NY: Routledge.

Cobb, P., Jackson, K., & Dunlap, C. (2017). Conducting design studies to investigate and support mathematics students' and teachers' learning. In J. Cai (Ed.), *First compendium for research in mathematics education* (pp. 208–233). Reston, VA: National Council of Teachers of Mathematics.

Cobb, P., & Steffe, L. P. (1983). The constructivist researcher as teacher and model builder. *Journal for Research in Mathematics Education, 14*(2), 83–94.

Cole, M. (2016). Designing for development: Across the scales of time. *Developmental Psychology, 52*(11), 1679–1689.

Cole, M., & Distributive Literacy Consortium. (2006). *The fifth dimension: An after-school program built on diversity.* New York, NY: Russell Sage Foundation.

Cole, M., & Packer, M. (2016). Design based intervention research as the science of the doubly artificial. *Journal of the Learning Sciences, 25*(4), 503–530.

Collins, A. (1990). *Toward a design science of education: Technical report*. New York, NY: Center for Technology in Education.

Collins, A. (1992). Towards a design science of education. In E. Scanlon & T. O'Shea (Eds.), *New directions in educational technology* (pp. 15–22). Berlin: Springer.

Collins, A., Joseph, D., & Bielaczyc, K. (2004). Design research: Theoretical and methodological issues. *Journal of the Learning Sciences, 13*(1), 15–42.

Confrey, J. (2006). The evolution of design studies as methodology. In R. K. Sawyer (Ed.), *The Cambridge handbook of the learning sciences* (pp. 137–143). New York, NY: Cambridge University Press.

Cronbach, L. J. (1975). Beyond the two disciplines of scientific psychology. *American Psychologist, 30*(2), 116–127.

De Jong, R., & Wijers, M. (1993). *Ontwikkelingsonderzoek: Theorie en praktijk [Developmental research: Theory and practice]*. Utrecht: NVORWO.

De Landsheere, G. (1985). History of educational research. *International Encyclopedia of Education, 3*, 1588–1596.

Design Based Research Collective (2003). Design based research: An emerging paradigm for educational inquiry. *Educational Researcher, 32*(1), 5–8.

Dewey, J. (1900). Psychology and social practice. *Psychological Review, 7*(2), 105–124.

Easley, J. A. (1977). *On clinical studies in mathematics education*. Columbus, OH: Ohio State University.

Elbers, E. (1993). Terugblik op de studiedag [Reflection on the conference day]. In R. De Jong & M. Wijers (Eds.), *Ontwikkelingsonderzoek: Theorie en praktijk [Developmental research: Theory and practice]* (pp. 131–138). Utrecht, the Netherlands: NVORWO.

Flis, I., & Van Eck, N. J. (in press). Framing psychology as a discipline (1950–1999): A large-scale term co-occurrence analysis of scientific literature in psychology. *History of Psychology*.

Freudenthal, H. (1968). Why to teach mathematics so as to be useful. *Educational Studies in Mathematics, 1*(1/2), 3–8.

Freudenthal, H. (1976). Preface. *Educational Studies in Mathematics, 7*(3), 189–190.

Freudenthal, H. (1977). *Weeding and sowing: Preface to a science of mathematical education*. Dordrecht, the Netherlands: Springer.

Freudenthal, H. (1987). Theorievorming bij het wiskundeonderwijs. Geraamte en gereedschap [Theory development in mathematics education. Framework and tools]. *Tijdschrift voor Nascholing en Onderzoek van het Reken-wiskundeonderwijs, 5*(3), 4–15.

Freudenthal, H. (1988). Ontwikkelingsonderzoek [Developmental research]. In K. P. E. Gravemeijer & K. Koster (Eds.), *Onderzoek, ontwikkeling en ontwikkelingsonderzoek [Research, development and developmental research]* (pp. 49–54). Utrecht: OW&OC.

Freudenthal, H. (1991). *Revisiting mathematics education: China lectures*. Dordrecht, the Netherlands: Kluwer Academic Publishers.

Ginsburg, H. P. (1997). *Entering the child's mind: The clinical interview in psychological research and practice*. New York, NY: Cambridge University Press.

Glaser, R. (1976). Components of a psychology of instruction: Toward a science of design. *Review of Educational Research, 46*(1), 1–24.

Goffree, F. (1979). *Leren onderwijzen met Wiskobas: Onderwijsontwikkelingsonderzoek 'wiskunde en didactiek' op de pedagogische akademie [Learning to teach Wiskobas. Educational development research]*. Utrecht, the Netherlands: Utrecht University.

Goffree, F. (1986). *Rekenen, realiteit en rationaliteit [Calculating, reality, and rationality]*. Inaugural speech.

Gravemeijer, K. P. E. (1988). Een realistisch researchprogramma? [A realistic research program?]. In K. Gravemeijer & K. Koster (Eds.), *Onderzoek, ontwikkeling en ontwikkelingsonderzoek [Research, development and developmental research]* (pp. 106–117). Utrecht, the Netherlands:Vakgroep OW&OC.

Gravemeijer, K. P. E. (1994). Educational development and developmental research in mathematics education. *Journal for Research in Mathematics Education, 25*(5), 443–471.

Gravemeijer, K. P. E. (1998). Developmental research as a research method. In A. Sierpinska & J. Kilpatrick (Eds.), *Mathematics education as a research domain: A search for identity* (pp. 277–295). Dordrecht, the Netherlands: Springer.

Gravemeijer, K. P. E., & Cobb, P. (2006). Design research from a learning design perspective. In J. van den Akker, K. P. E. Gravemeijer, S. McKenney, & N. Nieveen (Eds.), *Educational Design Research* (pp. 17–51). London, UK: Routledge.

Gravemeijer, K., & Koster, K. (Eds.) (1988). *Onderzoek, ontwikkeling en ontwikkelingsonderzoek [Research, development and developmental research]*. Utrecht, the Netherlands:Vakgroep OW&OC.

Gravemeijer, K. P. E., & Terwel, G. (2000). Hans Freudenthal:A mathematician on didactics and curriculum theory. *Journal of Curriculum Studies, 32*(6), 777–796.

Hoadley, C. P. (2002). Creating context: Design based research in creating and understanding CSCL. *Paper Presented at the Proceedings of the Conference on Computer Support for Collaborative Learning: Foundations for a CSCL Community.*

Jacob, E. (1992). Culture, context, and cognition. In M. D. LeCompte, W. L. Millroy, & J. Preissle (Eds.), *The handbook of qualitative research in education* (pp. 293–335). San Diego, CA:Academic Press.

Kanselaar, G. (1993). Ontwikkelingsonderzoek bezien vanuit de rol van advocaat van de duivel [Developmental research from the perspective of the devils' advocate]. In R. De Jong & M.Wijers (Eds.), *Ontwikkelingsonderzoek: Theorie en praktijk [Developmental research: Theory and practice]* (pp. 63–66). Utrecht, the Netherlands: NVORWO.

Koster, K. (1993). Ontwikkelingsonderzoek: Een overbodige categorie? [Developmental research:A superfluous category?]. In R. De Jong & M.Wijers (Eds.), *Ontwikkelingsonderzoek: Theorie en praktijk [Developmental research:Theory and practice]* (pp. 59–62). Utrecht, the Netherlands: NVORWO.

La Bastide-van Gemert, S. (2015). *All positive action starts with criticism. Hans Freudenthal and the didactics of mathematics.* Dordrecht, the Netherlands: Springer.

Laurel, B. (Ed.) (2003). *Design research: Methods and perspectives.* Cambridge, MA: MIT press.

Lave, J. (1988). *Cognition in practice: Mind, mathematics and culture in everyday life.* Cambridge, MA: Cambridge University Press.

McKenney, S., & Reeves, T. C. (2012). *Conducting educational design research.* London, UK: Routledge.

Moll, L. C., & Diaz, S. (1987). Change as the goal of educational research. *Anthropology & Education Quarterly, 18*(4), 300–311.

Nicolopoulou, A., & Cole, M. (2009). Design experimentation as a theoretical and empirical tool for developmental pedagogical research. *Pedagogies: An International Journal, 5*(1), 61–71.

O'Neill, D. K. (2012). Designs that fly: What the history of aeronautics tells us about the future of design based research in education. *International Journal of Research & Method in Education, 35*(2), 119–140.

Paas, F. (2005). Design experiments: Neither a design nor an experiment. In C. P. Constantinou, D. Demetriou, A. Evagorou, M. Evagorou, A. Kofteros, M. Michael, C. Nicolaou, D.

Papademetriou, & N. Papadouris (Eds.), *Integrating multiple perspectives on effective learning environments. Proceedings of 11th biennial meeting of the European Association for Research on Learning and Instruction* (pp. 901–902). Nicosia: University of Cyprus.

Papert, S. (1980). *Mindstorms: Children, computers, and powerful ideas*. New York, NY: Basic Books.

Pea, R. D. (1987). The aims of software criticism: Reply to professor Papert. *Educational Researcher, 16*(5), 4–8.

Penuel, W. R. (2014). Emerging forms of formative intervention research in education. *Mind, Culture, and Activity, 21*(2), 97–117.

Plomp, T., Feteris, A., Pieters, J. M., & Tomic, W. (Eds.) (1992). *Ontwerpen van onderwijs en trainingen* [Designing education and training]. Utrecht, the Netherlands: Lemma.

Plomp, T., & Nieveen, N. (2010). *An introduction to educational design research*. Enschede, the Netherlands: SLO.

Plomp, T., & Nieveen, N. (2013). *Educational design research: Introduction and illustrative cases*. Enschede, the Netherlands: SLO.

Prediger, S., Gravemeijer, K., & Confrey, J. (2015). Design research with a focus on learning processes: An overview on achievements and challenges. *ZDM Mathematics Education, 47*(6), 877–891. doi:10.1007/s11858-015-0722-3

Reinking, D., & Bradley, B. (2004). Connecting research and practice using formative and design experiments. In N. Duke & M. Mallette (Eds.), *Literacy Research Methodologies* (pp. 149–169). New York, NY: Guilford Press.

Reinking, D., & Bradley, B. A. (2008). *On formative and design experiments: Approaches to language and literacy research*. New York, NY: Teachers College Press.

Romberg, T. A. (1973). *Development research. Overview of how development-based research works in practice*. Madison, WI: Wisconsin Research and Development Center for Cognitive Learning.

Russell, T. L. (1999). *The no significant difference phenomenon: As reported in 355 research reports, summaries and papers*. Raleigh, NC: North Carolina State University.

Sandoval, W. A. (2004). Developing learning theory by refining conjectures embodied in educational designs. *Educational Psychologist, 39*(4), 213–223.

Schön, D. A. (1987). *Educating the reflective practitioner: Toward a new design for teaching and learning in the professions*. San Francisco, CA: Jossey-Bass.

Schoenfeld, A. H. (1992). Research methods in and for the learning sciences. *Journal of the Learning Sciences, 2*(2), 137–139.

Simon, H. A. (1967). *The sciences of the artificial*. Cambridge, MA: MIT Press.

Simon, H. A. (1996). *The sciences of the artificial* (3rd ed.). Cambridge, MA: MIT Press.

Steffe, L. P. (1991). The constructivist teaching experiment: Illustrations and implications. In E. Von Glasersfeld (Ed.), *Radical constructivism in mathematics education* (pp. 177–194). Boston, MA: Kluwer Academie Publishers.

Streefland, L. (1991). *Fractions in realistic mathematics education: A paradigm of developmental research*. Heidelberg, Germany: Springer.

Thompson, P. (1979). The constructivist teaching experiment in mathematics education research. *Paper Presented at the Annual Meeting of the National Council of Teachers of Mathematics*, Boston, MA.

Treffers, A. (1979). *Over onderzoek: Een samenvatting [About research: A summary]*. IOWO, Utrecht University. Utrecht. [unpublished manuscript]

Treffers, A. (1987). *Three dimensions. A model of goal and theory description in mathematics instruction. The Wiskobas project*. Dordrecht, the Netherlands: Kluwer.

Van den Akker, J. (1999). Principles and methods of development research. In J. van den Akker, R. M. Branch, K. Gustafson, N. Nieveen, & T. Plomp (Eds.). *Design approaches and tools in education and training* (pp. 1–14). Dordrecht, the Netherlands: Springer.

Van den Akker, J., Gravemeijer, K. P. E., McKenney, S., & Nieveen, N. (2006). *Educational design research.* London, UK: Routledge.

van den Akker, J., & Plomp, T. (1993, April). Development research in curriculum: Propositions and experiences. *Paper Presented at the AERA Annual Meeting.*

Van den Akker, J. J. H. (1988). *Ontwerp en implementatie van natuuronderwijs [Development and implementation of nature education].* Amsterdam, the Netherlands: Swets & Zeitlinger.

Van den Brink, J., & Streefland, L. (1979). Young children (6–8): Ratio and proportion. *Educational Studies in Mathematics, 10*(4), 403–420.

Van den Heuvel-Panhuizen, M. H. A. M. (1996). *Assessment and realistic mathematics education.* Utrecht, the Netherlands: University of Utrecht.

Van Die, H., & Knip, B. (1986). Conferentie ontwikkelingsonderzoek [Conference on developmantal research]. Panama-Post. *Tijdschrift voor nascholing en onderzoek van het reken-wiskundeonderwijs, 5*(3), 58–60.

van Parreren, C., & Carpay, J. (1972). *Sovjetpschyologen aan het woord [The voice of Soviet psychologists].* Zwolle, the Netherlands: Tjeenk Willink.

van Parreren, C. F. (1962). *Psychologie van het leren [Psychology of learning].* Deventer, the Netherlands: Van Loghum Slaterus.

van Parreren, C. F. (1988). *Ontwikkelend onderwijs [Developing education].* The Hague, the Netherlands: Acco.

Verschaffel, L. (1993). Inleiding [Introduction]. In R. De Jong & M. Wijers (Eds.), *Ontwikkelingsonderzoek: Theorie en praktijk [Developmental research: Theory and practice]* (pp. 9–15). Utrecht: NVORWO.

Wittmann, E. C. (1992). Didaktik der Mathematik als Ingenieurwissenschaft [Didactics of mathematics as an engineering science]. *Zentralblatt für Didaktik der Mathematik, 3,* 119–121.

Intermezzo I: a fictive dialogue between two research approaches

Two educational researchers, Arcy T. (RCT) and Daisy R. (DR), enter the stage. Arcy has mainly used randomized controlled trials in his research whereas Daisy considers herself a design researcher.

RCT The most important thing to know about an educational approach or tool is if it works.

DR This is an important thing to know, but how do you get to a good approach that is worth comparing with other approaches?

RCT Well, I am a researcher. Other people are designers. I study variables that matter, so that others can use the insights from research to design and implement good educational approaches.

DR This split between research and design has not been very productive in the past. I am the daughter of a researcher and a designer. My mother – a professor of education – was frustrated that insights from research were not picked up by practitioners, and my father – a curriculum designer – then always noted that research hardly ever produced insights that he could use in his design work. If ever the gap between research and design has to be closed then we need design based research and research-based design, and people who are trained as both designers and researchers. So here I am, a design researcher.

RCT The apple did not fall far from the tree, my grandfather used to say.

DR I don't claim to be original. Many people have done design research before it had that name. They talked about development or developmental research, which many people assumed to be about the psychology of child development.[1] The researchers using the terms development or developmental research just did not do a great job in branding and marketing their work.

RCT But what I don't understand is: If you intertwine design and research, how are you going to make scientific claims?

DR That depends on the stage in which the design and research are. In the beginning, I try to understand the problem, talk to potential users, do a needs analysis, formulate sensible learning goals, design something and improve it, see how useful people find it, and so on. My evaluations are then formative. And yes, if ever I get to the stage of summative evaluation, then I will separate design and research, and even ask someone else to evaluate my products and ideas. But mind you, your colleague Cronbach already wrote: Generalizations are always working hypotheses, not definitive conclusions.[2]

RCT OK, but that working hypothesis is then at least based on clear conditions.

DR But look at your other colleagues: They do experiments all the time before they know what matters; they sometimes naively[3] think that one or two variables are the key to improvement, and they hardly make an effort to measure validly. The control they need for warranted claims is impossible to achieve in ecologically valid situations. The frustrating thing for us is that your quantitatively oriented colleagues get away with it! They sweep problematic or contextual issues under the rug.

RCT Are you jealous? Our research is paid for by society. Policy-makers and stakeholders want to know what works. That is what the *What Works Clearinghouse*[4] is for.

DR Point taken, society pays, but now you give them false security. You just take advantage of silly rules such as the fact that 80% of the American research funding in education has to be spent on research following the so-called gold standard of randomized controlled trials, RCTs.

RCT Wait a minute! I can't help politics. And what do you mean, false security? RCTs are the only way to underpin causality. Experimentation, conducted well, is still the most rigorous research approach under the sun.

DR Rigorous in one particular sense yes, but relevant? I know few RCTs that are relevant to education. It is well known that RCTs are rare, uninformative, extremely expensive, have high internal but low external validity, and I could go on for a while.[5]

RCT OK, I know the critique, and sure, education is context specific and each person's development is unique. The debate between experimentalists and people who believe human development is idiosyncratic is as old as psychology.[6] But we do not have anything better. And mind you, I am not saying research is only research if it is experimental. In astronomy, experiments are impossible, yet it is a "hard science." RCTs are especially good if there are clear alternatives and, as in medical research, they need to be complemented with implementation research. Great to know that particular drugs work better than others, but if people do not take them properly, what can you do?[7]

DR The same story with Dupont's fertilizers. When farmers complained that their fertilizers did not work, the company eventually discovered that farmers were not driving at a constant speed when fertilizing their land.[8]

RCT I wanted to add that physicists and chemists also do a lot of tinkering, constructing laboratory set-ups, and make discoveries before they put their hypotheses to the test in a true experiment.

DR So you agree that a context of discovery is needed before there can be a context of justification?[9]

RCT Sure! Think of the discovery of penicillin – a matter of serendipity.

DR So what if we use an approach to research-based design in which each design cycle is evaluated in a formative sense? We start with checking the relevance of the design intentions, make sure that the design is consistent with what is known in the literature and with its purpose, test whether it is practical, and test whether learning goals are indeed achieved. Rather than keeping fingers crossed that findings from RCTs hold in other settings too, we would have filtered for instrumental effect – to use your methodological language.[10]

RCT Wonderful, I am glad to see that you can take my perspective. Perhaps large-scale testing is not even necessary anymore. If only design research was done in such a systematic way! But of course one day I want to know if it works better than something else.

DR I have to admit that you are more open-minded than I expected. Perhaps I was biased myself. But what do you mean by "it works?"

RCT If the educational approach is effective of course.

DR I already thought so, but an educational approach is not like a drug or a mobile phone that you can hand over to people. Knowing the mechanisms, how the approach works, under what conditions, what to watch out for, etc., are also important.

RCT Sure. Practical knowledge and experience are also an issue in science laboratories. If you want to do something special you hire postdocs who can do it. But that practical knowledge, which Aristotle called *phronesis*, is not published in *Nature* or *Science*.

DR I do not aim for such publications with sky-high impact factors. Let's return to education. Teachers need good designs and a lot of practical wisdom to use them well. How are we going to get them to develop these?

RCT That is what teacher educators do, right? And apart from scientific journals for research reports there are also professional journals and publications for practitioners, which reminds me: Reports from design research are so long and hard to read. Who is going to read these, let alone understand them?

DR Yeah, thick descriptions are often necessary to do justice to the complexity of the situation.

RCT And how do you generalize then?

DR We follow the validity and reliability criteria of qualitative research.[11] Our designs and accompanying knowledge need to inspire others to do something similar. Our findings are generalizable if they are transferable to other situations, where they have to be adjusted to local circumstances.

RCT Do you think teachers do that? In my experience they want ready-made materials that they can use.

DR I know the problem. When I took part in the redesign of a curriculum, our task was to make units that were teacher-proof. Very frustrating.

RCT Back to being understood. We agreed, I think at least, that society pays us to do research to improve education, in the short or long term. Policy-makers and other stakeholders want to understand the outcomes of research. RCT has a clear logic that everyone understands.

DR Sure. Similarly, Aristotle offered a clear logic of syllogisms that everyone understands: Socrates is a man, all men are mortal, so Socrates is mortal.

RCT He was a genius. It took centuries before logic made any serious progress.

DR I agree, but syllogisms have played no role in the progress of science.[12]

RCT Because they are trivial? And purely deductive?

DR The problem, in my view, is that the validity of syllogisms depends on their structural form only.

RCT I am not following you. What has this to do with RCTs?

DR The logic of RCTs depends on the structure of the research design only.

RCT Sorry to interrupt. Here is one source of confusion. We RCT adepts are used to thinking in terms of research design, and you promote design research. Fred Paas wrote a funny paper titled "Design Experiment: Neither Design Nor Experiment."[13]

DR Yeah, I know. He plays with words. Where design for him means research design, for us it means the thing or environment we design. Where experiment for him means an RCT, for the design researcher it means the teaching experiment, or trying out in practice. But you asked what syllogism has to do with RCT.

RCT Right, I am hanging on to every word.

DR The consumer of the results from RCT does not need to know anything about the content of what was investigated to understand what a higher learning gain in an experimental condition compared to a control condition means. The consumer, and reviewer for that matter, only focuses on the form of the argumentation.

RCT That is a good thing: rigorous and easy to understand. A clear argumentative grammar that is separate from content.[14] What more could science offer?

DR Well, listen and shiver. In the history of logic we see increasing attention for content rather than purely form. Induction is taking content into account. Abduction is hypothesizing to the best explanation. Pragmatic reasoning has become a topic of research. Walton and colleagues[15] have identified 96 argumentation schemes used in pragmatic reasoning. There are even inferences that are completely dependent on content, material inferences.

RCT An example?

DR "Namibia is west of Botswana" follows from "Botswana is east of Namibia." This inference is fully implied by the content of the concepts of east and west.

RCT I learned something today, thanks, but uhm . . .?

DR Well, I want to counterbalance your preference for argumentative grammar that depends on the structure of argumentation only.

RCT All right, but what would an argumentative grammar for design research look like then?

DR Here is a suggestion by Cobb and colleagues[16] for mathematics education:

> "1 Demonstrating that the students would not have developed particular forms of mathematical reasoning but for their participation in the design study.
>
> 2 Documenting how each successive form of reasoning emerged as a reorganization of prior forms of reasoning.
>
> 3 Identifying the specific aspects of the classroom learning environment that were necessary rather than contingent in supporting the emergence of these successive forms of reasoning."

RCT Let me see. I see the logic of the first, but it is hard to demonstrate this, right?

DR I admit it requires an informed reader who knows how students in a particular grade typically reason.

RCT Then the second. Methodologists will automatically ask loads of questions. How many students showed these successive forms? How many miles of video were not analyzed because little of interest happened? I have seen too much cherry picking in design research reports.

DR I must admit that quality is sometimes a concern. Too often people adopt the term design research when they have done design but not proper research. They have been tinkering around and collected some data. Ah, design research, sounds good. That is what I do!

RCT Then third: How can one distinguish necessary aspects of a learning environment from contingent ones? I immediately think of research designs required to get satisfactory conclusions.

DR Design researchers use cycles. In that way they have variation across settings. If a finding is robust across cycles then we know something more.

RCT Yeah, nice, but the variation is not planned? Shouldn't you use strict replication?

DR That sounds naïve to me. You are aware of contextual issues, right? In education, strict replication is hardly possible. Even in the natural sciences replication is sometimes impossible. Take the biologists from one continent who want to replicate an experiment with the same plant species from another continent. It may not work. The plant really has to be offspring from the local variant.[17] Replication is not as strict as some people think. Robustness across variable settings is more interesting.

RCT What about these MOOCs – massive open online courses?

DR What about them?

RCT Well, some MOOCs are attended by tens of thousands of students. You can test multiple design alternatives on a few thousand students, even simultaneously. In this way you can combine the power of RCTs with the rationale of design research.[18]

DR I love how you never give up! You are a genius.

RCT So you embrace me, in the end?

DR: I do, wholeheartedly!

Arcy T. and Daisy R. lived together happily ever after.

Notes

1 The phrase developmental research was used by Goffree (1979), Freudenthal (1988), Streefland (1991), Gravemeijer (1994), Yackel and Cobb (1996), Lijnse (1995); development research was used by Romberg (1973) and Van den Akker (1999). For the term developmental research in the psychological sense, see for example Bronfenbrenner (1974).
2 Cronbach (1975, pp. 124–125): "When we give proper weight to local conditions, any generalization is a working hypothesis, not a conclusion."
3 Salomon (1990)
4 https://ies.ed.gov/ncee/wwc/
5 Frick (1998) is an interesting resource here that argues experiments are not really about generalization to a population but rather an indication of propensities.
6 Cole's foreword to Bronfenbrenner (1979)
7 Medical Research Council (MRC) (2000)
8 Gravemeijer and Kirschner (2007) Pedagogische Studien
9 Reichenbach (1938).
10 Cobb, Confrey et al. (2003)
11 Guba (1981) and Lincoln and Guba (1985)
12 Lakatos (1999); see Chapter 6
13 (Paas, 2005)
14 Kelly (2004); see Chapter 6
15 Walton, Reed, & Macagno (2008)
16 Cobb, Jackson, and Dunlap (2014, p. 490)
17 See the replication crisis entry at Wikipedia.
18 This idea was suggested by Anthony Kelly (personal communication 2 December, 2016)

References

Bronfenbrenner, U. (1974). Developmental research, public policy, and the ecology of childhood. *Child Development, 45*(1), 1–5.
Bronfenbrenner, U. (1979). *The ecology of human development: Experiments by design and nature.* Cambridge, MA: Harvard University Press.
Cobb, P., Confrey, J., diSessa, A., Lehrer, R., & Schauble, L. (2003). Design experiments in educational research. *Educational Researcher, 32*(1), 9–13.
Cobb, P., Jackson, K., & Dunlap, C. (2014). Design research: An analysis and critique. In L. D. English & D. Kirshner (Eds.), *Handbook of international research in mathematics education* (pp. 481–503). New York, NY: Routledge.
Cronbach, L. J. (1975). Beyond the two disciplines of scientific psychology. *American Psychologist, 30*(2), 116–127.

Freudenthal, H. (1988). Ontwikkelingsonderzoek [Developmental research]. In K. P. E. Gravemeijer & K. Koster (Eds.), *Onderzoek, ontwikkeling en ontwikkelingsonderzoek [Research, development and developmental research]* (pp. 49–54). Utrecht: OW&OC.

Frick, R. W. (1998). Interpreting statistical testing: Process and propensity, not population and random sampling. *Behavior Research Methods, Instruments, & Computers, 30*(3), 527–535.

Goffree, F. (1979). *Leren onderwijzen met Wiskobas: Onderwijsontwikkelingsonderzoek 'wiskunde en didactiek' op de pedagogische akademie [Learning to teach Wiskobas: Educational development research]*. Rijksuniversiteit Utrecht, Utrecht.

Gravemeijer, K. P. E. (1994). Educational development and developmental research in mathematics education. *Journal for Research in Mathematics Education*, 443–471.

Gravemeijer, K. P. E., & Kirschner, P. A. (2007). Naar meer evidence-based onderwijs? [Towards more evidence-based education?]. *Pedagogische Studien, 83*, 463–472.

Guba, E. G. (1981). Criteria for assessing trustworthiness of naturalistic inquiries. *Educational Communication and Technology Journal, 29*(2), 75–91.

Kelly, A. E. (2004). Design research in education: Yes, but is it methodological? *Journal of the Learning Sciences, 13*(1), 115–128.

Lakatos, I., & Feyerabend, P. (1999). *For and against method*. Chicago, IL: Chicago University Press.

Lijnse, P. L. (1995). "Developmental research" as a way to an empirically based "didactical structure" of science. *Science Education, 79*(2), 189–199.

Lincoln, Y. S., & Guba, E. G. (1985). *Naturalistic inquiry*. Thousand Oaks, CA: Sage.

MRC. (2000). *A framework for development and evaluation of RCTs for complex interventions to improve health*. Retrieved from www.mrc.ac.uk/documents/pdf/rcts-for-complex-interventions-to-improve-health/

Paas, F. (2005). Design experiments: Neither a design nor an experiment. In C. P. Constantinou, D. Demetriou, A. Evagorou, M. Evagorou, A. Kofteros, M. Michael, C. Nicolaou, D. Papademetriou, & N. Papadouris (Eds.), *Integrating multiple perspectives on effective learning environments. Proceedings of 11th biennial meeting of the European Association for Research on Learning and Instruction* (pp. 901–902). Nicosia: University of Cyprus.

Reichenbach, H. (1938). *Experience and prediction: An analysis of the foundations and the structure of knowledge*. Chicago, IL: University of Chicago Press.

Romberg, T. A. (1973). *Development research: Overview of how development-based research works in practice*. Madison, WI: Wisconsin Research and Development Center for Cognitive Learning.

Salomon, G. (1990). Studying the flute and the orchestra: Controlled vs. classroom research on computers. *International Journal of Educational Research, 14*(6), 521–531.

Streefland, L. (1991). *Fractions in realistic mathematics education: A paradigm of developmental research* (Vol. 8). Heidelberg: Springer Science & Business Media.

Van den Akker, J. (1999). Principles and methods of development research. In J. van den Akker, R. M. Branch, K. Gustafson, N. Nieveen, & T. Plomp (Eds.), *Design approaches and tools in education and training* (pp. 1–14). Dordrecht, the Netherlands: Springer.

Walton, D., Reed, C., & Macagno, F. (2008). *Argumentation schemes*. Cambridge, UK: Cambridge University Press.

Yackel, E., & Cobb, P. (1996). Sociomathematical norms, argumentation, and autonomy in mathematics. *Journal for Research in Mathematics Education, 27*(4), 458–477. doi:10.2307/749877

Chapter 3

Design principles, conjecture mapping, and hypothetical learning trajectories

Summary

Design research aims to produce actionable knowledge that can be used to achieve some educational goal through design. Such advisory knowledge is often summarized in terms of design principles, conjecture maps, or hypothetical learning trajectories. What these have in common is that they sit in between educational theory and practice, and that they always stay hypothetical. This chapter gives examples of design principles and conjecture maps, and of their evolutions, and highlights the possible functions of hypothetical learning trajectories in different phases of design cycles, and the relations between these advisory ideas.

Actionable knowledge and theories of action

As observed by Argyris (1996), most scientific knowledge is descriptive or explanatory. This also holds for the social sciences, including educational sciences: Much is known about, for example, the influence of motivation, interest, and attitude on achievement (e.g., Ma & Kishor, 1997); such knowledge can be seen as "after-the-fact" theories. However, much less is known about how to make students more motivated or interested. Admittedly, one could argue that inquiry-based and context-based approaches can make students more motivated or interested in science or mathematics (Bennett, Lubben, & Hogarth, 2007; Savelsbergh et al., 2016), but then the question still remains: How do we create high-quality inquiry-based or context-based teaching approaches? This question is relevant because – to mention just two examples – the nature of guidance and the choice of context are crucial for anyone who would realize such teaching approaches (Fechner, 2009; Furtak, Seidel, Iverson, & Briggs, 2012).

So teachers and educators do not only need "after-the-fact" theories, but also "before-the-fact" theories. In Argyris's (1996) words, they need *actionable knowledge* – knowledge about which actions under what circumstances will lead to which kind of intended consequences. Mintrop (2016, p. 76) notes such knowledge is both normative (what people find important) and empirical (what works). Theories of action thus make explicit the relations between values in education and knowledge about how to change practice effectively in the valued direction (e.g., in Mintrop's case more equitable education).

An example from management may clarify why the generalized knowledge generated by descriptive or explanatory experimental research may not suffice (Argyris, 1996). Such research often produces knowledge of the following kind: In circumstances C, if you use intervention I, the outcome will be O. A commonly used abbreviation, promoting additional insight into the mechanisms behind the intervention, is CIMO, standing for Context, Intervention, Mechanism, and Outcome (Batterham et al., 2014). The problem with management – and the same holds for education – is the research does not offer insight into how these circumstances C could be created in the first place. Furthermore, the circumstances cannot be controlled in the way that experimental researchers control them, and procedures cannot be implemented as cleanly as in the research that generated the insights on the relation to possible effects. Additional research could in principle perhaps identify all kinds of variables and extra factors that are also relevant, but as Argyris notes, the model produced then becomes so complex that managers cannot apply it anymore. For knowledge to be actionable, it also has to be relatively simple.

Management is an interesting domain to learn from because it is about organizing and creating organizations, just like education. This is unlike biology, chemistry, and physics, where most of what is studied is not created by humans (synthetic biology is one exception). It is for such reasons that Simon (1967) characterized education as a design science (see also Cole & Packer, 2016).

Design researchers seek actionable knowledge and theories of action. They aim to yield useful knowledge (tied to design) that is sensitive to context and yet general enough to use in new situations. Such knowledge is often summarized in the form of design principles, conjecture maps, or hypothetical learning trajectories. These all serve a similar function in that they are intermediaries between educational theory and practice (Bell, Hoadley, & Linn, 2004; Euler, 2017). They are formulated from theory-informed experiences in practice and practice-informed theory development, and hence bear the potential to bridge theory and practice. Another key feature is that they have a hypothetical nature.

I therefore continue this chapter with a general reflection on the importance of hypotheses or conjectures in design research. I then discuss design principles and conjecture maps because these are typically the most general formulations of starting points and outcomes of design research. However, design research is often also about development over time, which leads to the discussion of hypothetical learning trajectories.

The role of conjectures or hypotheses in design research

Put simply, a scientific theory can explain particular phenomena and predict what will happen under specific conditions. When developing or testing a theory, scientists typically use hypotheses – conjectures that follow from some emergent theory that still needs to be tested empirically. This means that hypotheses should be formulated in a form in which they can be verified or falsified (Popper, 1963). The testing of hypotheses is typically done in an experiment: Reality is manipulated according to a theory-driven plan. If hypotheses are confirmed, this is support for the theory under construction (Confrey & Lachance, 2000; Sandoval, 2004).

It is not always possible to put reality to the test within a short time frame. In such cases *thought experiments* can help out. Albert Einstein is famous for his thought experiments on relativity. Already at the age of sixteen he imagined what he would perceive if he could chase a light beam at the speed of light. Such thought experiments can yield insight even if it is not possible to carry them out empirically.

As a starting point, design researchers can also use thought experiments – thinking through the consequences of particular design ideas. When preparing an empirical teaching experiment, design researchers typically do a thought experiment on how teachers or students will respond to particular tools or tasks based on their practical and theoretical knowledge of the domain (Freudenthal, 1991).

In empirical experiments, a hypothesis is formulated beforehand. A theoretical idea is operationalized by designing a particular setting in which only this particular feature is isolated and manipulated. Experimental researchers do not change conditions during an experiment, as this would spoil the research set-up that allows them to generalize. In design research, however, researchers continuously take their best bets (Lehrer & Schauble, 2001), even if this means that some aspect of the learning environment or ecology during or after a lesson has to be changed. In many examples, researchers are involved in the teaching, or work closely with teachers or trainers to optimize the learning environment (Hoyles, Noss, Kent, & Bakker, 2010; McClain & Cobb, 2001; Smit & Van Eerde, 2011). In the process of designing and improving educational materials, for example, it does not make sense to wait until the end of the teaching experiment before changes can be made. This would be inefficient.

Design research is therefore sometimes characterized as a form of what Freudenthal (1978) and many French educators called *didactical engineering* (Artigue, 2015; Margolinas & Drijvers, 2015): Something has to be made with whatever theories and resources are available. Lévi-Strauss (1962) called this *bricolage*. The products of design research are judged on innovativeness and usefulness, not just on the rigor of the research process that is more prominent in evaluating true experiments (Gutiérrez & Penuel, 2014; Plomp, 2010).

Design principles

Back to the three topics of this chapter, design principles, conjecture maps, and hypothetical learning trajectories aim to capture the thought experiments or testable conjectures formulated in design research.

Format and example

One of the clearest approaches to design principles is provided by Van den Akker (1999, p. 9), which he later extended to the following format:

- *If you want to design intervention X [for purpose/function Y in context Z]*
- *then you are best advised to give that intervention the characteristics C1, C2, . . . , Cm* [substantive emphasis]
- *and to do that via procedures P1, P2, . . . , Pn* [methodological emphasis]
- *because of theoretical arguments T1, T2, . . . , Tp*
- *and empirical arguments E1, E2, . . . , Eq*

(Van den Akker, 2013, p. 67, emphasis in original)

Because of the many letters in this approach, some people semi-jokingly refer to it as the *alphabet sentence*. Note how this format combines the *how* and the *why*, and thus allows the researcher to connect a value (*why* in terms of purpose) with actions (*how* in terms of design or procedures) underpinned by arguments (*why* in terms of scientific knowledge and practical experience). Here is a concrete example adapted from Vervoort (2013, p. 240) on working with student teachers (pre-service teachers, so students who are learning to become a teacher):

> If you want to design an intervention in which rich media cases are used to support student teachers putting innovative pedagogical insights into practice, you are advised to:
>
> - use exemplary cases that link practice to underlying theory, because this allows teachers to conceptualize feasible practice (Barnett-Clarke, 2001; Merseth, 1996, 2008).
> - connect the use of rich media cases to a guiding task, because this encourages active learning and focuses the teachers' attention on the content of a case (Blijleven, 2005).
> - encourage dialogue about the content of the rich media cases, because case-discussion is essential for meaning making (cf. Carter, 1999).

- initiate a dialogue between a student teacher and a mentor teacher on exemplary cases about innovative pedagogical insights, because mentor teachers are able to make their practical knowledge explicit. This contributes to the interpretation of the cases and the application of the case content in student teachers' teaching practice.

(p. 240)

One subtle point to note is that Vervoort did not use the term "best" in her formulation. I think this is wise since this term may suggest that alternatives, of which this version turned out to be the best, have been compared. In design research such comparisons across conditions are rare. Comparison is typically done within or between design cycles, within a local optimization process as common in engineering practices (cf. Glaser, 1976). Van den Akker (2013) writes about this:

> Design principles include not only statements about the (substantive) what and (methodological) how of the intended interventions, but also offer theoretical explanations and empirical underpinning to justify these knowledge claims. Obviously these heuristic principles cannot guarantee success, but they are intended to select and apply the most appropriate (substantive and methodological) knowledge for specific design and development tasks.
>
> (p. 67)

Van den Akker's proposal is a format with an underlying logic, but this does not mean that a design principle always has to be put on a Procrustean bed. It was not his intention that design researchers would try to fit their advice into one sentence. Rather, the format points to necessary ingredients of the argumentation around a design principle. For example, Mintrop (2016, p. 225) formulated a design principle in slightly looser terms without reference to arguments (these can also be formulated in the surrounding text). The design principle involves an initiative of forming grade-level teams in which senior teachers help a large group of novice teachers with their classroom management:

> If one wants to improve on teachers' individual and collective competence in managing student behavior in a context characterized by tenuous orderliness, high numbers of novice teachers, and a climate of distress, systematic development of leadership on the part of senior teachers is a promising approach. One should train senior teachers in ways to help grade-level teams self-organize and deliberately address issues of distress, disagreement, and conflict to strengthen collective responsibility for student discipline. Promising activities to do this are listed in the report. Another iteration is required to find out how to better combine work-team development with more effective task processing. Activities aimed at preparing senior teachers for their dual role as grade-level team leaders and informal socializing agents went in the right direction, but need to be strengthened.
>
> (p. 225)

Note that the last part of this quotation, from "another iteration is required . . ." onward, emphasizes the temporary and hypothetical nature of the principle.

A step back: different meanings of principles

I have also seen many people struggle with the concept of design principles, so it may be worth stepping back and situating Van den Akker's (1999, 2013) design principle format and concrete cases such as Vervoort (2013) in the wider landscape of types of design principles. One source of confusion is that the concept has so many different meanings. To name a few possible meanings I have encountered:

- Value, ethical norm
- Criterion
- Guideline, heuristic, advice
- Prediction.

The word *principle* often means something like a value or ethical norm. "This type of teaching is against my principles," typically means something like: "it is not the type of teaching I envision as desirable" or even "I find this way of teaching unethical," for instance because not all students get equal opportunities. As Biesta (2007) noted, education is a normative endeavor. People may formulate principles such as equity, democracy, or building on students' ideas, as values on which they do not want to compromise. So even if ensuring these values would mean lower learning gains, they would not want to give in. Principles in this meaning cannot be tested empirically or improved. They can only be more or less persuasive, but one can judge to what extent they are realized.

Sometimes, the term design principle is used in the meaning of a criterion. Famous examples can be found in Collins's (1990) early work. For example, "All technology used in projects must have the ability to stop work and restart easily on another machine (probability or restart capability) in [sic] to achieve *continued use*" (p. 5, emphasis in original). Nowadays, such a criterion may sound trivial or archaic, but back then this feature had to be facilitated deliberately.

Greeno (2016) treats design principles as predictions: "If <design feature D>, then <learning outcome L>" (p. 635). If you do this under similar circumstances, something similar will happen. In this form, a design principle comes close to the actionable knowledge that many of us seek, and it can be empirically tested in different contexts. However, depending on how strictly and literally the principle is taken, the risk of conceptualizing it as a prediction is that it is likely to fail: Education is so context-sensitive that predictions are unlikely to turn out true in many different situations. For any viable prediction there is most likely a factor that could undo it (Bakker, 2017; see also Chapter 6). Moreover, the distance between design features and learning outcomes may be too large to find effects. This is why it may be wise to distinguish between design conjectures and theoretical conjectures (Sandoval, 2014), as explained later in this chapter.

A common alternative is to conceptualize design principles as guidelines, advice, or heuristics – something to consider and try out, with the common sense understanding that no two situations will be identical and that adaptation to local circumstances is always necessary. Note that a design principle is not just a command – do this or don't do that – but is always accompanied with reasons that underpin it and goals that are intended to be achieved. Van den Akker's (2013) design principles have this heuristic nature.

Note that values are inevitably at stake too. A design principle can thus be seen as, in Penuel's words, "a kind of amalgam of value and knowledge." In the interview he continued:

> It's always a value. And so, therefore, difficult to convince people that their design principles are wrong. But it ought to have some evidence to support it and I think to be a principle it ought to meet different possible embodiments, different kinds of designs but with interpretable results that are somewhat [. . .] concordant or in that provides some evidence for how robust that principle is in terms of its utility for helping people think about how to design things that then produce the learning processes that are expected or hypothesized to come from those principles – the application of those principles. So for me it's both [. . .] fact and value, it should be evidence-based but it always is a value commitment.
>
> (Penuel, personal communication, December 19, 2016)

This implies that a design principle is (in my own terms) a generalized design practice, with norms and documented history in a generalized and argumentative form so that it can be re-enacted when and where appropriate.

It still seems advisable to analytically distinguish what role values play in your design principle: starting point, aim, nice to have, or need to have? One way to tackle this amalgamated nature of design principles is by defining layers. For example, Kali and Linn (2007) make a distinction between meta-principles and pragmatic principles, where meta-principle may sound more normative (e.g., "make science accessible to all students") or give a general direction ("make thinking visible"). Pragmatic principles are advice on what to do more specifically and concretely ("connect to personally relevant examples"; "enable three-dimensional manipulation").

Example of evolving design principles

So far I have given examples of design principles as formulated at the end of a design research project. How to arrive at such design principles in a methodologically sound way is quite a different story. As a step toward answering that question, I now first turn to how such principles may evolve. Validation, viability, or robustness is ensured when such principles are used in subsequent design iterations, by the same research team or by others. If they do not work they are discussed and adjusted, and potentially dropped as having little value in the design process. This implies that generalization is not ensured by a methodological decision upfront, such as working with random samples from a population, but is sought in the iterative process of having the design principles do real work in design practice.

Generalization is, in Penuel's words, "an accomplishment in practice, not a property of the research we do . . . The proof is in how others take up our work and make use of it. And they do so effectively. That's really all generalization is" (personal communication, December 19, 2016). In more formal terms, Gutiérrez and Penuel (2014) state: "we define the generalizability of findings and theories developed through research as contingent on the uptake of research by local actors who must sustain programs." It was for such reasons that Kali (2008) instigated a web-based community[1] where people can upload their design principles and receive feedback on how other members of the community used them and with what results (see also Plomp & Nieveen, 2013, part B with the 51 illustrative cases of educational design research).

To give a sense of how a design principle can evolve in design cycles, I use an example from a design principle on giving feedback to peers in a university course (Kali, 2008). Apart from showing how the evolution of a set of principles can take place, it shows how such principles can be empirically studied, and how they can be reported succinctly. Note also how all principles have been formulated in actionable language.

On the basis of then current literature of peer evaluation (evaluation of student work by fellow students), Kali formulated the following principles in the first iteration of a philosophy of education course:

Pragmatic Principle:	Enable students to give feedback to their peers
Specific Principle One:	Involve students in developing the evaluation criteria for the peer evaluation
Specific Principle Two:	Ensure anonymity to avoid bias in evaluating peers
Specific Principle Three:	Make the synthesis of the peer evaluation results visible for learners. (Kali, 2008, p. 429)

One key indicator for the quality of peer evaluation was how well scores given by students correlated with the scores given by the course instructor. In the first round, Kali found only a moderate correlation that was not statistically significant ($r = .43$, $p = .10$). Qualitative analysis of the discrepancies between instructor and peer evaluations pointed to the difficulty some students had in handling personal viewpoints on other students' "extreme" views on education. She therefore decided for the next iteration that extra design principles were needed to help students differentiate between more objective and their personal viewpoints.

> Specific Principle Four: "Enable students to state their personal non-objective viewpoints about their peers' work"
> Specific Principle Five: "Design features to foster discussion about non-objective evaluation criteria."
>
> (Kali, 2008, p. 432)

The term *features* here refers to features of the online peer evaluation environment. In this second iteration, the correlation between the instructor and students' scores had improved compared to the first iteration ($r = .62, p = .03$). Yet qualitative analysis of other data sources indicated that the scoring had been influenced by cultural and political values, and that classroom norms had not always been respected.

For the third iteration, Kali (2008) thus decided to add a sixth specific principle:

> Specific Principle Six: "When the contents being evaluated are socially or culturally sensitive, avoid grading students according to peer evaluation results. Rather, evaluate students as evaluators."
>
> (p. 433)

The instructor then decided to pay more attention to classroom norms. The correlation between instructor and student scoring went up further ($r = .70$, $p = .02$). This quantitative comparison was complemented with data from questionnaire data and assessment. These data showed that student satisfaction and learning gains remained high. For further details, see Kali and Ronen (2005).

Conjecture mapping

A design principle comes close to what Sandoval (2004, 2014) calls a *high-level conjecture* – a general idea of how particular theoretical characteristics when embodied in a design lead to certain mediating processes that then support desirable outcomes. An example that Sandoval gives is: "Scientific argumentation requires appropriation of discursive practices of making, justifying, evaluating claims" (2014, Figure 3.1, p. 27). The main difference is that design principles are formulated in action terms with their hypothetical nature being implicit, whereas high-level conjectures are explicitly hypothetical and predictive. Sandoval's example can be reformulated as a design principle in the following way: "If you want to promote scientific argumentation, you are advised to ensure that students appropriate discursive practices of making, justifying, evaluating claims."

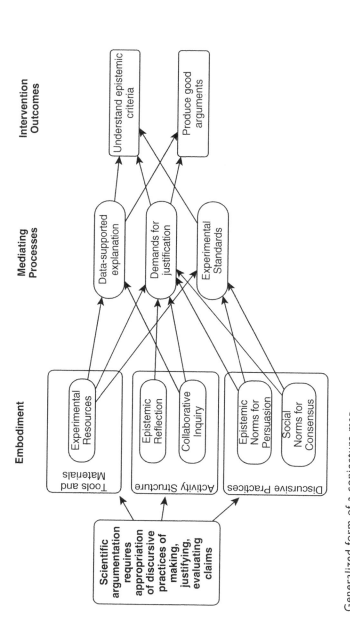

Figure 3.1 Generalized form of a conjecture map

Source: Sandoval (2014, p. 21). Reprinted with permission of the publisher.

One advantage of conjecture mapping is its link with methodology. It provides guidelines for how to approach design research ("method") and the underpinning logic ("-ology"), or in short, the *how* and the *why*. The idea of conjecture mapping stresses the importance of understanding the mechanisms that explain how particular design characteristics can lead to certain effects, processes, or outcomes. Without such insight there is no theory of improvement – no idea of how form and content of interventions contribute to the learning of teachers (theory of change) or students (theory of instruction) (Desimone, 2009; Van Veen, Zwart, Meirink, & Verloop, 2010). Many researchers consider the intermediate step of mediating processes important, because otherwise the distance between design characteristics and learning outcomes becomes too large to be investigable – a point I raised in relation to Greeno's design principles as predictions.

In Sandoval's framework, a *high-level conjecture* is a general idea about how to foster particular types of learning or achieve some educational goal. Such a high-level conjecture is *embodied* in a design, which should be conceptualized broadly to include tools and materials, but also activity structure, discursive practice, and even organizational infrastructure – for those who work at larger scale (Cobb & Jackson, 2011; Confrey, 2018; Penuel, Fishman, Cheng, & Sabelli, 2011). Characteristics of the design are assumed to lead to particular *mediating processes* (or mechanisms), which then are hypothesized to lead to certain intervention *outcomes* (learning goals, desirable change). Note that outcomes do not need to be only learning effects or products, but also can be intended procedures or processes.

I emphasize this point because design researchers in the arts and humanities sometimes stress that their learning goals are often not as clear-cut as in mathematics or science education. Yet I think the differences between the disciplines are not necessarily that big. Learning to speak Spanish (as an outcome) could indeed be practiced by speaking Spanish (as a mediating process), but the same holds for learning to model scientific phenomena (as an outcome), which is also often learned by engaging in modeling (as a mediating process). Of course it is not very helpful to make a conjecture map in which mediating processes and outcomes are the same (e.g., "speaking Spanish"). It makes more sense to specify both; for example, characterize the ways in which students practice speaking Spanish versus the quality of this skill (or particular aspects of it) as an intended outcome or learning goal.

One of the features of conjecture mapping that makes it a useful methodological tool in design research is that it distinguishes two types of conjectures that can be empirically tested. The first, *design conjectures*, have this form: "If learners engage in this activity (task + participant) structure with these tools, through this discursive practice, then this mediating process will emerge" (Sandoval, 2014, p. 24). In a conjecture map (examples in Chapters 18 and 19), design conjectures are the arrows between embodiment of a design and the mediating processes. So design conjectures make an explicit link between design characteristics and expected elicitation of mechanisms.

Theoretical conjectures, the second type of conjectures, have this form: "If this mediating process occurs it will lead to this outcome" (p. 24). So in a conjecture map the theoretical conjectures are the arrows between mediating processes and outcomes.

In my experience, trying to fit ideas for a design research project into this format is an excellent exercise to highlight the structure of what the design and research are about at a general level, in particular to stimulate thinking about mechanism or mediating processes (how the design works). However, as soon as the design researcher needs to hypothesize development at a smaller grain size, additional instruments or formats such as hypothetical learning trajectories may be necessary (see Chapters 18, 19, 21).

In my experience, Sandoval's conjecture mapping is not only a useful heuristic at the beginning of a project, but also at the end. Once you have arrived at a theoretically and practically informed high-level conjecture after cycles of empirical research, you can present the evolution of several conjecture maps in a row, succinctly pointing to the lessons learned during or after each cycle (as illustrated by Sandoval, 2014). Note that once you have such a conjecture map, you can also try to summarize it as a design principle in Van den Akker's (1999) format if you think that gets your message across to the reader more concisely or in more actionable terms (cf. Chapter 21).

What neither design principles nor conjecture maps capture explicitly is the micro-adjustment of a design and its accompanying conjectures. For example, in their explanation of conjecture-driven research design, Confrey and Lachance (2000) emphasize that conjectures evolve during and after teaching experiments. There can moreover be feedback loops between the design and conjectures, but also between design components (curriculum, classroom interaction, teacher role, assessment). This dialectical nature is not explicit in Sandoval's figures.

Another feature that is not captured in design principles or conjecture maps is that of development of learning or change. If your research is about a general strategy to be implemented, perhaps a repertoire of strategies where ordering the use of these strategies is left to the user, it may be sufficient to work with design principles or conjecture maps as illustrated in earlier sections. However, if sequencing is important, as in most domain-specific (didactical) instruction, something like hypothetical learning trajectories (HLTs) can be useful.

As Sandoval suggests, conjecture maps can provide useful input for HLTs that aim to predict how students could be supported from where they are to where teachers want them to be. The high-level conjecture formulates the general idea and the major design characteristics are specified, just like intended mediating processes and outcomes. What HLTs can specify is the means of support for moving from one stepping stone to the next. In that sense HLTs can be seen as more elaborate than conjecture maps.

Hypothetical learning trajectories

In an article on constructivist mathematics teaching, Simon (1995) introduced the idea of a mathematics teaching cycle. In short, the teacher has knowledge about mathematical learning goals and her students, and predicts in a so-called hypothetical learning trajectory how students may make progress from particular starting points to intended outcomes. During and after the lesson, the teacher assesses what students learn and checks if adjustments to the initial plan are needed. This feeds her knowledge about her students' mathematical knowledge, and the cycle can start again with a revised or new plan.

This idea of a teaching cycle is in line with the methodology of teaching experiments that involve "hypothesizing what the [learner] might learn and finding ways of fostering this learning" (Steffe, 1991, p. 177). Because both the concept of teaching experiment and HLT are sometimes misinterpreted, I cite Simon's original article at some length:

> The hypothetical learning trajectory is made up of three components: the learning goal that defines the direction, the learning activities, and the hypothetical learning process – a prediction of how the students' thinking and understanding will evolve in the context of the learning activities.
>
> (1995, p. 136)

Some people read the term to suggest that all students have to take one route, but Simon emphasized:

> "It characterizes an expected tendency. Individual students' learning proceeds along idiosyncratic, although often similar, paths. . . . The notion of a hypothetical learning trajectory is not meant to suggest that the teacher always pursues one goal at a time or that only one trajectory is considered. Rather, it is meant to underscore the importance of having a goal and rationale for teaching decisions and the hypothetical nature of such thinking.
>
> (pp. 135–136)

Although Simon originally used the term for lessons, nothing prevents us from using the idea for longer series of instructional activities (Clements & Sarama, 2004; Doorman, 2005; Drijvers, 2003). Another suggested adaptation was to include more explicitly hypotheses about teachers guiding students' learning processes, and therefore explicitly talk about hypothetical teaching-learning trajectories (Bakker & Van Eerde, 2015) or hypothetical teaching-learning strategies (Klaassen, 1995). The need for this was felt because in his teaching experiment Simon himself was the teacher, whereas many design researchers work with others as the teachers. Working as a researcher with a teacher (or teachers) generates a new layer of conjecture about what the teacher(s) might do or learn. For Simon, however, this inclusion of the word *teacher* is not necessary, because HLTs are part of the mathematics *teaching* cycle anyway (personal communication, February 1, 2017). In situations where readers may think that HLTs are about learning only, I am inclined to make it explicit that they are about teaching too, or insert the term *teaching* (HTLT).

A similar concept, more often used in science education, is that of a *didactical scenario* (Lijnse & Klaassen, 2004). *Learning progressions* are also worth mentioning, though they typically serve a different purpose, namely assessment, and cover longer-term learning processes (Wilson, 2009).

I stated that HLTs can not only summarize actionable knowledge about how to help students reach particular learning goals, but also have useful methodological functions. In the subsequent sections I discuss the functions HLTs can have in the various phases of design cycles.

Design cycles or iterations

What models of design research share is the emphasis on cycles or iterations. As Latour (2008) observed: "To design is always to redesign" (p. 4). The terminology to describe the different phases within such cycles differs. What seem quite general across design research projects are the following phases of each so-called macro-cycle of design research in terminology that can vary:

- Phase 1: preparation and design
- Phase 2: implementation (e.g., intervention, enactment, teaching experiment, trial)
- Phase 3: analysis and redesign.

Cobb, Confrey et al. (2003) emphasize the iterative nature of design research, but this does not mean that design researchers always repeat macro-cycles of design research. For example, Cobb, McClain, and Gravemeijer (2003) only used so-called micro-cycles in which they revised learning activities and tried revised versions in a next lesson. Their two-year study on statistical reasoning with mini-tools comprised a lesson series in Grade 7 and then one series in Grade 8. There was no repetition of macro-cycles within the study. However, ideas from this study were taken up by others (Bakker, 2004) and in subsequent projects directed by Cobb (Cobb, Zhao, & Dean, 2009; Henrick, Cobb, & Jackson, 2015).

I discuss the three phases now one by one, including the function of an HLT in each phase.

Phase 1: preparation and design

The first thing to decide is what exactly the design problem is. Do you want to solve a problem in education? Or do you have an idea of what may be feasible with new technology? Or are you convinced that other learning goals deserve more attention than they are currently given? At this stage precise research questions are not necessary, as long as you know your design problem. This is the phase to formulate an initial design principle, make a first conjecture map, or sketch a draft version of an HLT. The power of formulating an HLT in this early stage is that it forces you as a researcher to be as explicit as possible about your theoretical input and practical experiences, values, and goals. In my experience this helps communication with colleagues, but also starts a dialogue with yourself as a design researcher (Bakker, 2004).

It is evident that the relevant present knowledge about a topic should be studied. Inspired by Lévi-Strauss's (1962) idea of bricolage, Gravemeijer (1994) characterized the design researcher as a tinkerer or, in French, a *bricoleur*, who uses all the material that is at hand, including theoretical insights and practical experience with teaching and designing. This could include a historical study of the concepts you intend to teach as a source of inspiration of what obstacles students may encounter and what might be a suitable order of addressing topics in which kind of contexts (Bakker & Gravemeijer, 2006). In the first design phase, you decide what you want to design – tasks, sequences, learning environments – and what type of knowledge you want to generate.

Phase 2: intervention, trial, enactment, or teaching experiment

There are different levels at which you can intervene. Here I concentrate on teaching experiments – that is trials with individuals, pairs, small groups, or whole classrooms. For larger scale interventions see, for instance, the work by Cobb since 2009 (Cobb et al., 2009; Henrick et al., 2015). The function of an HLT at this stage is primarily to guide the enactment of the trial or teaching experiment and guide the data collection about phenomena in which you are most interested – related to mediating processes, mechanisms, and outcomes in your HLT.

The notion of a teaching experiment arose in the 1970s (Confrey, 2006). Its primary purpose was to experience students' learning and reasoning first-hand, and it thus served the purpose of eliminating the separation between the practice of research and the practice of teaching (Steffe & Thompson, 2000). Over time, teaching experiments proved useful for a broader purpose, namely as part of design research. During a teaching experiment, researchers and teachers use the activities and types of instruction that seem most appropriate at that moment. Observations in one lesson and theoretical arguments from multiple sources can influence what is done in the next session or lesson.

Hence, this type of research is different from experimental research designs in which a limited number of variables is manipulated and effects on other variables are measured. The situation investigated here, the learning of students in a new context with new tools and new end goals, is too complicated for such a set-up. Besides that, a different type of knowledge is sought, as pointed out earlier in this chapter: Design researchers do not only want to assess innovative material or a theory, but also need prototypical educational materials that could be tested and revised by teachers and researchers, and a domain-specific instruction theory that can be used by others to formulate their own HLTs adapted to local contingencies.

During a teaching experiment, data collection typically includes student work, tests before and after instruction, field notes, audio recordings of whole-class discussions, and video recordings of every lesson and of the final interviews with students and teachers. I further find mini-interviews with students, lasting from about twenty seconds to four minutes, very useful provided that they are carried out systematically (Bakker, 2004). These mini-interviews concentrate on key activities or points that are relevant to the HLT.

Phase 3: retrospective analysis

Dependent on your research question, different types of analysis can be useful in design research (Boeije, 2010; Ginsburg, 1997; Goldin, 2000; Mayring, 2015). Here I briefly allude to a task-oriented analysis and a more overall, longitudinal, cyclic approach. The first is to compare an HLT with the data on students' actual learning during the different tasks.

Dierdorp, Bakker, Eijkelhof, and van Maanen (2011) used an elaborate data analysis matrix (Table 3.1). The left part of the matrix summarizes the HLT and the right part is filled with excerpts from relevant transcripts and clarifying notes from the researcher, as well as a quantitative impression of how good the match was between the assumed learning as formulated in the HLT and

Table 3.1 Data analysis matrix for comparing HLT and actual learning trajectory (ALT)

Hypothetical Learning Trajectory			Actual Learning Trajectory		
Task number	Formulation of the task	Conjecture of how students would respond	Transcript excerpt	clarification	Match between HLT and ALT: Quantitative impression of how well the conjecture and actual learning matched (e.g., −, 0, +)

Table 3.2 Actual learning results compared with HLT conjectures for the tasks involving a particular type of reasoning

	5d	5f	6a	6c	7	8	9c	9e	10b	11c	15	17	23b	23c	24a	24c	25d	34a	42
+						x	x	x	x	x	x	x		x	x	x	x	x	x
±	x		x										x						
−		x		x	x														

Note: An x signifies how well the conjecture accompanying that task matched the observed learning (− refers to confirmation for up to 1/3 of the students, and + to at least 2/3 of the students)

Adapted from Dierdorp et al. (2011) with permission of the publisher.

the observed learning. With such an analysis it is possible to give an overview (Table 3.2), which can help to identify problematic sections in the educational materials. Insights into why particular learning does or does not take place help to improve the HLTs in subsequent cycles of design research. This iterative process allows the researcher to improve the predictive power of HLTs across subsequent teaching experiments.

An elaborated HLT would include assumptions about students' potential learning and about how the teacher would support students' learning processes. In the task-oriented analysis above no information is included about the role of the teacher. If there are crucial differences between students' assumed and observed learning processes or if the teaching has been observed to diverge from what the researcher had intended, the role of the teacher could be included in the analysis in search of explanations for these discrepancies.

A comparison of HLTs and observed learning is useful in the redesign process, and affords answers to research questions that ask how particular learning goals could be reached. However, in my experience additional analyses are often needed to gain more theoretical insights into learning processes (see also Chapter 21). A possible pitfall of working with detailed hypotheses is that design researchers may focus on small grain-size hypotheses that are very close to the data, with the additional risk of losing sight of other things that matter.

An example of a useful method for additional analysis is the *constant comparative method* (Glaser & Strauss, 1967; Strauss & Corbin, 1998) and Cobb and Whitenack's (1996) method of longitudinal analyses. I used this type of analysis in a study in the following way (Bakker, 2004): First, all transcripts were read and the videotapes were watched chronologically, episode-by-episode. With the HLT and research questions as guidelines, conjectures about students' learning and views were generated and documented, and then tested against the other episodes and other data material (student work, field notes, assignments). More concretely, this testing implied looking for confirmation and for counterexamples. The process of conjecture generating and testing was repeated for the whole data set. Seemingly crucial episodes were discussed with colleagues to test whether they agreed with our interpretation or could perhaps think of alternative interpretations. This process is called *peer examination*.

For the analysis of transcripts or videos it is worth considering computer software such as Atlas.ti (Van Nes & Doorman, 2010) or Nvivo for coding the transcripts and other data sources. As in all qualitative research, data triangulation (Denscombe, 2010) is commonly used in design based research.

Back to the challenge of summarizing the actionable knowledge generated

Although a useful methodological instrument in the various phases of design cycles, an HLT can get quite long and tedious, as you can infer from the example in Chapter 21. In my experience HLTs typically do not end up in journal articles, not even in online appendices. So, what would the average reader be interested in instead? One option is to focus HLTs on the main issues only. This is how Cobb uses HLTs (personal communication, July 25, 2016).

Another option is to turn to conjecture maps or design principles. Backed up by theoretically anchored and empirically grounded HLTs, one could formulate the main findings as a resulting conjecture map or design principle, as illustrated in Chapter 21.

Note

1 www.edu-design-principles.org

References

Argyris, C. (1996). Actionable knowledge: Design causality in the service of consequential theory. *The Journal of Applied Behavioral Science, 32*(4), 390–406.

Artigue, M. (2015). Perspectives on design research: The case of didactical engineering. In A. Bikner-Ahsbahs, C. Knipping, & N. Presmeg (Eds.), *Approaches to qualitative research in mathematics education* (pp. 467–496). New York, NY: Springer.

Bakker, A. (2004). *Design research in statistics education: On symbolizing and computer tools.* Utrecht: CD-β Press.

Bakker, A. (2017). Towards argumentative grammars of design research. In T. Dooley & G. Gueudet (Eds.), *Proceedings of the Tenth Congress of the European Society for Research in Mathematics Education (CERME10, February 1–5, 2017)* (pp. 2730–2737). Dublin, Ireland: DCU Institute of Education and ERME.

Bakker, A., & Gravemeijer, K. P. E. (2006). An historical phenomenology of mean and median. *Educational Studies in Mathematics, 62*(2), 149–168.

Bakker, A., & Van Eerde, H. A. A. (2015). An introduction to design based research with an example from statistics education. In A. Bikner-Ahsbahs, C. Knipping, & N. Presmeg (Eds.), *Approaches to qualitative research in mathematics education* (pp. 429–466). New York, NY: Springer.

Barnett-Clarke, C. (2001). Case design and use: Opportunities and limitations. *Research in Science Education, 13*(1), 309–312.

Batterham, R.W., Buchbinder, R., Beauchamp, A., Dodson, S., Elsworth, G. R., & Osborne, R. H. (2014). The OPtimising HEalth LIterAcy (Ophelia) process: Study protocol for using health literacy profiling and community engagement to create and implement health reform. *BMC Public Health, 14*(1), 694.

Bell, P., Hoadley, C. M., & Linn, M. C. (2004). Design based research in education. *Internet Environments for Science Education, 2004,* 73–85.

Bennett, J., Lubben, F., & Hogarth, S. (2007). Bringing science to life: A synthesis of the research evidence on the effects of context-based and STS approaches to science teaching. *Science Education, 91*(3), 347–370.

Biesta, G.J.J. (2007). Why "what works" won't work: Evidence-based practice and the democratic deficit in educational research. *Educational Theory, 57*(1), 1–22.

Blijleven, P.J. (2005). *Multimedia-cases: Naar een brug tussen theorie en praktijk [Multimedia cases: Toward a bridge between theory and practice].* Enschede, the Netherlands: University of Twente.

Boeije, H. (2010). *Analysis in qualitative research.* London, UK: Sage.

Carter, K. (1999). What is a case? What is not a case. In M. A. Lundeberg, B. B. Levin, & H. K. Harrington (Eds.), *Who learns what from cases and how? The research base for teaching and learning with cases* (pp. 165–175). Mahwah, NJ: Lawrence Erlbaum.

Clements, D. H., & Sarama, J. (2004). Learning trajectories in mathematics education. *Mathematical Thinking and Learning, 6*(2), 81–89.

Cobb, P., Confrey, J., diSessa, A., Lehrer, R., & Schauble, L. (2003). Design experiments in educational research. *Educational Researcher, 32*(1), 9–13.

Cobb, P., & Jackson, K. (2011). Towards an empirically grounded theory of action for improving the quality of mathematics teaching at scale. *Mathematics Teacher Education and Development, 13*(1), 6–33.

Cobb, P., McClain, K., & Gravemeijer, K. P. E. (2003). Learning about statistical covariation. *Cognition and Instruction, 21*(1), 1–78.

Cobb, P., & Whitenack, J.W. (1996). A method for conducting longitudinal analyses of classroom videorecordings and transcripts. *Educational Studies in Mathematics, 30*(3), 213–228.

Cobb, P., Zhao, Q., & Dean, C. (2009). Conducting design experiments to support teachers' learning: A reflection from the field. *Journal of the Learning Sciences, 18*(2), 165–199.

Cole, M., & Packer, M. (2016). Design based intervention research as the science of the doubly artificial. *Journal of the Learning Sciences, 25*(4), 503–530.

Collins, A. (1990). *Toward a design science of education: Technical report.* New York, NY: Center for Technology in Education.

Confrey, J. (2006). The evolution of design studies as methodology. In R. K. Sawyer (Ed.), *The Cambridge handbook of the learning sciences* (pp. 137–143). New York, NY: Cambridge University Press.

Confrey, J. (2018). Technological innovation and urban systemic reform: Designing for change. In L. S. Willams & M. Cozzens (Eds.), *Projecting forward: Learnings from educational systematic reform* (pp. 71–86). Bedford, MA: Comap.

Confrey, J., & Lachance, A. (2000). Transformative teaching experiments through conjecture-driven research design. In A. E. Kelly & R. Lesh (Eds.), *Handbook of research design in mathematics and science education* (pp. 231–265). Mahwah, NJ: Lawrence Erlbaum.

Denscombe, M. (2010). *The good research guide.* Maidenhead, UK: Open University Press.

Desimone, L. M. (2009). Improving impact studies of teachers' professional development: Toward better conceptualizations and measures. *Educational Researcher, 38*(3), 181–199.

Dierdorp, A., Bakker, A., Eijkelhof, H. M. C., & van Maanen, J.A. (2011). Authentic practices as contexts for learning to draw inferences beyond correlated data. *Mathematical Thinking and Learning, 13*(1–2), 132–151.

Doorman, L. M. (2005). *Modelling motion: From trace graphs to instantaneous change.* Utrecht, the Netherlands: CD-β Press.

Drijvers, P. H. M. (2003). *Learning algebra in a computer algebra environment: Design research on the understanding of the concept of parameter.* Universiteit Utrecht, Utrecht. CD-β Press.

Euler, D. (2017). Design principles as bridge between scientific knowledge production and practice design. *EDeR. Educational Design Research, 1*(1), 1–15. doi:10.15460/eder.1.1.1024

Fechner, S. (2009). *Effects of context-oriented learning on student interest and achievement in chemistry education* (Vol. 95). Berlin: Logos Verlag.

Freudenthal, H. (1978). *Weeding and sowing: Preface to a science of mathematical education.* Dordrecht, the Netherlands: Reidel.

Freudenthal, H. (1991). *Revisiting mathematics education: China lectures.* Dordrecht, the Netherlands: Kluwer Academic Publishers.

Furtak, E. M., Seidel, T., Iverson, H., & Briggs, D. C. (2012). Experimental and quasi-experimental studies of inquiry-based science teaching: A meta-analysis. *Review of Educational Research, 82*(3), 300–329.

Ginsburg, H. P. (1997). *Entering the child's mind: The clinical interview in psychological research and practice.* New York, NY: Cambridge University Press.

Glaser, B. G., & Strauss, A. L. (1967). *The discovery of grounded theory: Strategies for qualitative research.* Chicago, IL: Aldine.

Glaser, R. (1976). Components of a psychology of instruction: Toward a science of design. *Review of Educational Research, 46*(1), 1–24.

Goldin, G. A. (2000). A scientific perspective on structured, task-based interviews in mathematics education research. In A. E. Kelly & R. A. Lesh (Eds.), *Handbook of research design in mathematics and science education* (pp. 517–545). Mahwah, NJ: Lawrence Erlbaum Associates.

Gravemeijer, K. P. E. (1994). Educational development and developmental research in mathematics education. *Journal for Research in Mathematics Education, 25*(5), 443–471.

Greeno, J. G. (2016). Cultural-historical activity theory/design based research in Pasteur's Quadrant. *Journal of the Learning Sciences, 25*(4), 634–639.

Gutiérrez, K. D., & Penuel, W. R. (2014). Relevance to practice as a criterion for rigor. *Educational Researcher, 43*(1), 19–23.

Henrick, E., Cobb, P., & Jackson, K. (2015). Educational design research to support system-wide instructional improvement. In A. Bikner-Ahsbahs, C. Knipping, & N. C. Presmeg (Eds.), *Approaches to qualitative research in mathematics education* (pp. 497–530). New York, NY: Springer.

Hoyles, C., Noss, R., Kent, P., & Bakker, A. (2010). *Improving mathematics at work: The need for techno-mathematical literacies.* Abingdon, UK: Routledge.

Kali, Y. (2008). The design principles database as means for promoting design based research. In A. E. Kelly, R. A. Lesh, & J. Y. Baek (Eds.), *Handbook of design research methods in education: Innovations in science, technology, engineering, and mathematics learning and teaching* (pp. 423–438). Mahwah, NJ: Lawrence Erlbaum Associates.

Kali, Y., & Linn, M. C. (2007). Technology-enhanced support strategies for inquiry learning. In J. M. Spector, M. D. Merrill, J. J. G. V. Merriënboer, & M. P. Driscoll (Eds.), *Handbook of research on educational communications and technology* (3rd ed., pp. 145–161). Mahwah, NJ: Erlbaum.

Kali, Y., & Ronen, M. (2005). Design principles for online peer-evaluation: Fostering objectivity. *Paper Presented at the Proceedings of th 2005 Conference on Computer Support for Collaborative Learning: Learning 2005: The Next 10 years!*, Taipei, Taiwan.

Klaassen, C. W. J. M. (1995). *A problem-posing approach to teaching the topic of radioactivity.* Utrecht, the Netherlands: CD-β Press.

Latour, B. (2008). A cautious Prometheus? A few steps toward a philosophy of design (with special attention to Peter Sloterdijk). In J. Glynne, F. Hackney, & V. Minton (Eds.), *Proceedings of the 2008 annual international conference of the design history society* (pp. 2–10). Boca Raton, FL: BrownWalker Press.

Lehrer, R., & Schauble, L. (2001). Accounting for contingency in design experiments. *Paper Presented at the Annual Meeting of the American Educational Research Association*, Seattle, WA.

Lévi-Strauss, C. (1962). *The savage mind.* Chicago, IL: University of Chicago Press.

Lijnse, P. L., & Klaassen, K. (2004). Didactical structures as an outcome of research on teaching–learning sequences? *International Journal of Science Education, 26*(5), 537–554.

Ma, X., & Kishor, N. (1997). Assessing the relationship between attitude toward mathematics and achievement in mathematics: A meta-analysis. *Journal for Research in Mathematics Education, 28*(1), 26–47.

Margolinas, C., & Drijvers, P. H. M. (2015). Didactical engineering in France: An insider's and an outsider's view on its foundations, its practice and its impact. *ZDM, 47*(6), 893–903.

Mayring, P. (2015). Qualitative content analysis: Theoretical background and procedures. In A. Bikner-Ahsbahs, C. Knipping, & N. Presmeg (Eds.), *Approaches to qualitative research in mathematics education* (pp. 365–380). New York, NY: Springer.

McClain, K., & Cobb, P. (2001). Supporting students' ability to reason about data. *Educational Studies in Mathematics, 45*(1), 103–129.

Merseth, K. K. (1996). Cases and case methods in teacher education. In J. Sikula (Ed.), *Handbook of research on teacher education* (pp. 722–744). New York, NY: Macmillan.

Merseth, K. K. (2008). Using case discussion materials to improve mathematics teaching practice. *The Mathematics Educator, 11*(1), 3–20.

Mintrop, R. (2016). *Design based school improvement: A practical guide for education leaders.* Cambridge, MA: Harvard Education Press.

Penuel, W. R., Fishman, B. J., Cheng, B. H., & Sabelli, N. (2011). Organizing research and development at the intersection of learning, implementation, and design. *Educational Researcher, 40*(4), 331–337.

Plomp, T. (2010). Educational design research: An introduction. In T. Plomp & N. M. Nieveen (Eds.), *An introduction to educational design research.* Enschede: SLO.

Plomp, T., & Nieveen, N. (Eds.) (2013). *Educational design research: Part B: Illustrative cases.* Enschede, the Netherlands: SLO.

Popper, K. (1963). *Conjectures and refutations: The growth of scientific knowledge.* London, UK: Routledge.

Sandoval, W. A. (2004). Developing learning theory by refining conjectures embodied in educational designs. *Educational Psychologist, 39*(4), 213–223.

Sandoval, W. A. (2014). Conjecture mapping: An approach to systematic educational design research. *Journal of the Learning Sciences, 23*(1), 18–36.

Savelsbergh, E. R., Prins, G. T., Rietbergen, C., Fechner, S., Vaessen, B. E., Draijer, J. M., & Bakker, A. (2016). Effects of innovative science and mathematics teaching on student attitudes and achievement: A meta-analytic study. *Educational Research Review, 19*, 158–172.

Simon, H. A. (1967). *The sciences of the artificial.* Cambridge, MA: MIT press.

Simon, M. A. (1995). Reconstructing mathematics pedagogy from a constructivist perspective. *Journal for Research in Mathematics Education, 26*(2), 114–145.

Smit, J., & Van Eerde, H. A. A. (2011). A teacher's learning process in dual design research: Learning to scaffold language in a multilingual mathematics classroom. *ZDM The International Journal on Mathematics Education, 43*(6–7), 889–900.

Steffe, L. P. (1991). Operations that generate quantity. *Learning and Individual Differences, 3*(1), 61–82.

Steffe, L. P., & Thompson, P. W. (2000). Teaching experiment methodology: Underlying principles and essential elements. In R. Lesh & A. E. Kelly (Eds.), *Handbook of research design in mathematics and science education* (pp. 267–306). Hillsdale, NJ: Erlbaum.

Strauss, A., & Corbin, J. (1998). *Basics of qualitative research techniques and procedures for developing grounded theory* (2nd ed.). London, UK: Sage.

Van den Akker, J. (1999). Principles and methods of development research. In J. van den Akker, R. M. Branch, K. Gustafson, N. Nieveen, & T. Plomp (Eds.), *Design approaches and tools in education and training* (pp. 1–14). Dordrecht, the Netherlands: Springer.

Van den Akker, J. (2013). Curricular development research as specimen of educational design research. In T. Plomp & N. Nieveen (Eds.), *Educational design research. Part A: An introduction* (pp. 53–70). Enschede, the Netherlands: SLO.

Van Nes, F., & Doorman, M. (2010). The interaction between multimedia data analysis and theory development in design research. *Mathematics Education Research Journal, 22*(1), 6–30.

Van Veen, K., Zwart, R., Meirink, J., & Verloop, N. (2010). *Professionele ontwikkeling van leraren.* Leiden, the Netherlands: Universiteit Leiden.

Vervoort, M. (2013). *Kijk op de praktijk: Rich media-cases in de lerarenopleiding [A professional view on practice: Rich media cases in pre-service teacher education].* Enschede, the Netherlands: University of Twente.

Wilson, M. (2009). Measuring progressions: Assessment structures underlying a learning progression. *Journal of Research in Science Teaching, 46*(6), 716–730.

Intermezzo 2: design principles or learning trajectories?

Heather L. T. has a background in didactics (domain-specific pedagogy) and uses hypothetical learning trajectories (HLT). At a conference, she meets Desi P., who has a more general educational background and works with design principles (DP).

HLT Your talk about design principles was very interesting. I have done a lot of design research but never formulated a design principle.

DP Thanks! If not design principles, what do you work with instead?

HLT In the preparatory and design phase, I formulate hypothetical learning trajectories. I test them in trials – teaching experiments – and then compare my conjectures with what actually happened.

DP Interesting, but trajectories sound very linear.

HLT Yeah, I know, but they are not suggesting that all students follow the same path.[1]

DP I prefer landscape metaphors.[2]

HLT Sure, they are attractive, but you still need to shepherd students through a landscape. Would you be happier if I used the term hypothetical teaching-learning *strategy*?

DP I think so.

HLT But back to your presentation. I have never used the term design principle because I found it rather vague.

DP What's your problem with the term?

HLT Well, if I think back to how I have seen the term used, I can think of many different meanings. Some people use it to emphasize a value. For example, they do not want students to become robots that mechanically do rote learning. Some want to teach mathematics in a way that is accessible to all students rather than the happy few.

DP So principle in the sense of a valued choice, such as being a vegetarian, or an ethical norm such as "Thou shalt give thy students equal opportunities."

HLT Yes. Education is full of implicit norms of what people find important. For some, inquiry-based learning is important in itself, because they want students to engage actively in whatever they are doing and learning. They may want students to develop a better sense of the nature of science. Or they value interest, motivation, or a positive attitude as valuable in their own right. If they talk of design principles, these sound like something they want to achieve, irrespective of whether the approach is more effective in terms of achievement than alternative approaches.

DP Yep, as Biesta[3] argues, educational research is too often about effectiveness without proper discussion of what we value in education.

HLT All fine, but then some people use the term design principle as something that can be empirically tested. Sometimes principles sound like criteria – something required; this can indeed be empirically tested. For example, students should see the relevance of what they are learning, or have a motive to do or learn something. And sometimes principles sound like a prediction: If you do this, then that will happen.[4]

DP I have seen that too. Not sure if such claims can be made.

HLT I am relieved, because your "alphabet sentence" sounded a bit like such a prediction. Is it a prediction, a guideline, an advice, or a heuristic?

DP *Opens her laptop and shows a quote:*

"If you want to design intervention X [for the purpose/function Y in context Z], then you are best advised to give that intervention the characteristics A, B, and C [substantive emphasis], and to do that via procedures K, L, and M [procedural emphasis], because of arguments P, Q, and R" (Van den Akker, 1999).

DP The sentence literally says, "you are best advised to," but you are right: It has a heuristic nature. Whoever uses the design principle should treat it as a heuristic: something to use prudently, sensitive to local circumstances, with an eye on the argumentation and empirical examples. The design principle tries to generalize the lesson learned from the case in such a way that it can be transferred to another situation.

HLT The sentence sounds a bit abstract. What was your example again?

DP Here is Vervoort's example that I used in my presentation:

If you want to design a learning arrangement with multi-media cases to promote didactics–informed reasoned action by future primary teachers (purpose), in a competence-oriented program (context), then you can best stimulate a professional dialogue between student and mentor about innovative didactics (procedural emphasis). Then she continues to give procedural characteristics and arguments. For example, she advices to give explicit tasks to students when they watch multi-media cases of teachers teaching in classrooms. The argument is based on literature: Without such explicit tasks, students are inclined to skim through the videos.[5]

HLT Cool, I am convinced that the alphabet sentence can work!

DP It indeed took her a lot of work to get to this stage. But I heard from colleagues that they cannot always fit their ideas into this template.

HLT I indeed feared it could be a Procrustean bed.

DP What's that?

HLT Procrustes was a Greek mythical figure who stretched people if they did not fit his iron bed, or cut off parts of their bodies if they were too tall.

DP Horrible image.

HLT It is often used when people try to squeeze things into a rigorous template.

DP The alphabet sentence is meant to inspire, not to be an iron bed of one single size.

HLT Phew! But then, the sentence uses the phrase "best" as in "you are best advised to." How can you underpin such a claim if you do not compare alternatives?

DP "Best" here means the best advice that we can give now. But you are right, it may pretend more than it means. But it only means "best given our current knowledge." You want me to take out the "best?"

HLT Yes, then it is clearer to me that you are not making a predictive or comparative claim, but giving a heuristic or guideline.

DP Consider it done! *Types in the Powerpoint.*
But now I am curious what you use in your research.

HLT I do domain-specific pedagogy, or as Europeans say: didactical research. I am interested in how to teach specific topics in a discipline such as mathematics or science. So I have learning goals in mind: say B, and I study students' prior knowledge on that topic, say A, and I design ways of getting from A to B. I try to formulate possible routes in the form of a hypothetical learning trajectory (HLT), or hypothetical teaching-learning strategy – HTLS, if you like – that is both theoretically and empirically underpinned.

DP Makes sense. Sounds a bit like a design principle but then more detailed for specific topics and with a time dimension.

HLT I guess so.

DP And how do you use such an HLTs?

HLT That depends on the phase of the research. In the preparatory and design phase, it helps me make explicit what we think and try to achieve. I say "we," because we hardly ever work alone. I prefer to work with teachers and colleagues. In the trial phase, where we test the designed instructional sequence, the accompanying HLTs function as a guideline for teachers on what to focus and, for the research, on what to collect data. Then last, in the analysis phase, I compare the HLTs with what actually happened in the classroom. If conjectures were not supported, then I try to explain why and improve the tasks of the instructional sequence. If conjectures are supported, I keep them in.

DP That sounds quite systematic. All these hypotheses being tested. But might it become pseudo-scientific? What if most of your conjectures are refuted? Is your design bad or are your ambitions too high?

HLT Good point! In one case I concluded that I should work with older students, because some students complained that I tried to teach them "adult things," so my ambitions were too high. In other cases, I redesigned the tasks, for example when the context chosen did not evoke the type of reasoning I had hoped for.

DP So a percentage of conjectures being refuted does not say much. It really requires the judgment of a well-informed stakeholder to interpret the outcomes.

HLT Indeed, it is not like an RCT in which one or two main hypotheses are tested. The main goal of HLTs is to understand how tasks, tools, or instructional strategies help to foster certain types of learning.

DP They sound very local. To what extent are they generalizable?

HLT Whoever uses them elsewhere, or parts of them, has to adjust them to the local context. That is why the theoretical contributions of such research are often called humble. Still, I have seen examples of ideas successfully being used elsewhere. They turned out to be transferable.

DP Can you give an example?

HLT Bakker (2004) formulated the idea of growing samples as part of his HLT. Students are asked what they would do to find out something about children of their age – say weight, favorite song, or whatever characteristic they are interested in. They typically suggest measuring a few students – say two boys and two girls. Data are collected and a discussion is stimulated about how solid this information is. What would the data of a whole class look like? Would that be different? Then they predict the data for all students of that grade or all students in the country in that grade. In this process of growing samples, making and checking predictions with data, students reasoned about a lot of issues that matter from a statistical point of view. Plus they reasoned with emerging statistical concepts in relation to each other: population, sample, data, mean, mode, distribution, inference, prediction, different, coincidence, etc. This set-up worked very well in Bakker's design research in Grades 7 and 8, but others have tried it out too. Ben-Zvi[6] used it in Israel with younger students. German colleagues successfully implemented it with pre-service teachers. So the didactical idea was transferred, and turned out to be generalizable. But of course, the idea always has to be adjusted to local contexts.

DP Just like with design principles! But I do see a few differences. One is that your HLT is more explicitly concerned with a progression from students' prior knowledge to a particular learning goal.

HLT Yes, and HLTs are more explicitly formulated in terms of conjectures that can be tested, so my audience is researchers and teachers working with the design. Design principles seem to have a different audience: People who may want to apply the principles. Still I can imagine that the general idea behind an HLT can be reformulated as a design principle.[7]

DP That would be worth trying. Thanks for the chat!

Notes

1 Simon (1995)
2 See Fosnot and Dolk (2001); Bakker (2002)
3 Biesta (2009)

4 Greeno (2016)
5 Vervoort (2013)
6 Ben-Zvi et al. (2012)
7 See Chapter 21.

References

Bakker, A. (2002). Route-type and landscape-type software for learning statistical data analysis. In B. Phillips (Ed.), *Proceedings of the Sixth International Conference on Teaching Statistics Cape Town, South Africa*. Hawthorn: Swinburne Press.

Bakker, A. (2004). Reasoning about shape as a pattern in variability. *Statistics Education Research Journal, 3*(2), 64–83. Retrieved from http://www.stat.auckland.ac.nz/~iase/serj/SERJ3(2)_Bakker.pdf

Ben-Zvi, D., Aridor, K., Makar, K., & Bakker, A. (2012). Students' emergent articulations of uncertainty while making informal statistical inferences. *ZDM, The International Journal on Mathematics Education, 44*(7), 913–925.

Biesta, G. J. J. (2009). Good education in an age of measurement: On the need to reconnect with the question of purpose in education. *Educational Assessment, Evaluation and Accountability, 21*(1), 33–46.

Fosnot, C. T., & Dolk, M. (2001). *Young mathematicians at work: Constructing number sense, addition, and subtraction*. Portsmouth, NH: Heinemann.

Greeno, J. G. (2016). Cultural-historical activity theory/design based research in Pasteur's Quadrant. *Journal of the Learning Sciences, 25*(4), 634–639.

Simon, M. A. (1995). Reconstructing mathematics pedagogy from a constructivist perspective. *Journal for research in Mathematics Education, 26*(2), 114–145.

Van den Akker, J. (1999). Principles and methods of development research. In J. van den Akker et al. (Eds.), *Design approaches and tools in education and training* (pp. 1–14). Dordrecht, the Netherlands: Springer.

Vervoort, M. (2013). *Kijk op de praktijk: Rich media-cases in de lerarenopleiding [A professional view on practice: Rich media cases in pre-service teacher education]*. (Thesis), University of Twente, Enschede, the Netherlands.

Chapter 4

Research questions in design research

Summary

In this chapter I first make a distinction between a researcher's question and a research question. Then I address the issue of what counts as a good research question, summarize some of the discussions about research questions in design research, and propose a structure of a main research question and subquestions that may be suitable for a design research project or design study.

This chapter focuses on research questions in design research – a topic that has received little attention in the literature, even though research questions are at the heart of any research project. In Chapter 1, I characterized design research as focusing not on what was or is, but what *could be* (cf. Jacob, 1992, p. 321). This emphasis on future possibilities has consequences for the types of questions that design research aims to answer. As Reinking and Bradley (2004) write:

> To oversimplify for the sake of comparison, a controlled experiment might ask: "Which intervention is better on average, *X* or *Y*?" (What is best?) A naturalistic study might ask: "When implementing intervention X (or Y), what happens? (What is?) A formative [or design] experiment, on the other hand, is best suited for the following type of question: "Given that intervention *X* (or pedagogical theory *Y*) shows promise to bring about a valued pedagogical goal, can it be implemented to accomplish that goal, and, if so, how? (What could be?) (p. 153)

In some types of research, formulating the research question is rather straight-forward. For example, in experimental studies researchers are often interested in the effects of particular educational approaches. In a meta-analysis of experimental studies we conducted (Savelsbergh et al., 2016), phrasing the research question thus took little effort. We wanted to know: What are the effects of innovative teaching approaches on student attitudes in primary or secondary science or mathematics education? This is the question we stuck with all the way to the end of the project.

However, in design research it is often much harder to settle on a suitable question. Like in much qualitative research, it often changes even after the data have been collected. In my experience, many design researchers struggle with formulating good research questions, and in many cases the debate on formulations continues until the end of a project. In my interviews with experts several design researchers emphasized it is fine in design research to formulate research questions at a rather late stage of the project. New designs often lead to the discovery of new phenomena or problems worth investigating, so it is hard to predict what is worth asking at the start of the design and research process. However, experts also noted that they had seen examples of students who did not know what they were studying and used design research as an excuse for not yet having a research question.

If you start a design research project, my advice would be: list the questions you have – things you genuinely want to know – irrespective of whether they are suitable as research questions. Whether they are your own questions or proper research questions can be decided later, but at least make sure you have a well-defined design problem (see Chapter 9). Yet researchers have responsibilities toward funders and participants, so it is worth seriously *trying* to develop proper questions early on to guide your reading of the literature and data collection. This chapter provides some starting points.

Researcher's question or research question?

When you start your research project, you have many questions. These could for instance be about the theoretical framework you need, the methods and techniques you may use, or how to design for the learning goals you have in mind. In my experience, many students and early career researchers formulate initial questions such as these:

> How can playful narratives be conceptualized from a media and literary perspective?
> What is a useful framework for studying students' conceptions of the nature of science?
> What is a good definition of gamification in the context of second-language learning?

These are all theoretical questions. If you indeed intend to do a theoretical study, and the answer is unknown in the literature, then such theoretical questions could be good research questions. Answering a theoretical question could be done by means of a literature review with the aim of defining a problematic key concept that has so far been underdeveloped. Here is one example: Around 2008, in a project on promoting boundary crossing between school and work, my colleague Sanne Akkerman and I were dissatisfied with how the concept of boundary crossing was used in the literature. We decided to do a review study (Akkerman & Bakker, 2011) as a stand-alone study before we started to develop an intervention to improve students' boundary crossing. Theoretical clarification felt necessary to be able to make a genuine contribution to the interventionist literature based in vocational education. The review study formed that basis for a small-scale design study (Bakker & Akkerman, 2014).

However, in most cases questions like the aforementioned ones are what I call the *researcher's questions*. These are questions that the starting researcher should indeed ask, but the answer is not going to end up in the results section of a scientific publication. Rather, the hard work of conceptualizing, selecting a framework, or defining your key concepts typically goes into the theoretical background section of such a publication.

Something similar holds for methodological questions that students have. In initial research proposals, students often formulate questions such as these:

How can we determine students' ability to recontextualize cellular respiration to other contexts? (Wierdsma, 2012, p. 34)

How can the processes of learning and teaching during module X with characteristic C be described?

How can students' attitudes toward music apps be measured?

In most cases, these are questions that the researcher needs to answer in order to do the research. Hence the results of your hard work in deciding how to describe, measure, or compare end up in a methods section of an empirical paper. If the aim of your research is, for example, to describe characteristics of a design then you should not ask how these can be described. One way to phrase this point of criticism more generally is that the research function (see Chapter 1) should not be part of your research question. In this question, the function of describing is part of the question: How can X be characterized? The latter formulation is ambiguous because it suggests a process question and possibly a methodological question, whereas some students who ask this question intend it to be about the result of characterizing. In that case it is better to ask simply: What are the characteristics of X?

In design research proposals students often formulate questions such as the following:

How can an inquiry-based teaching and learning strategy for topic T in Grade 7 be designed?

How can game elements be designed into an open learning second-language environment?

If you take these questions literally, and this is what scientists are good at, then these questions are about the process of designing. Again, these are questions in which the function of the research is part of the question. Such formulations are not advised unless you do indeed want to study – in this case – the design process itself. However, the knowledge that design researchers in education typically aim for instead is insight into how particular learning and teaching processes can be supported, stimulated, elicited, promoted, fostered, or whatever is your preferred term. A better formulation for an empirical design study in education would be:

> What inquiry-based teaching-learning strategy in Grade 7 can help students learn topic T?
> How can an inquiry-based strategy support students to learn topic T?
> Which game elements enhance an open environment for second-language learning?

But what if you *are* interested in the design process and think you can contribute to the literature on this topic? Just as it is possible to write a theoretical or a methodological paper, it is possible to write a design paper in which you take the design process as the object of research. In that case, you probably need to draw on a different body of literature (see Laurel, 2003) than you do when you are mainly interested in how to foster particular types of learning. For example, in the sociology of science or in the field of adult expertise, scholars may be interested in the professional expertise of designers. They may be interested in how educational designers, scientists, and teachers collaborate in shaping a new course in which gamification is the key idea, and how they deal with dilemmas they face. Before you are tempted to embark on such an exciting project, make sure you can anchor your question in the right body of literature and preferably find a supervisor who is well versed in this discipline. However, if you do research in the educational or learning sciences, you probably will avoid a question like, "how can X be designed?" Some students said to me that these deliberations sounded like playing with words. Thinking of Oost's (1999) analysis of problem statements, I do not agree. A formulation such as "how can X be designed" is ambiguous as it could be about the process of designing or its product.

When researchers have made their theoretical, methodological, and design decisions, the answers to their own researchers' questions end up in the theoretical background and methods sections, not in the results sections of your publications; unless of course these answers turn out to be worth studying in their own right and justify a separate scientific publication. Then the questions are true research questions.

Criteria for research questions

The most important criterion is of course to formulate a genuine question – about something you really want to know. This curiosity is the driver of your project. At some point, and make sure you do not get paralyzed by scientific norms, you need to check if your questions meet the standard criteria (cf. Oost, 1999).

What counts as a good research question?

1   It addresses a *knowledge gap* (it makes no sense to ask a question if the answer is already known).
2   The question should be pragmatically and theoretically *relevant* (why put so much effort and resources into the research?).
3   Its main concepts are *precise and anchored* in the literature (how could we build on existing work?).
4   It should be *manageable*: It is answerable by means of research within a reasonable time frame and with available resources.
5   Its formulation should help the reader envision the *type* of research carried out (descriptive, evaluative, design oriented, advisory, etc.).

If you use subquestions, make sure that these, taken together, lead to an answer of the main research question. In some situations, subquestions are not required. Avoid more than four subquestions because readers find it hard to digest too many questions. Not every step in the project needs its own research subquestion.

Most researchers prefer one main question rather than two or more. They argue that one is always more general or important than the other(s). However, in some cases, it is artificial to formulate one question, for example if two questions can be answered by means of two subsequent studies. In that case, it may be possible to formulate one overall research aim rather than one main research question.

In the case of doing or reporting on a design study I think it wise to decide whether you are going for a descriptive, evaluative, predictive, design oriented, or advisory answer. Asking about characteristics of a design, a strategy, or learning process is a descriptive question. Asking about how an educational goal can be accomplished is an advisory question. As explained in Chapter 1, readers will expect different methodological approaches and types of results depending on the type of research question. Case studies go well with descriptive questions. Experiments and comparisons are often evaluative (what is better?). If you are after a design principle in the form of "if you want X, you are advised to do Y," then formulate your research question so that it will be recognized as an advisory one.

What- versus how-questions

You may wonder what type of question would then be suitable as the main question of a design research project. I have had several debates with colleagues and students about this. There seem to be two broad types of research questions in design research, and I have noticed that groups of design researchers often have a preference for one or the other type of formulation. The first is to ask about characteristics of some kind of intervention that has the intended effects. I call these *what*-questions. For example:

> What are characteristics of a valid and effective teaching and learning strategy to teach students about correlation and regression in such a way that they experience coherence between mathematics and the natural sciences? (Dierdorp, 2013, p. 12)
>
> What are the design characteristics for a practicable and effective learning, supervising, and teaching strategy that enables VMBO [pre-vocational] students to recognize the functionality of biological knowledge of reproduction in work placement sites? (Mazereeuw, 2013, p. 14)

At first sight this kind of formulation sounds attractive because it is through such characteristics that generalization can presumably take place: If a researcher knows the key characteristics that make a strategy (unit, module, instructional sequence, learning environment) work, then another researcher can try to make other strategies for other topics or domains with similar characteristics. It is assumed that similar results can then be expected. However, it is difficult to identify the key characteristics that really matter – a point I return to later in this chapter.

The second type of research question in design research is the *how*-question, for example:

> How can a learning-and-teaching strategy, aimed at the flexible use of biological concepts through recontextualizing, be structured? (Wierdsma, 2012)

I prefer to reformulate this question as something like this:

> How can a learning-and-teaching strategy focusing on recontextualising biological concepts support pre-university students (aged 15–16) in the flexible use of the concept of cellular respiration?

One advantage of such a how-question is that it asks what most design researchers want to know: how particular learning goals can be achieved or how an educational problem can be solved. In most cases, design researchers are dissatisfied with how particular topics are typically taught or introduced in the curriculum. They have an innovative idea about how to teach them alternatively, or they may even argue that new learning goals need to be achieved. If there are no satisfying examples in natural settings that can be studied, then the envisioned teaching and learning needs to be designed first.

A common critique of how-questions is that learning goals can be achieved in thousands of ways; why would one be happy with this particular way? How-questions are so open and broad. Even if it is not possible to find the best way, do you not want to find at least an effective and efficient way? The design researcher could answer, okay, but in our case, one solution to the problem is already an accomplishment. And there is nothing to compare it with, so the design researcher may be happy with anything that works. Only then can we compare with other ways of achieving educational goals, but first we need a route to particular, possibly innovative, endpoints. Such design researchers are successful once they have provided a proof of principle that, or how, something is possible (see Chapter 6). The next step is to improve effectiveness and efficiency, scale up, compare your own design with alternatives, etc. But the initial phase should not be skipped. It is only in the later stage, when designs are of sufficient quality and when enough is known about the relevant mechanisms, that evaluative or comparative research is sensible, and that randomized controlled trials (RCTs) are useful. Otherwise one may waste a lot of money on collecting data from a large sample, possibly finding very small effects, but having little idea as to what factors the differences can be attributed (cf. the no significant difference phenomenon described by Russel, 2001).

A common critique of a *what-are-the-characteristics*-question is: How do you know which characteristics ensure the success of your intervention? Can the results really be attributed to the characteristics you identified? Moreover, design researchers typically try to enact particular characteristics they think are worth exploring or enacting. In that case it could lead to circular reasoning when they ask about characteristics of a design that were intended. It may also sound odd to ask about characteristics of a design that does not yet exist. Nevertheless, as Euler (2017) argued, this is what design research often does: "The DBR research process begins with the following question: How can an aspired, initially vaguely formulated goal be reached by a yet to be developed design?" (p. 4). Last, educational units designed to have similar characteristics can have very different effects. Many different factors or characteristics are at stake that co-determine whether a design is effective (cf. Salomon, 1990).

In whatever formulation, what or how, one needs to consider upfront whether finding an answer is doable with the intended data collection and analysis, and one should give an answer to the question. The characteristics variant is a descriptive question and requires a descriptive answer: a well-argued list of characteristics that matter. The how-question requires a design oriented, predictive, or advisory answer: a well-argued strategy with empirical support for its accompanying hypothetical learning trajectory, conjecture map, or design principles.

Most experts I interviewed considered the aforementioned examples of what- and how-questions presented to them too broad for a PhD study. Some found the formulations across PhD projects rather similar, because one wants to know similar things in both formulations. However, several scholars preferred the how-questions because these emphasize the process of achieving particular learning goals or solving a particular problem. In terms of Cobb, Confrey et al. (2003), design research typically aims to provide insight into how particular means can support particular learning. This hints at the type of actionable knowledge claims that design research purports to deliver (Chapter 3). One disadvantage of the what-are-the-characteristics formulation is that it suggests descriptive research whereas design research ultimately has a different research function (to predict, design, or advise).

Would it be possible to combine strengths of both formulations? Yes, I think so. I have a preference for how-questions but with predefined characteristics of the strategy being specified, because this makes the question less open and allows for theoretical generalization based on characteristics. The two afore-mentioned versions of research questions can be combined, and in my view improved, by using the following format:

> How can a teaching-learning strategy with characteristics C_i support students to learn G?

If you do not design a strategy or do not work with students, the format can be adjusted to whatever design you work on and whatever learners or stakehold-ers you focus on or collaborate with. The learning goal can also be replaced by a broader educational goal (e.g., a more systemic change at a school or even national level).

If you look back at Wierdsma's (2012) original research question, you may notice something discussed before. First of all, the term *structured* is not so clear. To me it sounds similar to *designed*, in which case the research function is more clearly incorporated into the research question. Second, *students* are not speci-fied. Hence my attempt to reformulate:

> How can a learning-and-teaching strategy focusing on recontextualising biological concepts support pre-university students (aged 15–16) in the flexible use of the concept of cellular respiration? (a reformulation of Wierdsma's, 2012, research question)

Note that I also tried to formulate the characteristic of the strategy (recon-textualizing) closer to the strategy, and put the learning goal at the end of the sentence. Why do I care about this? I have often seen research questions like these: How can students learn G by approach or strategy A? Such formulations sound odd because the answer to the question "How can students learn G" is given in the question. If you are in the process of formulating a research ques-tion, also consider reading Chapter 19 because it discusses several versions of research questions in a design study.

Several experts stressed that such what- and how-questions are suitable only after a lot of research on the topic. In many cases, design researchers encounter problems or discover new interesting phenomena that catch their attention, so they never get to the stage where problems are resolved or the effectiveness of new designs can be tested. In such cases, you can use research questions that are similar to ones used in descriptive research such as case studies. Chapter 20 provides an example of a problem that design researcher Konrad initially experienced in implementing her ideas. She then felt forced to change her research topic and focus on teaching band classes rather than analyzing in detail what students had learned. So make your problems and frustrations the object of a new research phase or analysis, and they suddenly are an interesting phenomenon rather than problems!

Stumbling upon new problems or phenomena does not have to hinder the progress of research. A view expressed during the interviews by Abrahamson and diSessa was that design research provides a generative context. Because new types of learning are promoted, new phenomena can emerge and become the object of investigation. This view fits with the image of design research as a context of discovery. Once such phenomena can be evoked, they can be theorized or studied as interesting in their own right, with no or little reference to the broader design research context, using conventional research methods. For example, inspired by theories on embodied cognition and using design research, Abrahamson designed embodied tablet applications in which students have to solve proportional tasks. After some minor redesign and enrichment of the original design, we needed years of descriptive and explanatory research to understand how students solved these embodied tasks (e.g., Abrahamson, Shayan, Bakker, & Van der Schaaf, 2016; Duijzer, Shayan, Bakker, Van der Schaaf, & Abrahamson, 2017) before we felt ready to draw tentative conclusions about the benefits of variants within the tablet application.

A possible structure of research questions in a design study

So far I have concentrated on a format for the main question of a substantial design research project (design study). However, to answer such a big question, subquestions are often necessary. In this section, I propose a structure that seems to work for design research projects as carried out by master's and PhD students at our institute in classroom-based research.[1] Whether it works for professional development or different scale projects needs to be thought through and tested empirically.

When focusing on particular learning goals, the main question of a design research project could be formulated using the following format:

> *How can a teaching-learning strategy with characteristics C_i support students to learn G?*

Such a question asks about a structure between a goal G, a strategy to achieve that goal (design in which theoretical characteristics C_i are embodied). An answer also requires an evaluation of whether the goal has indeed been achieved. To answer this main question, a list of research question types to choose from could therefore be (for the logic behind it also see Chapter 6):

1   What is an appropriate learning goal for a particular group of students?
2   What is a teaching-learning strategy (design) that would help students to achieve this goal (or help teachers to support students in achieving that goal)?
3   How (well) was this strategy (design) implemented?
4   What were the effects/results of implementing this strategy (design)?
5   What would an improved design look like?

The first question is only necessary if such a learning or educational goal needs to be formulated. For example, in their early work in statistics education, Cobb and colleagues (Cobb, 1999; McGatha, Cobb, & McClain, 2002) did thorough reading to arrive at statistical distribution as a suitable learning goal. Bakker (2004) concluded after several cycles of design research that sampling should be added to this learning goal to prevent the one-sidedness in the Cobb et al. research. If you have a wild idea, you may first have to argue why you think your idea is worth pursuing. Or, as in design based implementation research (Chapter 1), you need a phase of negotiation with stakeholders about what the aims of the design research are, and what are the constraints and wishes.

Some design researchers may consider question two to be the heart of their work. Arriving at an answer is certainly a time-consuming and creative process of research-based design. The answer typically takes the form of a strategy description, a scenario, sometimes accompanied by a hypothetical learning trajectory (HLT), conjecture map, or design principle. The descriptive formulation chosen above (what is a design that. . .?) works better for me than, for example: "Can we design and effectuate a learning trajectory that guides students meaningfully through the multi-level mechanistic relationship between cell activities and molecular interactions?" (Van Mil, 2013, p. 23).

First of all, the use of "we" is problematic. The guidelines of the American Psychological Association (APA, 2010) state that "we" should only refer to the authors, not to some general but vague population of researchers or readers. Moreover, research is a collective endeavor, so it is not important if particular researchers (the authors) can design something, but whether it is possible in general. The second problematic feature is that the design function (design, effectuate) is part of the question.

Note that the word *effectuate* suggests enactment or implementation – the topic of the third type of subquestion I propose. Design research is more than design – it is predominantly research, so it is still an empirical question about how the strategy works in practice. At this point it is good to make a distinction between two approaches. The classical view on interventions is that implementation fidelity should be high. This means that we need to check whether the design (strategy, scenario, HLT) was implemented as intended. If not, then it is impossible to attribute effects to the design. If yes, by and large, then the effects found can be linked to the strategy. As O'Neill (2012) wrote:

> While reproducibility is a central value in basic science [. . .], it is problematic to adhere to in design fields like education because there are so many ways for the application of good ideas to be marred by poor implementation. In education as in aeronautics, one cannot prove that an idea will not work by implementing it badly, the way Robert Esnault-Pelterie [an airplane builder] appeared to have done with his copies of the Wright Flyer.
>
> (p. 134)

However, there is also a second approach to implementation, which treats implementation of a design or intervention not as the independent variable, but as a dependent variable. In naturalistic studies, formative interventions (Engeström, 2011) and sometimes also design research, what happens in practice as a consequence of using a new design is studied as a result rather than a condition. An in-between position – in line with design researchers' emphasis on ecological validity – has been put forward by Collins, Joseph, and Bielaczyc (2004):

> There is a web of interrelations between independent and dependent variables. The division between the two depends on what outcomes one is interested in. But changes in any variable can have effects on other variables through complex feedback loops. Hence, changes in a dependent variable may lead to changes in an independent variable, as when increases in engagement lead to increases in attendance. The language of dependent and independent variables is only meant to capture the distinction between outcomes we should consider and those variables that may affect the outcomes.
>
> (p. 38)

The next step does not depend much on which approach you take to implementation – independent, dependent, or viewing them as an ecology of factors: For the main question to be answered, the design researcher needs to check if intended goals have been achieved, otherwise she has no knowledge about how something can be achieved. Reaching a goal or achieving effects ideally include more than learning results on some tests (e.g., pre- and post-tests). Researchers may also have other aims such as raising interest or improving attitude, motivation, engagement, or particular forms of interaction that they value (e.g., scaffolding or dialogic teaching).

So far I have focused on design research that aims to support learners to achieve something. However, in some cases, the main question may also take the shape of solving a particular problem: How can educational problem Y be solved? When translated to solving an educational problem, the list of questions or studies could be as follows:

1 Problem or needs analysis.
2 Initial formulation of a potential solution to the problem.
3 Implementation of the intended solution.
4 Evaluation of to what extent the intended solution indeed solved the problem.
5 Advice on how to further resolve the problem (better or at a larger scale).

Such questions seem to work better for design research at a larger scale or more general orientation than the domain-specific pedagogical and didactical examples I have given so far. Think of curriculum change or professional development at scale (e.g., Confrey, 2018; McKenney, Raval, & Pieters, 2011) Cobb and colleagues work with districts to improve mathematics teaching at a large scale (e.g., Cobb, Jackson, Smith, & Henrick, 2017). Improving research-practice partnerships is also an increasingly common goal (Coburn & Penuel, 2016; Henrick, Munoz, & Cobb, 2016; Penuel, Fishman, Cheng, & Sabelli, 2011; Penuel & Gallagher, 2017). The design based school improvement discussed by Mintrop (2016) focuses often on equity-related improvements in education. For more background to the structure of questions proposed here, see Chapter 6 on argumentative grammars.

Let me return to the debate about what would be a suitable main question for a design study. Some design researchers are fine with a design oriented question as the main question, but to me this would be a research-based design. Design research aims to provide new scientific knowledge, not just a product (e.g., tools, educational materials, educational infrastructure). In my view, the main question of a design research project should therefore not be a design oriented question. But in design based research and design research, a new design is required to generate new knowledge with and about a new design. Hence, it is in my view fine to have a *subquestion* that is design oriented. The answer to this subquestion could be a description of the design (e.g., a unit, strategy, course, learning or teaching trajectory or approach).

In this section I presented an overall structure of a main question and subquestions. However, it may turn out that answering the main question is not feasible within one project. Perhaps one subquestion is too challenging or justifies a complete PhD project. It is also possible to divide the different subquestions between several collaborating master's students to keep the work manageable (see also Chapter 8). Chapter 6 dives deeper into the logic behind the structure proposed here.

Note

1 I thank Prof. Karel Stokking for interesting conversations on this topic. I also thank Christine Knippels and Paulien Postma for discussing and testing the structure as well as many different versions of research questions.

References

Abrahamson, D., Shayan, S., Bakker, A., & Van der Schaaf, M. (2016). Eye-tracking Piaget: Capturing the emergence of attentional anchors in the coordination of proportional motor action. *Human Development, 58*(4–5), 218–244.

Akkerman, S. F., & Bakker, A. (2011). Boundary crossing and boundary objects. *Review of Educational Research, 81*, 132–169.

APA. (2010). *Publication manual of the American Psychological Association* (6th ed.). Washington, DC: American Psychological Association.

Bakker, A. (2004). *Design research in statistics education: On symbolizing and computer tools.* Utrecht, the Netherlands: CD-β Press.

Bakker, A., & Akkerman, S. F. (2014). A boundary-crossing approach to support students' integration of statistical and work-related knowledge. *Educational Studies in Mathematics, 86*(2), 223–237.

Cobb, P. (1999). Individual and collective mathematical development: The case of statistical data analysis. *Mathematical Thinking and Learning, 1*(1), 5–43.

Cobb, P., Confrey, J., diSessa, A., Lehrer, R., & Schauble, L. (2003). Design experiments in educational research. *Educational Researcher, 32*(1), 9–13.

Cobb, P., Jackson, K., Smith, T., & Henrick, E. (2017). Supporting improvements in the quality of mathematics teaching on a large scale. In S. Doff & R. Komoss (Eds.), *Making change happen* (pp. 203–221). Wiesbaden: Springer.

Coburn, C. E., & Penuel, W. R. (2016). Research – Practice partnerships in education: Outcomes, dynamics, and open questions. *Educational Researcher, 45*(1), 48–54.

Collins, A., Joseph, D., & Bielaczyc, K. (2004). Design research: Theoretical and methodological issues. *Journal of the Learning Sciences, 13*(1), 15–42.

Confrey, J. (2018). Technological innovation and urban systemic reform: Designing for change. In L. S. Willams & M. Cozzens (Eds.), *Projecting forward: Learnings from educational systematic reform* (pp. 71–86). Bedford, MA: Comap.

Dierdorp, A. (2013). *Learning correlation and regression within authentic practices* (Doctoral dissertation), Utrecht University, Utrecht.

Duijzer, A. C. G., Shayan, S., Bakker, A., Van der Schaaf, M. F., & Abrahamson, D. (2017). Touchscreen tablets: Coordinating action and perception for mathematical cognition. *Frontiers in Psychology, 8*(144). doi:10.3389/fpsyg.2017.00144

Engeström, Y. (2011). From design experiments to formative interventions. *Theory & Psychology, 21*(5), 598–628.

Euler, D. (2017). Design principles as bridge between scientific knowledge production and practice design. *EDeR. Educational Design Research, 1*(1), 1–15. doi:10.15460/eder.1.1.1024

Henrick, E., Munoz, M. A., & Cobb, P. (2016). A better research-practice partnership. *Phi Delta Kappan, 98*(3), 23–27.

Jacob, E. (1992). Culture, context, and cognition. In M. D. LeCompte, W. L. Millroy, & J. Preissle (Eds.), *The handbook of qualitative research in education* (pp. 293–335). San Diego, CA: Academic Press.

Laurel, B. (2003). *Design research: Methods and perspectives.* Cambridge, MA: MIT press.

Mazereeuw, M. (2013). *The functionality of biological knowledge in the workplace. Integrating school and workplace learning about reproduction.* (Doctoral dissertation), Utrecht University.

McGatha, M., Cobb, P., & McClain, K. (2002). An analysis of students' initial statistical understandings: Developing a conjectured learning trajectory. *The Journal of Mathematical Behavior, 21*(3), 339–355.

McKenney, S., Raval, H., & Pieters, J. (2011). Understanding the design research process: The evolution of a professional development program in Indian slums. *Paper Presented at the AERA Annual Meeting*, New Orleans.

Mintrop, R. (2016). *Design based school improvement: A practical guide for education leaders.* Cambridge, MA: Harvard Education Press.

O'Neill, D. K. (2012). Designs that fly: What the history of aeronautics tells us about the future of design based research in education. *International Journal of Research & Method in Education, 35*(2), 119–140.

Oost, H. (1999). *De kwaliteit van probleemstellingen in dissertaties: Een evaluatie van de wijze waarop vormtechnische aspecten van probleemstellingen worden uitgewerkt.* Utrecht: WCC.

Penuel, W. R., Fishman, B. J., Cheng, B. H., & Sabelli, N. (2011). Organizing research and development at the intersection of learning, implementation, and design. *Educational Researcher, 40*(4), 331–337.

Penuel, W. R., & Gallagher, D. J. (2017). *Creating research practice partnerships in education.* Boston, MA: Harvard Education Press.

Reinking, D., & Bradley, B. (2004). Connecting research and practice using formative and design experiments. *Literacy Research Methodologies*, 149–169.

Russel, T. L. (2001). *The no significant difference phenomenon: A comparative research annotated bibliography on technology for distance education* (5th ed.). Chicago, IL: The International Distance Education Certification Center.

Salomon, G. (1990). Studying the flute and the orchestra: Controlled vs. classroom research on computers. *International Journal of Educational Research, 14*(6), 521–531.

Savelsbergh, E. R., Prins, G. T., Rietbergen, C., Fechner, S., Vaessen, B. E., Draijer, J. M., & Bakker, A. (2016). Effects of innovative science and mathematics teaching on student attitudes and achievement: A meta-analytic study. *Educational Research Review, 19*, 158–172.

Van Mil, M. H. W. (2013). *Learning and teaching the molecular basis of life.* (Doctoral dissertation), Utrecht University, Utrecht.

Wierdsma, M. D. M. (2012). *Recontextualising cellular respiration: Designing an learning-and-teaching strategy for developing biological concepts as flexible tools.* Utrecht: Utrecht University.

Chapter 5

Research quality in design research

Summary

This chapter is about the quality of research. It starts with technical criteria for a problem statement and continues with the concepts of validity and reliability in design research.

Some supervisors of design research advise their students to focus on design first, and then gradually learn more and more about research. In this way students and early career researchers keep their passion for what they care about, better education and high-quality design, while learning to think methodologically. Reading this chapter can be postponed until the reader is ready to think deeper about research quality. A possible disadvantage of starting with all these normative issues and criteria is that lists of norms and criteria can be quite intimidating and paralyzing. My advice to design researchers who come from a discipline outside education therefore is to take some time to get acquainted with the methodology. In the beginning common sense is good enough, but gradually you need to be able to write succinctly according to scientific practice about how you ensured issues such as validity and reliability.

Quality of a research project is not a singular characteristic. There are multiple criteria that good research should meet. For example, a research study should meet certain *technical* criteria (Oost, 1999) that relative outsiders can judge fairly well, but also methodological criteria such as validity and reliability. Moreover, funders or readers can expect the research to be innovative, or the products to be practically useful (Kelly, 2006; Phillips, 2006).

Technical criteria

In an analysis of 341 PhD dissertations, Oost (1999) judged their quality on the following technical criteria (standards of quality):

1   The problem addressed in the study should be *relevant* (both theoretically and practically).
2   It should be clearly *anchored* in a discipline (e.g., the learning sciences in general, geography education in particular).
3   It should be *precise*. This includes issues such as using key concepts (e.g., dialogic teaching, embodiment, modeling, problem solving, scaffolding) according to the state-of-the-art literature. Moreover, it should be clear what is known and unknown about your topic of investigation.
4   The methodology should be *functional*. This means that the proposed or used methodological approach and techniques help to answer your research question.
5   The key elements of your project should be *consistent*, meaning that they fit together in a logical way.

Only around 25% of these dissertations scored sufficient on all five criteria. In many cases, authors seem to assume that it is clear in which discipline their research is anchored, or they assume the problem addressed to be clearly relevant to the reader.

Oost (2003) later added another standard of quality (criterion): *exposition*.

6   The presentation of your work should be transparent. Good writing is essential here, just like clear data collection procedures, data analysis, and systematic data storage (when possible anonymous, but open access). Chapter 7 elaborates on writing up design research.

Methodological criteria: validity and reliability

The key concepts of research methodology are validity and reliability. Like quality, these are not singular concepts. First of all, within quantitative measurement they have a particular technical meaning that cannot easily be transferred to qualitative research. Some scholars have even suggested different terminology for qualitative investigation (e.g., Guba, 1981; Lincoln & Guba, 1985). To make communication among educational researchers easier, I prefer to specify what we mean by the key concepts of validity and reliability in the context of design research rather than use different terms.

In its simplest version, validity refers to the question of whether you are really measuring what you intend to measure. Reliability is primarily about whether findings are independent of the researcher, or more generally whether similar results can be expected under similar circumstances. A silly example may clarify the difference. Assume you want to test the quality of students' historical reasoning by means of a test. Someone proposes to give every student a 7 out of 10. This is indeed a very reliable procedure: A machine could do the grading, and it does not depend on who applies this rule. It is very simple to follow. However, it is clearly not a valid procedure. Most likely, students' abilities to reason historically are different, and thus require different grades. Two criteria need to be fulfilled: the attribute (in this case the ability to reason historically) really exists and variations in this attribute lead to variations in the measurement (Borsboom, Mellenbergh, & Van Heerden, 2004).

In quantitative measurement, the difference between validity and reliability is relatively straightforward. A measurement is valid if the mean of measurements is correct. It is reliable if the variation of measurements is small. Figure 5.1 shows the traditional bullseye metaphor to explain the different concepts. Another way of phrasing the difference is that reliability refers to the absence of unsystematic bias, whereas validity means the absence of systematic bias (Maso & Smaling, 1998). For example, in the bullseye with measurements spread out but with the correct mean, there is no systematic bias, only unsystematic variation. In the image with all measurements in the wrong place but closely together there is little unsystematic variation, but a clear systematic bias (too much to the top right).

So far, I have only referred to a very specific aspect of variability and reliability, namely measurement. In fact, the type of validity addressed so far is typically called *construct* validity, because it is about how well a particular construct (e.g., ability) is measured. Yet there are more steps in any research study that could endanger the validity and reliability of the study as a whole (see Table 5.1). After all, the study is as strong as its weakest link. To clarify this, let us consider some general steps in a design research project.

Whatever theoretical construct you focus on, it has to be a sensible one that is well defined, or at least at the frontline of where research in your field is, otherwise your study's validity may be at risk. One famous example is that of learning styles. Although they have been popular for a long time, several

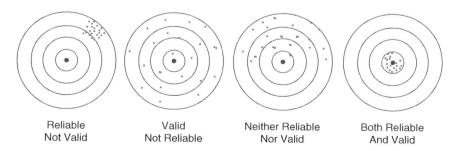

| Reliable | Valid | Neither Reliable | Both Reliable |
| Not Valid | Not Reliable | Nor Valid | And Valid |

Figure 5.1 Bullseye metaphor to explain valid and reliable measurement

Table 5.1 Aspects of validity and reliability in a research study

Aspect of the study	Validity issue	Reliability
Theoretical constructs	Well defined in line with the literature?	Can the sources be found?
Research design and procedure	Is the research design suitable for the question raised?	Can the procedure be (virtually) replicated?
Sampling procedure	Representative sample? (generalization; external validity) What is it a case of?	Can the sampling procedure be replicated; is it clear?
Instruments	Is it a valid instrument? (construct validity; consequential validity)	A reliable instrument?
Data collection	Are the data of high quality? (internal validity)	Making audio and/or video recordings to avoid memory problems Making transcripts
Data analysis	Has data triangulation or member checking been applied? (internal validity)	Using a coding scheme and measuring interrater agreement (interrater reliability)
Drawing conclusions	Have conclusions been drawn in a valid way? (Inferential validity)	Is the argumentation transparent? Does another researcher arrive at the same conclusions?

scholars have criticized the validity of the construct or have shown that empirical studies have not been able to show that differentiating for learning style has a positive effect (Kirschner & van Merriënboer, 2013). So it is advisable to be aware of the state-of-the-art discussion about the construct you are studying or taking as the point of departure (e.g., twenty-first century skills, attitudes, gamification, inquiry, modeling).

An obvious remark on reliability (transparency) here is that sources should be traceable. It is therefore advisable to cite sources in a widely read language in journals or books or documents available on the internet rather than sources in a language that few people read or documents that are hard to trace. If you write in English and cite a text in another language, it is advisable to add a translation of the title into English. See the guidelines of the American Psychological Association (APA, 2010) for details about citing and references (and many other issues about research).

In some cases, key ideas or phenomena still need to be defined. For example, the phenomenon of mothers scaffolding their children had already been described by Bruner (1975) as well as Wood and Middleton (1975) before it was clearly defined (Wood, Bruner, & Ross, 1976). When scholars wanted to use the concept for whole-class situations rather than dyads of parent and child or teacher and student, theoretical work had to be done to ensure that this was possible and justified (e.g., Smit, Van Eerde, & Bakker, 2013, a theoretical paper based on design research). Another example comes from statistics education: Many scholars considered informal statistical inference an important skill to be developed, but it took until 2009 before a satisfactory definition was proposed (Makar & Rubin, 2009).

A key concern in any quantitative study is the representativeness of the sample. If it is unclear how the sample was taken, it is unclear to what extent results can be statistically generalized beyond the sample studied. Therefore, researchers typically ask for random samples from a clearly defined population. Generalization is considered an issue of external validity. In qualitative studies, statistical generalization is typically impossible. In such cases, analytic or theoretical generalization is still possible and desirable. For example, a case study can be of such quality that its findings can be generalized in a theoretical sense (Yin, 1994).

In design research, such *analytic* or *theoretical generalization* is also feasible. For example, Smit and colleagues' (2013) research on whole-class scaffolding led to the identification of the phenomenon's features that other people recognize, and that we think also hold for scaffolding in other situations, even in the original situation of mothers scaffolding their children in solving a puzzle (Bakker & Smit, 2017).

When collecting data, you strive for the best possible quality of these data (an issue of internal validity). Think for a moment about conducting interviews about students' prior knowledge or their evaluation of a teaching experiment in terms of validity and reliability. What might systematic and unsystematic bias look like? An example of systematic bias would be a biased interviewer who steers answers in a particular direction or interprets them in a particular way. To avoid unsystematic bias, it helps to have well-prepared interview questions so that the same questions are asked in each interview. In semi-structured interviews it is possible to have the same set of questions, but with the freedom to follow interesting threads. An obvious way to improve reliability is to record the interviews on audio or video. This precaution avoids bias due to memory, and it allows for analysis by other researchers (reliability in the sense of independence of the researcher).

A common way to further improve internal validity is by means of *triangulation*. This can be done in multiple ways. Here I focus on data triangulation. If different types of data lead to the same conclusion, this enforces the validity of the findings. For example, in my own PhD dissertation (Bakker, 2004), I concluded from my observations in class (field notes), student work, and audio- and video-recording that our Grade 8 students did not expect variation between industrial products such as batteries in terms of life span. They thought that sampling one or two batteries would suffice to identify the brand's life span. Although one data source (video of students working on this task, field notes, student written work) would probably have been enough to draw this conclusion, the conclusion was stronger because of the underpinning from multiple data sources.

In the data analysis phase, conclusions of course have to be drawn in a valid way (*inferential validity*). In quantitative studies, the correct statistical techniques have to be used under the right conditions. In qualitative studies, the argumentation should be valid too.

Turning to reliability, an important test to check if the conclusions are independent of the researcher is to ask a second rater (or judge) to use the same coding scheme or book to check to what extent you agree. The percentage of agreement is a rather shallow measure of agreement. This becomes clear if you think of situations where agreement by chance is quite high, for example if there are only two codes (innocent vs. guilty; correct vs. incorrect). With two codes, the chance that raters agree merely by chance is already 50%. For this reason, Cohen has proposed a descriptive statistic, kappa (κ), which accounts for the chance of a code being attributed to a situation.

It is not so straightforward to interpret the height of kappas. There are some general rules of thumb such as ".8 is high." However, one should also take into account the wider context. A kappa of .71 about something as straightforward as mathematical answers being correct would make the experienced reviewer frown (Murphy, 1982). But a kappa of .68 for a situation in which something elusive was measured might be convincing enough. One further consideration is the number of fragments (excerpts, units) to be coded by a second coder. For this to be done well, scholars have proposed rules of thumb. One that gives a rough sense of the realistic number compared to the number of codes is Cicchetti's (1976) $2n^2$ rule: If n is the number of codes, ask your second rater to code at least $2n^2$ fragments. Some scholars prefer to use an alternative measure of interrater agreement, such as Krippendorff's alpha or the intra-class correlation (e.g., when having more than two raters). Note, however, that not all qualitative researchers find reliability checks so important. For example, Thomas (2013) writes they are overrated, but in my experience reviewers increasingly ask for interrater reliability measures.

Textbox 5.1

Question: Do I have to ask a second rater and measure interrater reliability?

Response: I advise this for analyses that really matter in justifying your main conclusions. However, if you are still at the stage of improving your design, it may be a waste of time.

In an era in which integrity and conscientiousness of scientific research are high on the agenda of both academia and politics, there is increased attention for ways to make research more transparent and replicable. Social psychology currently suffers from a bad reputation because so many studies do not yield the same results when replicated (Anderson & Maxwell, 2016; Open Science Collaboration, 2015). The replication crisis is much broader than in social psychology (see the replication crisis entry in Wikipedia).

Can design studies be replicated? After all, a design is typically developed for a particular learning context or culture, and offers creative solutions for an idiosyncratic situation. It thus seems impossible to replicate design studies. In qualitative studies it is therefore common to interpret replicability as virtual replicability, the ability to follow the whole research process so that the main ideas can be used in different situations with the necessary adjustments.

However, there are forms of replication that do make sense in my view. In Chapter 6, I refer to the Design Principles Database (Kali, 2008) as an initiative to use the same principles in various contexts to see how robust they are. It is also possible to try out the same didactical idea in various settings to see what its scope may be. As an example, I can mention an activity that I designed called *growing samples* (Bakker, 2004), which was inspired by an idea from Konold and Pollatsek (2002) and which others successfully used in a different country with a different type of students and even a different computer application (Ben-Zvi, 2006; Ben-Zvi, Aridor, Makar, & Bakker, 2012). I would call such traveling of ideas replication for variation rather than what is mostly meant by replication: reproducing a study in exactly the same conditions. Replication with variation tells us more about the robustness of design ideas and the scope of their usability.

So far I have addressed multiple aspects of validity and reliability. Over time, more and more distinctions have been made, with the risk of getting lost in details. One interesting, more holistic way to monitor the whole research process for methodological quality is through an *audit* (Akkerman, Admiraal, Brekelmans, & Oost, 2008). An outsider is asked to check a portfolio of all main elements of a study including its data, analyses, and findings, and report on the quality of how the study was carried out. This is a lot of work for both the researcher and auditor, but, if conducted properly, yields a convincing argument for the overall quality of the study.

References

Akkerman, S. F., Admiraal, W., Brekelmans, M., & Oost, H. (2008). Auditing quality of research in social sciences. *Quality & Quantity, 42*(2), 257–274.

Anderson, S. F., & Maxwell, S. E. (2016). There's more than one way to conduct a replication study: Beyond statistical significance. *Psychological Methods, 21*(1), 1.

APA. (2010). *Publication manual of the American Psychological Association* (6th ed.). Washington, DC: American Psychological Association.

Bakker, A. (2004). *Design research in statistics education: On symbolizing and computer tools.* Utrecht: CD-β Press.

Bakker, A., & Smit, J. (2017). Theory development in design based research: An example about scaffolding mathematical language. In S. Doff & R. Komoss (Eds.), *Making change happen* (pp. 111–126). Wiesbaden, Germany: Springer.

Ben-Zvi, D. (2006). Scaffolding students' informal inference and argumentation. *Paper Presented at the Proceedings of the Seventh International Conference on Teaching Statistics*, Salvador de Bahia, Brazil.

Ben-Zvi, D., Aridor, K., Makar, K., & Bakker, A. (2012). Students' emergent articulations of uncertainty while making informal statistical inferences. *ZDM Mathematics Education, 44*(7), 913–925.

Borsboom, D., Mellenbergh, G. J., & Van Heerden, J. (2004). The concept of validity. *Psychological Review, 111*(4), 1061.

Bruner, J. S. (1975). The ontogenesis of speech acts. *Journal of Child Language, 2*(1), 1–19.

Cicchetti, D.V. (1976). Assessing inter-rater reliability for rating scales: Resolving some basic issues. *The British Journal of Psychiatry, 129*(5), 452–456.

Guba, E. G. (1981). Criteria for assessing trustworthiness of naturalistic inquiries. *Educational Communication and Technology Journal, 29*(2), 75–91.

Kali, Y. (2008). The design principles database as means for promoting design based research. In A. E. Kelly, R. A. Lesh, & J.Y. Baek (Eds.), *Handbook of design research methods in education: Innovations in science, technology, engineering, and mathematics learning and teaching* (pp. 423–438). Mahwah, NJ: Lawrence Erlbaum Associates.

Kelly, A. E. (2006). Quality criteria for design research. In J. van den Akker, K. P. E. Gravemeijer, S. McKenney, & N. Nieveen (Eds.), *Educational design research* (pp. 107–118). London, UK: Routledge.

Kirschner, P. A., & van Merriënboer, J. J. G. (2013). Do learners really know best? Urban legends in education. *Educational Psychologist, 48*(3), 169–183.

Konold, C., & Pollatsek, A. (2002). Data analysis as the search for signals in noisy processes. *Journal for research in Mathematics Education, 33*(4), 259–289.

Lincoln, Y. S., & Guba, E. G. (1985). *Naturalistic inquiry.* Thousand Oaks, CA: Sage.

Makar, K., & Rubin, A. (2009). A framework for thinking about informal statistical inference. *Statistics Education Research Journal, 8*(1), 82–105.

Maso, I., & Smaling, A. (1998). *Kwalitatief onderzoek: Praktijk en theorie [Qualitative research: Practice and theory].* Amsterdam, the Netherlands: Boom.

Murphy, R. J. L. (1982). A further report of investigations into the reliability of marking of GCE examinations. *British Journal of Educational Psychology, 52*(1), 58–63.

Oost, H. (1999). *De kwaliteit van probleemstellingen in dissertaties: Een evaluatie van de wijze waarop vormtechnische aspecten van probleemstellingen worden uitgewerkt.* Utrecht, the Netherlands: WCC.

Oost, H. (2003). *Circling around a question: Defining your research problem.* Utrecht, the Netherlands: Utrecht University.

Open Science Collaboration. (2015). Estimating the reproducibility of psychological science. *Science, 349*(6251), aac4716.

Phillips, D. (2006). Assessing the quality of design research proposals. In J. Van den Akker, K. P. E. Gravemeijer, S. McKenney, & N. Nieveen (Eds.), *Educational design research* (pp. 93–99). London, UK: Routledge.

Smit, J., Van Eerde, H. A. A., & Bakker, A. (2013). A conceptualisation of whole-class scaffolding. *British Educational Research Journal, 39*(5), 817–834.

Thomas, G. (2013). *How to do your research project: A guide for students in education and applied social sciences* (2nd ed.). London, UK: Sage.

Wood, D., Bruner, J. S., & Ross, G. (1976). The role of tutoring in problem solving. *Journal of Child Psychology and Psychiatry, 17*(2), 89–100.

Wood, D., & Middleton, D. (1975). A study of assisted problem-solving. *British Journal of Psychology, 66*(2), 181–191.

Yin, R. (1994). *Case study research: Design and methods.* Thousand Oaks, CA: Sage.

Chapter 6

Argumentative grammars used in design research

Summary

Argumentative grammars connect the research question, via data collection and analysis, to warranted claims. In design research, argumentative grammars typically follow a different structure than that of, say, a randomized controlled trial or a case study. This chapter aims to spell out some of the possible argumentative grammars for design research. The simplest version is a proof of principle to show that something is possible. I also suggest an argumentative grammar that can assist in answering a research question of the following form: How can an intervention with characteristics C support learners to achieve learning goal G? This is a proof of principle for how something can be achieved.

The need for an argumentative grammar of design research[1]

Research reports such as scientific articles can be seen as a chain of reasoning: They first try to convince the reader of the relevance of filling a particular knowledge gap and of achieving a research aim that logically follows from this lack of knowledge. From this aim, connections are made with theory and research questions, which are addressed by using particular research methods. The analyses of collected data lead to warranted claims that answer the research question and are then discussed.

The previous chapters address elements of this chain of reasoning. Chapter 3 highlights the type of actionable knowledge that design researchers are after in terms of design principles, conjecture maps, or hypothetical learning trajectories. Chapter 4 discusses possible research questions that are suitable within design studies (specific investigations using the general orientation of design research). Chapter 5 dives into methodological issues involved in doing design research. The current chapter focuses on the "-logy" of methodology in terms of argumentative grammars, so the logic (from the Greek word logos, λόγος) behind using particular research methods. Awareness of different types of reasoning can also assist in writing clearly (Chapter 7).

An argumentative grammar in the words of Kelly (2004) is "the logic that guides the use of a method and that supports reasoning about its data" (p. 118). In the special issue on design research in the *Journal of the Learning Sciences*, he argues that design research is a valuable emerging set of methods in education, but he has methodological concerns. In his view, "the next task is to establish the logos of design research so that we can argue, methodologically, for the scientific warrants for its claims" (p. 115). He proposes that to become a methodology (method + logos), design research needs an argumentative grammar.

A methodology that already has a clear argumentative grammar is that of randomized field trials as introduced by Sir Ronald Fisher in the 1920s for agriculture. In such trials, also called randomized controlled trials (RCTs), researchers randomly attribute objects or subjects to an experimental or control condition so that they can assume that these two groups are equal on average except for receiving the treatment or not. Any differences between these two groups as measured through pre- and posttests can therefore be attributed to the difference in treatment. In terms of Toulmin's (1958) argumentation scheme, the grammar of RCTs can be represented as in Figure 6.1. One advantage of this methodology is that its argumentative grammar is a structure that "can be described *separately* from its instantiation in any given study so that the logic of a proposed study and its later claims can be criticized." (Kelly, 2004, p. 118, emphasis in original).

Kelly and other critical friends such as Shavelson, Phillips, Towne, and Feuer (2003) thus push design researchers to make warranted claims and go beyond purely narrative accounts. With Cobb and colleagues (2014, 2017), I think design researchers should indeed work toward argumentative grammars to increase the methodological quality of their research (see also Cobb & Gravemeijer, 2008). This chapter aims to sketch several options for such grammars.

The proposal made by Cobb and colleagues is (2014):

- Demonstrating that the students would not have developed particular forms of mathematical reasoning but for their participation in the design study.
- Documenting how each successive form of reasoning emerged as a reorganization of prior forms of reasoning.
- Identifying the specific aspects of the classroom learning environment that were necessary rather than contingent in supporting the emergence of these successive forms of reasoning.

(p. 490)

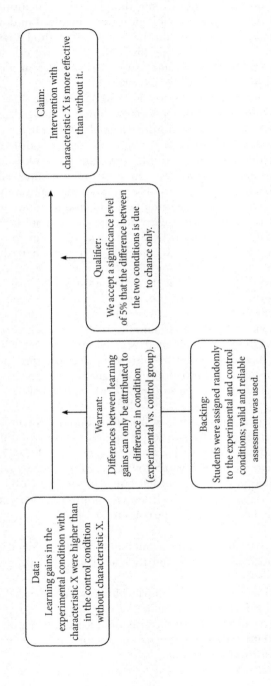

Figure 6.1 Argumentation scheme underlying a randomized controlled trial

Although these are important aims, it is hard to achieve them, in particular the first and the third. As one of my colleagues, Tommy Dreyfus, said: It is like proving you do not have a sister. Where demonstrating that you do have one can be quite easy ("here she is!"), the counterfactual case is difficult to prove. Assume you want to prove that B would not have happened without A. The assumed gold standard for showing causal relationship is the RCT, but this approach is certainly not without problems (e.g., Biesta, 2007; Olson, 2004; Smedslund, 2016; Worrall, 2002). Alternatively, in a single-subject design (where subjects serve as their own control), one could create conditions in which A does not happen, and check if B does not happen either (Horner et al., 2005; Kazdin, 1982). However, a rebuttal could be that there may be carry-over effects from an earlier to a later phase, and that there may be order effects.

The issue of causality in the social sciences is actually a very deep one that is outside the scope of this book, but interested readers are referred to Maxwell (2004) and Packer (2017). At the end of the chapter, I problematize Kelly's focus on the *structure* of argumentation. But first I propose simpler reasoning structures to alert early career design researchers to the types of claims they are able to make.

An example from mathematics: proof of existence

To develop a sense of what an argumentative grammar is all about, I start with the simplest relevant example I can think of: a proof of existence. In several disciplines, existence proofs are quite common. If biologists find a new species of orangutans, morphometric, behavioral, and genomic analysis can show that a specimen really has different features than species that were known until then (Nater et al., 2017). If a mathematician has to prove there are natural numbers bigger than 1 that are the sum of the digits to the third power, then it is sufficient to provide one number that fulfills this criterion.[2]

I use Toulmin's (1958) argumentation scheme as a way to summarize argumentative grammars. An advantage of this scheme is that it is simple and many people know it (its limitations are of little relevance to my purpose here). Spelling it out may come across as a bit exaggerated for an existence proof, but this is only preparation to focus more on the structure of argumentation in design research.

In Figure 6.2 the claim C we want to make is that there are natural numbers (more precisely: integers larger than 1, which is a trivial solution: $1^3 = 1$) equal to the sum of the cubes of their own digits. The presentation of one such number already proves this claim. A famous example is 153, which is considered data to underpin the claim. To warrant the connection between this data and the claim, we need to ensure that 153 does fulfill the criterion. Here comes the backing for this warrant: $1^3 + 5^3 + 3^3 = 1 + 125 + 27 = 153$. *Quod erat demonstrandum* (what was to be proved).

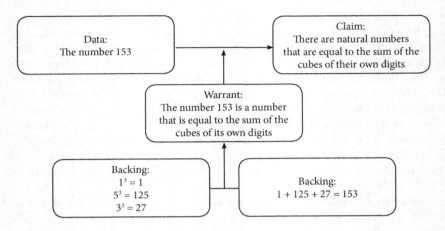

Figure 6.2 A proof of existence in mathematics

Argumentative grammar 1: proof of principle that something is possible

In education, an existence proof or proof of principle (or proof of concept) shows *that* something is possible. For example, when a professional development program with particular characteristics turns out to have positive impact on teacher learning, it is commonly considered a proof of principle or an existence proof (Borko, 2004). Such research shows what is possible, though it preferably also provides useful information that the reader can infer from the example (Clement, 2000). As Shulman (1983) wrote, existence proofs "evoke images of the possible . . . not only documenting that it can be done, but also laying out at least one detailed example of how it was organized, developed, and pursued" (p. 495). As common with much qualitative research, what can be learned from it is to a large extent left to the reader (cf. Easley, 1977).

Design researchers often use this argumentative grammar of a proof of principle. They show it is possible to help, say, students of a particular age to learn particular content, or teachers to learn to effectively apply particular strategies. Perhaps conditions were favorable, but who cares for now? At least we have learned *that* it was possible. Figure 6.3 provides an argumentative structure of a proof of principle for the claim *that* it is possible for a specific group of learners to achieve a particular learning goal. For proofs of principle of *how* something is possible, I refer to argumentative grammars later in this chapter.

I have so far presented Toulmin's scheme in its simplest form. It is however often enhanced (e.g., Mislevy, 2003) with so-called qualifiers (nuancing claims), alternative explanations, and rebuttals (counterarguments). In any real situation, it is probably more appropriate to add qualifiers such as: "Most of the learners

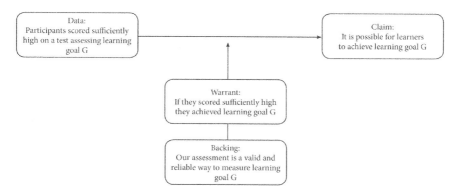

Figure 6.3 An example of a proof of principle that something is possible in education

achieved the learning goal to a satisfactory degree." Or one may add rebuttals such as: "Learners perhaps already knew G before they enrolled in the program." A response may then be: "Analysis of a pretest indicates that learners did not already know G before the program."

During conferences, I have often heard heated debates between design researchers who worked with new technology and bright students to study how particular statistical reasoning could be promoted (e.g., Ben-Zvi, Aridor, Makar, & Bakker, 2012). In the cited example we were interested in what was possible with the tool when working in favorable conditions (good teacher, productive classroom culture, suitable learning activities), and we were interested in the development of types of student reasoning that thus far had not been observed. This type of design research is truly science faction about how education could be (cf. Chapter 1). New types of learning are promoted so they can be studied in such a way that they can be replicated once better understanding of the means of supporting students' development has been gained. This type is meant to be inspirational: Isn't this wonderful? Try something similar yourself too! Informed readers make many judgments about the study (e.g., didactical quality of the tasks, progress of students compared to their own experience with that age group) that help them decide what and how they can use the findings in their own context.

However, a response from some colleagues is then: How useful is it to provide only a proof of principle? Why not work in common classrooms with average students on a larger scale? One cannot generalize what is possible to what can be done on a larger scale. These colleagues' primary concern is improving practice, not understanding cutting-edge learning processes or mechanisms.

In my view, both views are legitimate at different stages of research and design. Compare them with the chain of making new drugs, where fundamental researchers explore fundamental mechanisms of the interaction between bacteria and particular chemical structures, and others are concerned with the production of drugs at a larger scale. The development of new drugs, from identification of a working mechanism via prototyping, clinical trials, to large-scale production can easily take decades. Why couldn't educational research cover a similar range from fundamental to large-scale evaluation?

Existence proofs are very important and common in educational research more broadly: It is hard to think of innovative programs without a proof of principle. Yet, whatever your taste and personal preference for a particular phase of research and design, it is quite commonly accepted that design research should not restrict itself to proofs of principle (Bielaczyc, 2013; Schwartz, Chang, & Martin, 2008). I therefore also mention a few more possible argumentative grammars that may be useful in design research.

Argumentative grammar 2: small changes per iteration

An argumentative grammar that comes close to experimental approaches rests on a structure in which only few variables are changed in each iteration of design research. Its grammar rests on the same logic as in quasi-experiments, see Figure 6.4. When one can work with similar students each year, and designs do not have to be changed too drastically, such logic is easy to follow, rather convincing, and relatively easy to publish in a concise form. Good examples of such logic can be found in the earlier research by Kali (Kali, 2008; Kali, Levin-Peled, & Dori, 2009). The characteristics on which she and her colleagues focused were design principles that she enacted in the new iteration on the basis of progressive insight (see also Chapter 3).

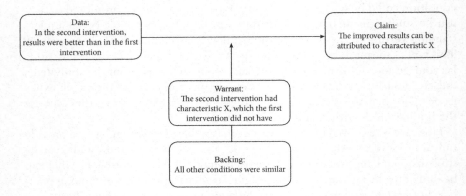

Figure 6.4 Argumentative grammar belonging to small changes per iteration

Argumentative grammar 3: experience of the design community

As Bell, Hoadley, and Linn (2004) write, design principles can be seen as:

> an intermediate step between scientific findings, which must be general-ized and replicable, and local experiences or examples that come up in practice. Because of the need to interpret design principles, they are not as readily falsifiable as scientific laws. The principles are generated inductively from prior examples of success and are subject to refinement over time as others try to adapt them to their own experiences. In this sense, they are falsifiable; if they do not yield purchase in the design process, they will be debated, altered, and eventually dropped.
>
> (p. 83)

In line with this view, Kali (2006, 2008) and colleagues (Kali & Linn, 2007) took an interesting initiative: They built a design principles database that formed the infrastructure for a larger community of people who contributed design prin-ciples they had used. The database was set up so that design principles were connected to their theoretical background but also accompanied with practical considerations (limitations, pitfalls, tradeoffs). In this way, design principles were shared and used across contexts. The argumentative grammar belonging to this initiative could be summarized in the following way (Figure 6.5):

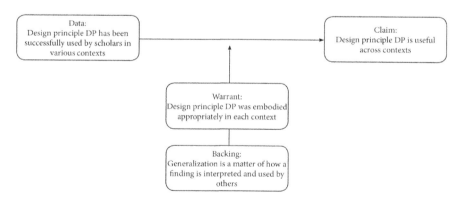

Figure 6.5 Argumentative grammar belonging to the design principles used in a collaborative community

Note, however, that such grammar is only a bare structure of a much more refined web of reasons – a point that I return to later in this chapter.

Argumentative grammar 4: conjecture mapping

There is also a logic to Sandoval's (2014) conjecture mapping (Chapter 3). Reduced to its simplest form, the argumentation behind conjecture maps could be something like this (see Figure 6.6):

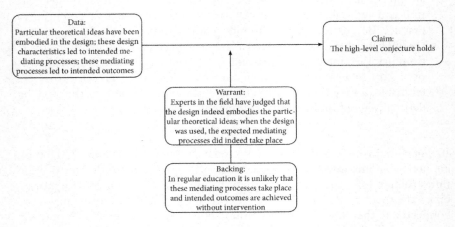

Figure 6.6 Argumentative grammar belonging to conjecture mapping

Of course, the argumentation is not like a mathematical proof. There may be confounding variables such as contextual circumstances that have contributed to the observed processes and outcomes. However, if theoretical features have been embodied in the design, and design and theoretical conjectures had been confirmed, it has at least been shown *that* and *how* the intended outcomes were achieved. Whether others can repeat the success in other circumstances is still another issue. Yet insight into the whole process is valuable information for anyone who would like to achieve something similar.

Argumentative grammar 5: answering the how-question

I now turn to the argumentative grammar underlying the structure I propose in Chapter 4 to answer a main research question of the following format: *How can a teaching-learning strategy with characteristics C_i support students to learn G?* One could see this type of research as aiming for a proof of principle of *how* rather than only *that* something is possible.

As possible research questions that together may answer this main question, you may think of questions like these:

1. What is students' prior knowledge, and what is an appropriate learning goal for this particular group of students?

2. What is a teaching-learning strategy (design) that would help students to achieve this goal (or help teachers to support students in achieving that goal)?
3. How (well) was this strategy (design) implemented?
4. What were the effects/results of implementing this strategy (design)?
5. What would an improved design look like?

In the current section, I discuss the logic behind studies that address such questions to ensure an answer to the main how-question and thus provide a proof of principle for how something can be achieved.

I often think of educational design as helping learners to get from A to B. A could be students' or teachers' current knowledge or expertise, and B the desired outcome. This could be an instructional sequence that helps students get from their prior situation (attitude, interest, motivation, skill) to the learning goals. But it may also be a repertoire of strategies that teachers can employ while teaching (e.g., waiting a few seconds longer with responding, scaffolding, establishing ground rules of classroom interaction). Or A could be a problematic situation, and B the solution. Perhaps A is the current educational infrastructure, and B the more effective or efficient one. So more generally, design is what helps people get from A to B.

To answer the question of how to get from A to B, it makes sense to underpin A and B. Table 6.1 offers some suggestions for how to study either A (e.g., problem analysis) or B (underpinning of learning goals). Next, you need design ideas and criteria to delimit the problem space of possible candidates for the trajectory from A to B. There are many options: study of existing curricula, tools, interventions, and their effects. One source of inspiration I found useful was the history of the ideas I intended to promote in students (Bakker & Gravemeijer, 2006) because history tells us what scientists in the past have wrestled with when inventing these ideas.

Once there is a design, it can be judged on several criteria Plomp (2013, p. 129): proposed relevance, consistency, practicality, and effectiveness (see also Nieveen, 1999). Relevance relates to what I have called the underpinning of A and B: Is there really a problem, lack of knowledge, or skill? Is it worth solving this problem or pursuing this educational goal? Consistency is about the internal coherence between theoretical ideas and features of the design, similar to Sandoval's focus on whether a design really embodies theoretical ideas. Practicality points to feasibility: Can practitioners work with this? This can be evaluated in an implementation phase. Effectiveness speaks for itself: Have the educational goals been achieved? Has the initial problem been solved? Given the situated nature of the findings, it is acknowledged that they are all provisional. Most likely improvements can still be made. This is not unique to design research. As Cronbach (1975) wrote about experimental and correlational studies: "When we give proper weight to local conditions, any generalization is a working hypothesis, not a conclusion" (p. 125).

Table 6.1 Options for studies within a design research project focusing on a how-question

	Type of study or activity	Possible methods
Start (A) or end (B)	Problem analysis, needs analysis, assessment of prior knowledge, underpinning of learning goals	Survey, Delphi study, assessment, literature review
Design (A to B)	Identification of design criteria, co-design, formulation of conjectures or something like a hypothetical learning trajectory	(Group) interview with experts, historical analysis, review of intervention characteristics, mechanisms, and effects, survey of curricula (document analysis)
Implementation	Enactment of the design and observation of resulting processes	Observation, survey, case study
Evaluation	Evaluation of mediating processes and outcomes, or whether the problem has been solved	Evaluation study
Redesign	Reflection and looking ahead	Synthesis of ideas for redesign based on earlier information, possibly discussed with stakeholders or external experts

One may add other criteria, for example that the design is innovative or empirically and theoretically underpinned. With regard to the implementation, there is an additional point to consider. You may want to study a particular phenomenon that first needs to be realized, for example whole-class scaffolding (Bakker & Smit, 2017) or embodied learning (Abrahamson, 2009), because there are no naturalistic settings in which you can observe this phenomenon. In such cases, it is necessary to evaluate whether the phenomenon has been realized before conclusions about it can be drawn. For example, Smit and Van Eerde (2013) analyzed the classroom interaction in their design study for three defining characteristics (diagnosis, responsiveness, handover to independence) to evaluate if it could be characterized as scaffolding. Only then were we able to make claims about the phenomenon of whole-class scaffolding as realized in that project (Smit, Van Eerde, & Bakker, 2013). In regular experimental research, the criterion would be formulated as "implementation fidelity," which is necessary to check to ensure that any effects can be attributed to the intervention having particular characteristics (cf. Sandoval, 2014).

One key characteristic of design research compared to a typical experiment is that design researchers allow for intermediate adjustment of their design. If the implementation does not work as intended they typically take the freedom to improve the design or its enactment. Waiting for the trial to be over is a waste of time; the early airplane builders would make some adjustments to make their constructions fly better (Collins, 1990, 1992; diSessa & Cobb, 2004; O'Neill, 2012) – this strategy saves time and provides insight into how to make something work.

Of course, there is also a downside: It is impossible to make claims about the effectiveness of the design as such (without local adaptations). However, design researchers typically do not want to make such claims, because design is not like a pill that one can take. Designs are always part of an ecology with human agents that are to some extent free and unpredictable.

Problematizing the need of a *separate* argumentative structure

At the beginning of this chapter, I cited Kelly (2004) on the presumed advantage of RCT's dependence on a structure of argumentation that can be judged separately from its instantiation in a particular study. The argumentative grammars I have proposed so far seem to fulfill this criterion: The logic of the methods used can be judged separately from the content of the study. However, in some of the aforementioned examples, trying to formulate an argumentative grammar felt like a reduction that does not do justice to the richness of the argumentation behind the proposed approach (e.g., the community logic and conjecture mapping).

In this section I argue that this quest for a logic that can be judged separately from the content of a study should not be taken too far when we head toward a stronger methodology of design research (which many think is necessary; e.g., Cobb, Jackson, & Dunlap, 2014; Cobb, Jackson, & Dunlap, 2017; Collins, Joseph, & Bielaczyc, 2004; Kelly, 2004). I use the history of logic to argue that logic based only on the structure and not on its content is of limited scientific value. I propose that design research requires argumentative grammars that acknowledge content as part of their logic, where content can refer to many things including key concepts used in the research, information on local circumstances (context), and the content of what is learned or aimed to achieve. Focus on the *structure* of argumentation may eventually hold back educational research.

The discipline of logic started in Aristotle's *Prior Analytics* with syllogisms such as "All men are mortal; Socrates is a man; therefore Socrates is mortal." This logic purely depends on the structure of the inference: The non-logical terms such as "mortal," "Socrates," and "man" can all be replaced by other terms without loss of validity. The interpreter does not even need to know the meaning of these terms to judge the validity of the reasoning. This reasoning is thus rigorous but irrelevant in scientific reasoning:

> This kind of logic based on syllogisms came into disrepute in the seventeenth century when science was born. Scientists like Descartes found that all interesting propositions, all interesting inferences are in fact nonsyllogistic.
> (Lakatos, 1999, p. 39)

Logic as a discipline has developed in multiple ways. One nonsyllogistic type of reasoning relevant to science is called *nonmonotonic*. This means that new conditions can turn a valid inference into an invalid one. Brandom (2000, p. 88) gives an example from physics:

1   If I strike this dry, well-made match, then it will ignite. $(p{\rightarrow}q)$
2   If p and the match is inside a very strong electromagnetic field, then it will *not* ignite." $(p\&r{\rightarrow}\neg q)$ [The sign before q negates q, so $\neg q$ means *not q]*
3   If p and r, but the match is in a Faraday cage, then it will light. $(p\&r\&s{\rightarrow}q)$
4   If p and r and s and the room is evacuated of oxygen, then the match will not light. $(p\&r\&s\&t{\rightarrow}\neg q)$

Scientific reasoning in educational research is clearly nonmonotonic: There are overwhelming numbers of factors that can influence learning and development (Collins, 1992; Smedslund, 2016). Any relevant positive factor can probably be counteracted by a negative one. Given the pragmatic nature of education, it is also worth mentioning progress on pragmatic reasoning: Walton, Reed, and Macagno (2008), for example, identified 96 argumentation schemes that people use in reasoning.

It has also become evident that valid argumentation does not depend purely on structure but also on content (and context). So-called *material inferences* even depend purely on content. Brandom (2000, p. 85) uses the inference from "Pittsburgh is to the west of Philadelphia" to "Philadelphia is to the east of Pittsburgh," as an example of an inference that is materially valid because it depends only on the content of the concepts of east and west.

These brief observations from logic suggest that scientific progress relies not only on the structure of argumentation, but also on content. Why then should research methodology in education be judged by the separate structure of its argumentation? What would an alternative look like? I think the aforementioned argumentative grammars should always be used in relation to content in the broad sense: a judgment of context; the content taught; the didactical quality of the design; linkage between theory, design, and teaching-learning processes, etc.

Reflective comments

In this chapter I argue it is unreasonable to expect that educational research including design research should use an argumentative grammar that depends solely on structure, rather than also content (quality of the design, learning content, context, etc.). Moreover, scientific results purely based on the validity of the structure of argumentation may not be very interesting; see also Ausubel's, 1961 criticism of "sterile empiricism" (p. 21) – a term also used in Chapter 2 to criticize much experimental research that led scholars in the Netherlands to do design research. Examples from logic illustrate the importance of types of reasoning that are also based on content. Argumentative grammars for design research should thus in my view acknowledge content too.

Rather than trying to generalize from sample to population, design studies typically aim for theoretical generalization: insight into how particular interventions work in terms of mediating processes or mechanisms can help others do similar things. Design research thus is typically meant to be inspirational rather than purely descriptive or evaluative. This is by no means unique to design research; much qualitative research in education shares this feature. As Easley (1977) wrote, much of the judgment is left to the reader, rather than claimed by the author. For example, what design researchers sometimes do is to present their work in a descriptive manner in the context of something they designed, and leave it to the reader to infer how this design contributed to the observations made in the research.

My proposal for a proof of principle for *how* something can be achieved focused on a grammar of a design research project with the aim to contribute to knowledge about *how* particular educational goals could be achieved in general (or problems solved). It could thus be seen as a proof of principle about *how* rather than purely *that* something is possible.

The structures proposed here never should become straightjackets. Rather they may function as starting points for design researchers if they ponder what to do. They are intended to help communicate in publications what design researchers have done. Without making explicit what the authors are claiming (and not), readers from a different commissive space may expect particular other reasoning patterns than the authors use. For example, with my coauthors I have had reviewers of manuscripts who criticized the lack of a control group. However, in these manuscripts we argued that, when helping students achieve a new learning goal, it does not make sense to compare their results with those of a control group: What characteristic should we have compared if regular education works toward other learning goals? Moreover, we did not make any claims about our approach being better than anything else.

I hope that specifying possible argumentative grammars may help design research become more accessible to educational researchers not used to this genre of approaches. Valuable resources for further development of argumentative grammars are Cole et al. (2014), and Penuel and Frank (2015). It has taken some time for case studies, ethnographies, and other qualitative approaches to become widely known in educational research. I expect that design research does not need quite as long, but will soon be a standard approach discussed in the well-known methodology books rather than conceptualized as complementary (e.g., Schoenfeld, 2006).

Notes

1 Parts of this chapter are based on Bakker (2017). I thank Chris Rasmussen for alerting me to the work of Mislevy (2003), who used Toulmin's scheme for similar purposes as I do here, but in the context of educational assessment.
2 Such numbers are a special case of so-called narcissistic numbers; see https://en.wikipedia. org/wiki/Narcissistic_number. Other examples are 370, 371, and 407. Proof that there are no other such natural numbers larger than 1 is more laborious than the existence proof provided here.

References

Abrahamson, D. (2009). Embodied design: Constructing means for constructing meaning. *Educational Studies in Mathematics, 70*(1), 27–47.

Ausubel, D. P. (1961). Learning by discovery: Rationale and mystique. *The Bulletin of the National Association of Secondary School Principals, 45*(269), 18–58.

Bakker, A. (2017). Towards argumentative grammars of design research. In T. Dooley & G. Gueudet (Eds.), *Proceedings of the Tenth Congress of the European Society for Research in Mathematics Education (CERME10, February 1–5, 2017)* (pp. 2730–2737). Dublin, Ireland: DCU Institute of Education and ERME.

Bakker, A., & Gravemeijer, K. P. E. (2006). An historical phenomenology of mean and median. *Educational Studies in Mathematics, 62*(2), 149–168.

Bakker, A., & Smit, J. (2017). Theory development in design based research: An example about scaffolding mathematical language. In S. Doff & R. Komoss (Eds.), *How does change happen?* (pp. 109–124). Wiesbaden, Germany: Springer.

Bell, P., Hoadley, C. M., & Linn, M. C. (2004). Design based research in education. In M. C. Linn, E. A. Davis, & P. Bell (Eds.), *Internet environments for science education* (pp. 73–85). Mahwah, NJ: Erlbaum.

Ben-Zvi, D., Aridor, K., Makar, K., & Bakker, A. (2012). Students' emergent articulations of uncertainty while making informal statistical inferences. *ZDM, 44*(7), 913–925.

Bielaczyc, K. (2013). Informing design research: Learning from teachers' designs of social infrastructure. *Journal of the Learning Sciences, 22*(2), 258–311.

Biesta, G. (2007). Why "what works" won't work: Evidence-based practice and the democratic deficit in educational research. *Educational Theory, 57*(1), 1–22.

Borko, H. (2004). Professional development and teacher learning: Mapping the terrain. *Educational Researcher, 33*(8), 3–15.

Brandom, R. (2000). *Articulating reasons: An introduction to inferentialism.* Cambridge, MA: Harvard University Press.

Clement, J. J. (2000). Analysis of clinical interviews: Foundations and model viability. In A. E. Kelly & R. A. Lesh (Eds.), *Handbook of research design in mathematics and science education* (pp. 547–589). Mahwah, NJ: Lawrence Erlbaum.

Cobb, P., & Gravemeijer, K. P. E. (2008). Experimenting to support and understand learning processes. In A. E. Kelly, R. A. Lesh, & J. Y. Baek (Eds.), *Handbook of design research methods in education: Innovations in science, technology, engineering, and mathematics learning and teaching* (pp. 68–95). London: Routledge.

Cobb, P., Jackson, K., & Dunlap, C. (2014). Design research: An analysis and critique. In L. D. English & D. Kirshner (Eds.), *Handbook of international research in mathematics education* (pp. 481–503). New York, NY: Routledge.

Cobb, P., Jackson, K., & Dunlap, C. (2017). Conducting design studies to investigate and support mathematics students' and teachers' learning. In J. Cai (Ed.), *First compendium for research in mathematics education* (pp. 208–233). Reston, VA: National Council of Teachers of Mathematics.

Cole, M., Engeström, Y., Sannino, A., Gutiérrez, K., Jurow, S., Packer, M., Penuel, W. R., et al. (2014). Toward an argumentative grammar for socio-cultural/cultural-historical activity approaches to design research. In J. L. Polman, E. A. Kyza, D. K. O'Neill, I. Tabak, W. R. Penuel, A. S. Jurow, K. O'Connor et al. (Eds.), *ICLS Proceedings* (pp. 1254–1263). Boulder, CO: ICLS.

Collins, A. (1990). *Toward a design science of education – Technical Report No. 1.* Retrieved from ERIC.

Collins, A. (1992). Towards a design science of education. In E. Scanlon & T. O'Shea (Eds.), *New directions in educational technology* (pp. 15–22). Berlin: Springer.

Collins, A., Joseph, D., & Bielaczyc, K. (2004). Design research: Theoretical and methodological issues. *Journal of the Learning Sciences, 13*(1), 15–42.

Cronbach, L. J. (1975). Beyond the two disciplines of scientific psychology. *American Psychologist, 30*(2), 116–27.

diSessa, A. A., & Cobb, P. (2004). Ontological innovation and the role of theory in design experiments. *Journal of the Learning Sciences, 13*(1), 77–103.

Easley, J. A. (1977). *On clinical studies in mathematics education.* Columbus, OH: Ohio State University.

Horner, R., Carr, E., Halle, J., Mcgee, G., Odom, S., & Wolery, M. (2005). The use of single-subject research to identify evidence-based practice in special education. *Exceptional Children, 71*(2), 165–179.

Kali, Y. (2006). Collaborative knowledge-building using the Design Principles Database. *International Journal of Computer Support for Collaborative Learning, 1*(2), 187–201.

Kali, Y. (2008). The Design Principles Database as means for promoting design based research. In A. E. Kelly, R. A. Lesh & J. Y. Baek (Eds.), *Handbook of design research methods in education: Innovations in science, technology, engineering, and mathematics learning and teaching* (pp. 423–438). Mahwah, NJ: Lawrence Erlbaum Associates.

Kali, Y., Levin-Peled, R., & Dori, Y. J. (2009). The role of design principles in designing courses that promote collaborative learning in higher-education. *Computers in Human Behavior, 25*(5), 1067–1078.

Kali, Y., & Linn, M. C. (2007). Technology-enhanced support strategies for inquiry learning. In J. M. Spector, M. D. Merrill, J. J. G. van Merriënboer, & M. P. Driscoll (Eds.), *Handbook of research on educational communications and technology* (3rd ed., pp. 445–461). Mahwah, NJ: Erlbaum.

Kazdin, Alan (1982). *Single-case research designs.* New York: Oxford University Press.

Kelly, A. (2004). Design research in education: Yes, but is it methodological? *The Journal of the Learning Sciences, 13*(1), 115–128.

Lakatos, I., Feyerabend, P., & Motterlini, M. (1999). *For and against method: Including Lakatos's lectures on scientific method and the Lakatos-Feyerabend correspondence.* Chicago, IL: University of Chicago Press.

Maxwell, J. A. (2004). Causal explanation, qualitative research, and scientific inquiry in education. *Educational Researcher, 33*(2), 3–11.

Mislevy, R. J. (2003). Substance and structure in assessment arguments. *Law, Probability and Risk, 2*(4), 237–258.

Nater, A., Mattle-Greminger, M. P., Nurcahyo, A., Nowak, M. G., de Manuel, M., Desai, T., . . . Krützen, M. (2017). Morphometric, behavioral, and genomic evidence for a new orangutan species. *Current Biology, 27*(22), 3487–3498.e3410. doi:10.1016/j.cub.2017.09.047

Nieveen, N. (1999). Prototyping to reach product quality. In J. van den Akker, R. M. Branch, K. Gustafson, N. Nieveen, & T. Plomp (Eds.), *Design approaches and tools in education and training* (pp. 125–136). Boston, MA: Kluwer Academic.

Olson, D. R. (2004). The triumph of hope over experience in the search for "what works": A response to Slavin. *Educational Researcher, 33*(1), 24–26.

O'Neill, D. K. (2012). Designs that fly: What the history of aeronautics tells us about the future of design based research in education. *International Journal of Research & Method in Education, 35*(2), 119–140.

Packer, M. J. (2017). *The science of qualitative research* (2nd ed.). Cambridge, UK: Cambridge University Press.

Penuel, W. R., & Frank, K. A. (2015). Modes of inquiry in educational psychology and learning sciences research. In L. Corno & E. M. Anderman (Eds.), *Handbook of educational psychology* (3rd ed., pp. 16–28). London, UK: Routledge.

Plomp, T. (2013). Educational design research: An introduction. In T. Plomp & N. Nieveen (Eds.), *Educational design research: Part A: An introduction* (pp. 10–51). Enschede, the Netherlands: SLO.

Sandoval, W. (2014). Conjecture mapping: An approach to systematic educational design research. *Journal of the Learning Sciences, 23*(1), 18–36.

Schoenfeld, A. H. (2006). Design experiments. In J. L. Green, G. Camilli, & P. B. Elmore (Eds.), *Handbook of complementary methods in education research* (pp. 193–206). London, UK: Routledge.

Schwartz, D. L., Chang, J., & Martin, L. (2008). Instrumentation and innovation in design experiments: Taking the turn towards efficiency. In A. E. Kelly, R. A. Lesh, & J. Y. Baek (Eds.), *Handbook of design research methods in education: Innovations in science, technology, engineering, and mathematics learning and teaching* (pp. 47–67). London, UK: Routledge.

Shavelson, R. J., Phillips, D. C., Towne, L., & Feuer, M. J. (2003). On the science of education design studies. *Educational Researcher, 32*(1), 25–28.

Shulman, L. S., & Sykes, G. (1983). *Handbook of teaching and policy*. New York, NY: Longman.

Smedslund, J. (2016). Why psychology cannot be an empirical science. *Integrative Psychological and Behavioral Science, 50*(2), 185–195.

Smit, J., & van Eerde, H. A. A. (2013). What counts as evidence for the long-term realisation of whole-class scaffolding? *Learning, Culture and Social Interaction, 2*(1), 22–31.

Smit, J., Van Eerde, H. A. A., & Bakker, A. (2013). A conceptualisation of whole-class scaffolding. *British Educational Research Journal, 39*(5), 817–834.

Toulmin, S. E. (1958). *The uses of argument*. Cambridge, UK: Cambridge University Press.

Walton, D., Reed, C., & Macagno, F. (2008). *Argumentation schemes: Fundamentals of critical argumentation*. New York, NY: Cambridge University Press.

Worrall, J. (2002). What evidence in evidence-based medicine? *Philosophy of Science, 69*(3), 316–330.

Chapter 7

Writing an empirical design research paper

Summary

This chapter provides advice on how to write up your design study. After discussing the elements of a paper, from introduction to discussion, I focus on how to make your text coherent by ensuring that all relevant inferential and referential relationships are clear.

Writing an academic paper is quite a challenge for most design researchers, but the good news is that it can be learned by following a few guidelines and studying successful examples. In this chapter, I provide general advice on writing empirical papers, with special attention to reporting findings from design research. As McKenney and Reeves (2012) observe, writing, reviewing, and publishing occurs in commissive spaces of people who more or less agree on the ground rules of their discipline. The disadvantage of design researchers is that they have to explain more to their non-design oriented colleagues about their approach than vice versa. Several decades ago, scholars who published case studies or ethnographies were in a somewhat similar position (Easley, 1977); a substantial part of their papers was dedicated to why they used these research approaches. This implies that design researchers have to choose their journals carefully. Some journals welcome long manuscripts (e.g., *Cognition & Instruction*; *Journal of the Learning Sciences*); other journals explicitly welcome design studies (*Educational Designer*; *Educational Design Research – An International Journal for Design Based Research in Education*; *Educational Technology Research and Development*); several mathematics education research journals regularly publish design research papers. Special issues can also be a venue for design researchers, provided that the guest editors and reviewers have at least some sympathy for what design researchers aim to do. However, the most important task is to write not merely well, but very well.

Chain of reasoning

Each research project has a particular logic, and a paper about it should reflect this logic. Krathwohl (1998) compared a research report with a chain of reasoning that is as strong as its weakest link. For example, you might address a particular problem and propose a potential solution. The research project's goal is to figure out how to make your idea work, so you have a conjecture or a research question on some specific aspect of the potential solution (say a teaching strategy). You apply particular research methods to test the high-level conjecture or answer your question, which leads to results. The results are then discussed in the final section, where one also reflects on how well the question was answered and what the implications of your findings are.

I always advise my students to start with what I call a skeleton, a one-page outline of your paper's chain of reasoning. And I often also make such skeletons myself. The ingredients of a skeleton are: title, problem, solution direction, knowledge gap, research aim, research question, relevance of answering the question, and methodological approach. The advantage of having this on one page is that you can easily see whether concepts in the title recur in the rest of the story and whether the research aim is linked well with the initial problem. It may also become visible that your envisioned methods are suitable for an evaluative experiment, but not for the how-question you intend to answer. So here is the first guideline for writing (G):

> G1: Make a one-page outline of your paper's chain of reasoning to check if it makes sense (skeleton).

The general "shape" of a paper

The general shape of a research paper can be visualized as zooming in and out. The start of a paper should be broad enough to seduce readers into your topic (zooming in), except when your first sentences state the purpose of your paper. How broad you start depends on the scope of the journal or the audience. If you write for a special issue on a particular topic, there is no need to start much broader, but if you write for a general educational journal, you might need to speak to a wider field before you zoom in on your specific subfield or topic. You relate your work to that of others and identify the knowledge gap.

The narrowest part of the paper is the middle – the methods and results sections, which are specific to your own project. In the results section, you do not (or hardly) refer to other people's work.

In the discussion, you zoom out again and relate to the broader field of study. Implications for practice and limitations of your approach are discussed (zooming out). You relate your findings to the work of others or future research to be done. For a feeling of closure, it is worth trying to return to the title or topic of your first paragraph. This gives the reader a sense of the text being a whole.

> G2: Ensure that your paper starts broad enough. Zoom in on the knowledge gap and your goal or research question. In the discussion, you zoom out again.

Ingredients of a paper

The guidelines of the *Publication Manual of the American Psychological Association* (6th edition; APA6) are worth studying in detail. For advice on each section of a paper, even on titles, also see for instance Wallwork (2011), but note that he wrote for disciplines other than education. Here I summarize the main topics that keep recurring in my educational research methods courses and research projects.

Title

The most important function of a title is that it catches the attention of the right audience. It should contain the key concepts or the key message of your research. Keep the title relatively short. APA6 recommends up to 12 words.

In educational research you will often see catchy titles, sometimes with student quotes. If these do capture your key messages, fine, but if the reader has little clue in what subdomain of educational research this is situated, then it may be better to use a "boring" but informative title. In some disciplines, the colon (:) is avoided, but in educational research, it is common and useful.

From a coherence perspective, it is key that the title fits the purpose, question, and the rest of the publication's skeleton. It will typically cover a slightly broader topic than your specific focus to draw a potentially wider interested readership. For design studies I often like titles that link a design idea to an intended outcome, for example "Seeding Evolutionary Thinking by Engaging Children in Modeling its Foundations" (Lehrer & Schauble, 2012).

Note that most journals also ask for a running head, which is a summary of the title in often up to 50 characters. The running head is used as a header in the paper or chapter itself.

Abstract

The abstract is perhaps the most important single paragraph of your paper. It is read more than any other paragraph, and it is pivotal in readers' decision whether or not to download and read the paper.

Having done several review studies, I know how frustrating it is if abstracts do not contain the relevant information that a scholar needs to judge if a paper fits particular search criteria. Also make sure the abstract is self-contained, which means it can be read as a stand-alone text, preferably without any references to other publications. The APA6 (2010) guidelines are again useful here. In an empirical paper make sure you address:

- The problem in one sentence
- Participants (age, grade, . . .)
- Research approach
- Key findings
- Brief discussion or implication.

If you have more space than say 120 words, also add a research goal or question, or any other relevant information (knowledge gap, definitions). Sometimes design researchers start their abstract with the goal, for example: "The goal of this classroom study of third-grade students was to support and document the emergence of multiple senses of mathematical similarity" (Lehrer, Strom, & Confrey, 2002, p. 359).

Introduction

There are two common shapes for introductions: the funnel (start of the aforementioned zooming in) and what I call the reverse pear (see Figures 7.1 and 7.2). The funnel is the most common one (Swales & Feak, 2004).

The *funnel* shape introduction involves the following steps:

1   Introduction of an interesting topic or societal problem (the reader needs to be convinced of the practical and/or theoretical relevance of the paper). In design research, the problem is often a gap between the current and desirable situation (McKenney & Reeves, 2012). Many papers start with a problem, such as low interest in STEM subjects, need for teacher professional development, or poor preparation for what students need in the twenty-first century. The challenge could also be to contribute to more equitable or accessible education (e.g., Mintrop, 2016).
2   Narrow down to a specific aspect or potential solution (zoom in). In design research this often means you sketch solution that have been tried so far, or argue that new opportunities have arisen to tackle a persistent problem (e.g., new technology, new theory, new learning arrangements).
3   Identification of a knowledge gap; formulation of purpose, hypothesis, or research question of the paper. Identify or carve out your niche: convince the reader that it is necessary to fill the gap. It is not enough to state that little is known or little research has been done on this topic. The key issue is that more or better insight into the topic is needed to resolve the aforementioned problem.

Figure 7.1 Funnel

4   State the research aim, and possibly also the research question, which natu-
    rally follows from the knowledge gap. My personal preference is to end the
    introduction with the research aim or question. This is where experienced
    readers expect such key information to be placed (if not already presented
    at the beginning of the introduction). One could add a sentence on how
    an answer to this research question will help to resolve the aforementioned
    problem. This gives the introduction a well-rounded feeling.

Sometimes people add a description of what the reader can expect in the publication. This is not really necessary if the paper follows the standard format of
empirical research papers. Such advance organizers may be appreciated if you
decide to deviate from standard practice.

   In medium-sized papers of about 6,000 to 8,000 words, the introduction is
typically about four paragraphs – one for each step. If you need to discuss why
a solution or instructional idea did not quite work and why you will try something else, you might need an extra paragraph, or perhaps you need an extra

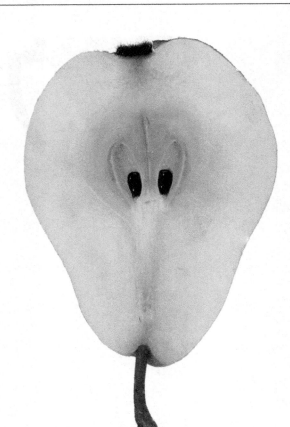

Figure 7.2 Reverse pear

paragraph to define a key concept (e.g., scaffolding, drawing-based modeling, inquiry-based learning, connectivism).

What I call the *reverse pear* introduction is almost the same, except that it starts with the aim of the paper – the top of the reverse pear, after which the funnel starts. The advantage of such a start is that the quick reader immediately knows what the paper is about, which is important in times when people read a lot online and are always in a hurry (Wallwork, 2011). However, this approach can only be applied if the concepts used to describe the purpose need little explanation. If you need to explain technical concepts, it might be necessary to introduce these before the purpose can be stated. In the context of a special issue on statistics education, this held for the following first sentence: "The purpose of this paper is to provide an analysis of fifth-grade students' emergent expressions of uncertainty in the context of drawing inferences informally from growing data sets" (Ben-Zvi, Aridor, Makar, & Bakker, 2012, p. 913).

> G3: The function of an introduction is to convince your readers of the relevance of your topic, the need to fill a knowledge gap, and to narrow down to the aim of your paper. The aim of your paper is typically the end of the funnel but could also be the very first sentence.

Theoretical background

In some disciplines and with short papers in education, there is no need to have a separate section titled "Theoretical Background" or "Conceptual framework." If the key concepts and the survey of what is known and unknown about your topic are clear in a relatively short introduction, then there is no reason to go deeper or broader in a second section. In some cases, it is easier to go straight to writing the methods section, because it can be challenging to split up what you want to tell from a helicopter view in the introduction and what you want to discuss in-depth in the theoretical background section.

For a theoretical background you can think of at least three basic structures, which can also be combined (Weissberg & Buker, 1990):

1   *Historically or chronologically.* For example, if you want to develop an alternative approach to transfer, you may want to go back to the origin of this concept over a hundred years ago (Tuomi-Gröhn & Engeström, 2003).
2   *From broad to narrow.* If your topic is, say, drawing-based modeling in astronomy (van Joolingen, Aukes, Gijlers, & Bollen, 2015), you can start with the importance of modeling in science, argue for the potential of drawing-based modeling, and zoom in via physics on the domain of astronomy.
3   *By theme.* Assume that your purpose and/or main research question entails two key concepts; then it makes sense to address these two one by one. For example, if you use a modeling approach to teaching about evolution, you can address the learning goal and the teaching approach one by one (Lehrer & Schauble, 2012).
4   *Rationale behind design.* In design research specifically, you can use the theoretical background to explicate the main reasons behind your design. We have done this in, for example, Smit, Bakker, Van Eerde, and Kuijpers (2016). The advantage is that a description of an intervention, tool, or whatever you have designed is often too complex for a subsection of the methods section.

If the main research question has not already been formulated in the introduction, the end of the theoretical background is the logical place to put it, possibly complemented with subquestions. This position is natural because the next step in the paper is to argue what steps you took to answer the question(s).

Methods section

In reports from design research it is wise to start the methods section with a brief explanation of why the question raised, often a how-question, requires design research. Typical argumentation goes as follows: Given that the intended or desirable learning process X could not be observed in regular educational settings, we had to design something to ensure that X would happen. To this end, we deployed the approach of design research (or "conducted a design study"). If you have not used a control or comparison group because your aim is to prove that something is possible, or if any solution is already better than none, then you may have to explain to readers from other commissive spaces that a control group was not used because you aimed for different learning goals than in regular education, or because your aim was to explore the potential of idea Y, not to prove that it worked better than Z. It may also be wise to describe the procedure to give the reader a sense of what you have done to get your results.

After a brief general introduction on the research approach or strategy (Denscombe, 2010), the following ingredients are common. Terminology varies widely across research traditions, so before you submit to a journal check if yours fits with that of most authors.

1   *Setting/context*: Design researchers are well aware of the importance of context. Hence a description of the setting in which the research took place is crucial. It is up to you which characteristics you think are important. In some countries, these include whether the school was urban, suburban, or rural. In my own country, this feature is not so informative. More informative is probably if the educational setting has a long tradition of using technology, collaborative learning, puts professional development high on its agenda, etc.

2   *Participants*: In design research, I mostly prefer using a term like "participants" to avoid connotations that a "sample" has. When readers see the term sample, they will immediately wonder: Was this sample taken randomly? Do you aim for statistical generalization?

3   *Instruments/design/tasks*: Think of interview schemes, assessment, and questionnaires, but also design specific instruments such as a hypothetical learning trajectory (conjecture map, scenario, learning progression, etc.). The design itself is also sometimes seen as an instrument. You may have to explain the tasks or learning activities.

4   *Data collection*: Which data did you collect and how? How did you ensure quality assurance? Avoid overlap with the previous subsection: If you only do interviews, it looks artificial to separate the description of your interview scheme from the interviews themselves. This is also the place to tell whether audio recordings were transcribed (verbatim or otherwise).

5   *Data analysis*: How did you analyze the data? Did you use validation procedures such as member checking? How did you make this process reliable?

This is also the place to report Cronbach's alpha or similar measures for assessment or questionnaires, and Cohen's kappa for interrater reliability. Such measures tell something about the quality of the data analysis and are not considered to be part of the results, hence they are reported in the methods section. The same holds for checking whether conducting particular statistical analyses is appropriate (normality, collinearity, homogeneity, etc.).

Results

There are a few pieces of advice here that are worth sharing. First, early career researchers sometimes stick too close to their data (see Chapter 21 for an example). They cite from their transcripts to illustrate particular points or describe interesting phenomena without rising enough to a more theoretical perspective. If you present a case, what is it a case of?

Readers should never wonder "Why am I reading this?" This means you have to provide a good story with sufficient theoretical explanation and practical detail. It is through theoretical generalization that illustrations are powerful.

A common dilemma is how much to discuss the findings already in the results section. In general, you will find very few references to other work in results sections and little discussion, but there are situations where the readability deteriorates if you postpone remarks or discussion points to the last section. As with other guidelines on writing, they should never become a straightjacket, but rather be a heuristic for what to do when in doubt.

In design research, it is especially important to highlight the mechanisms that you think describe *how* learning or teaching proceeds, and how these may be connected to particular design features.

Discussion

The most common structure of the last section is to repeat the purpose or main question of the study and summarize how you achieved this purpose or answered this question. You may need to summarize answers to subquestions too. Then you can discuss the relevance and meaning of your findings. In a design study report, it may be necessary to demarcate explicitly which claims can be made and which claims cannot. Typical subsections include: limitations, recommendations for practice, and future research.

Making your writing coherent

So far I have concentrated on the subsequent elements of an empirical research paper. However, one of the most important features of a good manuscript is coherence.

Lack of coherence

Lack of coherence is much more apparent than coherence itself. Do you recognize any of the following feedback on your own texts?

- This comes out of the blue.
- What is the line of reasoning/thread exactly? The argumentation could be tighter.
- What is the focus of your paper?
- What has X to do with Y?
- What is your main message?
- Do you really need this concept/theory/passage?
- Your goal and research question are not really in line.
- Your research question is not really answered.
- Are the subquestions really helping to answer the main research question?
- How is this study related to the bigger project?
- You do not refer to all figures/tables.
- There are missing references and references you do not cite in the text.
- What does "this" refer to? What is this issue/this research?

All these questions and comments refer to some lack of coherence. Some refer to missing links at the micro or sentence level (what does the word "this" refer to?), while others have to do with the macro level or overall structure of the paper. Some questions have to do with references within the text; others with the logic of the paper.

In the remainder of this chapter, I classify different types of coherence. But let me first address the question: What does coherence mean? Dictionaries state something like the following: Forming a whole that fits together. Your writing is coherent if everything is logically laid out and connected.[1] Coherence leads to continuity (flow): Some papers read seamlessly from the first sentence to the last because all information is concisely formulated and all connections are aptly expressed.

Why is coherence so important?

Educational research has shown that people find it easier to read a coherent text than a less coherent one and they remember better what the text is about (Kamalski, Sanders, & Lentz, 2008; McNamara, Kintsch, Songer, & Kintsch, 1996; Sanders, Land, & Mulder, 2007). Thus a coherent text communicates your message better than a text with some missing connections. It is therefore not surprising that coherence is something that editors, reviewers, and supervisors look for. A lack of coherence is easily spotted and often criticized.

I once sat next to two students, Joan and Norman (pseudonyms), who read each other's introductions to research proposals. Norman could easily summarize Joan's proposal, whereas Joan complained she did not really know what

Norman's proposal was about. "It is odd how some texts are easy to follow. I don't know what causes that." Surprise, surprise; this has to do with coherence.

A coherent text focuses on what it is about. Ideas are easy to follow, and links are as expected or logical: The text is transparent. The spectacles metaphor can illuminate this notion: When your spectacles are dirty, you are distracted; you see the glasses themselves (Roth, 2003). But once you can see through them, they help you see something outside, and you do not notice the spectacles anymore. This is why a coherent text mostly does not draw any attention to itself: The reader can focus on the content instead. Readers are not disturbed by missing reasoning steps or lack of clarity over what the authors are talking about.

What makes a text fit together?

Using Brandom's (2000) semantic theory of inferentialism, I distinguish two types of relations that keep ideas and texts together: inferential and referential relations (cf. Bakker & Derry, 2011). Inferential relations have to do with logic and reasoning. Referential relations link something in the text to something else in or outside the text (see Table 7.1).

Inevitably, when I make such distinctions, there are also boundary cases in which a relation can be both inferential and referential. Let me start with the inferential relations because they are the most important and difficult type of "glue" that makes papers fit together.

Guidelines for improving inferential relations

Focus

Focus is very important for a paper to be coherent: The text has to be at the service of one main message that the reader can remember and tell somebody else in a one-minute elevator chat.

G4: Try to summarize the main message of your paper in 12 to 16 words.

Table 7.1 Examples of inferential and referential relations

Inferential relations	Referential relations
• Question – answer • Premise – conclusion (if – then) • Goal – achievement • Means – end • X is a reason for Y • After X one expects Y • X is necessary information to understand Y	• Reference to a larger project or field of research • Reference to another publication • Reference to table or figure • Reference to something in the text (problem, challenge, section, demonstrative pronoun such as "this")

Do not rest until you have one focus. If you have two goals, try to see if one is at the service of the other (e.g., identify problems at the service of identifying potential solutions). The most common criticism I have seen in reviews is that the focus is not clear or not consistent. A good way to check the focus of your paper is to highlight all sentences that could be interpreted as indicating the focus: title, core sentences in the abstract, and sentences that capture the aim, research question, or conclusion. Then read all highlighted text in one go to see if all these sentences are consistent.

Identify the main research function

A research project has a main function (Plomp, 2013), for example to

- describe or define
- compare
- evaluate
- explain
- design
- advise.

It is very common for research projects to have phases with different functions, one of which can be to design, such as in design research. Oftentimes, it is necessary to describe a situation before it can be evaluated, and to evaluate before advice for improvement can be asserted. The main research goal is then to advise researchers – the other phases are at the service of this higher goal. In such a case, the research question is typically evaluative, because a piece of advice is mostly based on something that has been evaluated as effective.

Research questions should reflect the research function (otherwise your text is inconsistent at this point):

- To describe (e.g., what conceptions of sampling do Grade 7 students have?)
- To compare (e.g., does method A lead to better test scores than method B?)
- To evaluate (e.g., how well do students develop an understanding of distribution in this instructional sequence?)
- To explain or to predict (e.g., why do so few students choose a bachelor's degree in mathematics or science? What will students do when using a particular software package?)
- To design (e.g., what constitutes a learning trajectory in which students use modeling to learn about evolution? How can teachers learn to scaffold their students' mathematical language?)
- To advise (e.g., how can secondary school students be supported to learn about correlation and regression?).

For example, a what-question is often descriptive (what are characteristics of . . .). Evaluative questions often include language like "how well." Explanatory questions can generally be recognized by formulations such as "why" or "what are explanations for . . ." Advice questions often start with "how should . . ." Or "what is a good/the best way to . . .?"

> G5: Identify the main research function addressed in your paper and ensure that the formulation of your question is consistent with this function.

Sticking to such conventions helps the reader to identify the type of research carried out, and foresee the kind of research methods used. Sometimes, I see descriptive research questions in a context that clearly suggests the researchers actually want to evaluate or give advice.

Only introduce what you need

The Russian playwright Anton Chekhov is well known for his one-liner: "One must never place a loaded rifle on the stage if it isn't going to go off. It's wrong to make promises you don't mean to keep" (Goldberg, 1976, p. 163). Students often feel the need to show they know the theories or concepts used in a particular area. Or they identify knowledge gaps that are not filled in this particular paper. If you identify something in your introduction that is unsolved or unknown, the reader will expect your paper to contribute to a solution. In other words:

> G6: Only introduce elements (concepts, theories) that you will need to position your research, clarify key concepts, or analyze your data. Otherwise, you raise expectations you cannot fulfill.

Guidelines for improving referential relations

Relations with a larger project

One of the key challenges for PhD students is to "cut up the elephant" (an expression I first heard from Albert Pilot). Unless a research project is split into well-defined smaller studies, it can be hard to demarcate what should be addressed in a single paper and what should be left out. This challenge is especially prominent in design based research and large projects with many facets. Think carefully about how you phrase the goal of the larger project and, in relation to that, how the goal of the specific study you report on fits into the bigger picture. Chapters 6 and 8 address aspects of this challenge.

Relations with objects outside the text

A common source of confusion is that authors use different terms for the same thing (e.g., instructional materials, educational sequence, module, unit). Like Wallwork (2011) says, my advice is:

> G7: Vary words that are not technical (especially within one paragraph), but stick to the same word for each technical or scientific object of interest.

Hence it is fine to use synonyms for terms such as importance (value, need, requirement), but if your paper is about an educational unit, use the same term consistently throughout your text. Otherwise, readers might think you mean something different as soon as you use the term module or sequence. If you use the word "purpose" in your introduction, use the same word again in your discussion: If you use synonyms such as "goal" or "aim," readers will take an extra thinking step or might even wonder for a second whether you mean something else than in the introduction.

Relations within the text

Relations within the text might sound rather trivial. Yet flaws in this area are common.

References to sources of information:

1   Make sure you refer to all figures and tables in the text.
2   Make sure your list of references is complete, and all references are cited in the text.
3   If you refer to a section, make sure you use the right number or title of the section.

References at the sentence and paragraph level:

> Ensure that each sentence links with the next (Wallwork, 2011). Sentences start with a topic and end with the focus on what you want to write about it. This focus becomes the topic of the next sentence. The end of a paragraph should link with the start of the following paragraph. If you are tempted to copy and paste text from other positions, ensure that links with the surrounding text are restored. In my experience, this mostly requires full rewriting of what was copied and pasted initially.

> G8: Avoid copying and pasting text, because it mostly leads to incoherence. Flow is best achieved by writing without interruption.

One of the most common flaws in referring to terms is the use of demonstrative pronouns such as *this*. Whenever you use or read this word, ask yourself: Is what it refers to clear? Take an excerpt in a fictional paper like this one (Lehrer & Schauble, 2012). This research . . . When writing *this*, students mostly refer to their own research, not to the aforementioned research cited in the reference. To avoid confusion, I recommend something like the following: "The research project reported in this paper" or avoiding a reference to some-one else's work just before "this."

The APA guidelines also advise using "I" or "we" ("my," "our," etc.) to make references clear. Another advantage of I and we is that they make it easier to use the active voice. Note, however, that "we" should refer to the authors, not to some general "we," because it is often not clear what this "we" refers to: author and reader together, society, or people in the discipline?

Textbox 7.1

Question: Is a coherent text a good text?

Response: Not necessarily. A coherent text may be superficial, too limited, or without enough substance. A good manuscript may have some flaws in coherence, which are compensated by depth, quality of the research, interesting results, or implications of the ideas presented.

Textbox 7.2

Question: What if an interesting idea or observation in the study does not fit the research goal or research question? Would writing about it make my paper less coherent?

Response: Yes, when aiming for coherence, I would say: Leave this idea out and try to get it across in another paper. However, you may have limited time to write papers, or you may lack empirical data to jus-tify another paper on the same topic. One solution then could be to weave your idea into the discussion section of your paper, because this is the place for generating hypotheses and potential explana-tions. At the end of the paper you have more freedom to bring in ideas that are not strictly tied to the research aim and question.

Note

1 wiki.answers.com

References

APA (2010). *Publication manual of the American Psychological Association* (6th ed.). Washington, DC: American Psychological Association.

Bakker, A., & Derry, J. (2011). Lessons from inferentialism for statistics education. *Mathematical Thinking and Learning, 13*, 5–26.

Ben-Zvi, D., Aridor, K., Makar, K., & Bakker, A. (2012). Students' emergent articulations of uncertainty while making informal statistical inferences. *ZDM Mathematics Education, 44*(7), 913–925.

Brandom, R. B. (2000). *Articulating reasons: An introduction to inferentialism.* Cambridge, MA: Harvard University Press.

Denscombe, M. (2010). *The good research guide.* Maidenhead, UK: Open University Press.

Easley, J. A. (1977). *On clinical studies in mathematics education.* Columbus, OH: Ohio State University.

Goldberg, L. (1976). *Russian literature in the 19th century: Essays.* Jerusalem, Israel: The Magnes Press, Hebrew University.

Kamalski, J., Sanders, T., & Lentz, L. (2008). Coherence marking, prior knowledge, and comprehension of informative and persuasive texts: Sorting things out. *Discourse Processes, 45*(4–5), 323–345.

Krathwohl, D. R. (1998). *Methods of educational and social science research: An integrated approach* (2nd ed.). New York, NY: Longman.

Lehrer, R., & Schauble, L. (2012). Seeding evolutionary thinking by engaging children in modeling its foundations. *Science Education, 96*(4), 701–724.

Lehrer, R., Strom, D., & Confrey, J. (2002). Grounding metaphors and inscriptional resonance: Children's emerging understanding of mathematical similarity. *Cognition and Instruction, 20*(3), 359–398.

McKenney, S., & Reeves, T. C. (2012). *Conducting educational design research.* London, UK: Routledge.

McNamara, D. S., Kintsch, E., Songer, N. B., & Kintsch, W. (1996). Are good texts always better? Interactions of text coherence, background knowledge, and levels of understanding in learning from text. *Cognition and Instruction, 14*(1), 1–43.

Mintrop, R. (2016). *Design based school improvement: A practical guide for education leaders.* Cambridge, MA: Harvard Education Press.

Plomp, T. (2013). Educational design research: An introduction. In T. Plomp & N. Nieveen (Eds.), *Educational design research: Part A: An introduction* (pp. 10–51). Enschede, the Netherlands: SLO.

Roth, W.-M. (2003). Competent workplace mathematics: How signs become transparent in use. *International Journal of Computers for Mathematical Learning, 8*(2), 161–189.

Sanders, T., Land, J., & Mulder, G. (2007). Linguistics markers of coherence improve text comprehension in functional contexts. *Information Design Journal, 15*(3), 219–235.

Smit, J., Bakker, A., Van Eerde, D., & Kuijpers, M. (2016). Using genre pedagogy to promote student proficiency in the language required for interpreting line graphs. *Mathematics Education Research Journal, 28*(3), 457–478.

Swales, J. M., & Feak, C. B. (2004). *Academic writing for graduate students: Essential tasks and skills* (2nd ed.). Ann Arbor, MI: University of Michigan Press.

Tuomi-Gröhn, T., & Engeström, Y. (2003). Conceptualizing transfer: From standard notions to developmental perspectives. In T. Tuomi-Gröhn & Y. Engeström (Eds.), *Between school and work: New perspectives on transfer and boundary-crossing* (pp. 19–38). Amsterdam, the Netherlands: Pergamon.

van Joolingen, W. R., Aukes, A. V. A., Gijlers, H., & Bollen, L. (2015). Understanding elementary astronomy by making drawing-based models. *Journal of Science Education and Technology, 24*(2), 256–264. doi:10.1007/s10956-014-9540-6

Wallwork, A. (2011). *English for writing research papers.* New York, NY: Springer.

Weissberg, R., & Buker, S. (1990). *Writing up research.* Englewood Cliffs, NJ: Prentice Hall.

Chapter 8

Supervising design research in education

Summary

This chapter focuses on the supervision of design research projects (design studies), with acknowledgment of the variety of roles that early career researchers can have (e.g., master's, PhD, EdD student, or postdoc). Although primarily written for supervisors, the chapter may be useful for the researchers themselves too when they want to reflect on their own learning or feel the need to reorient their supervisors.

There are at least three ways to get into design research in education. One is as part of a master's, EdD (Doctor of Education), or PhD program. In master's programs, students pay for their education. In some countries, such as the US and UK, students sign up for a PhD or EdD program, often paying for it themselves or possibly through a bursary, or scholarship(s). They often take part in a larger research program led by a professor, and find their own niche in a long-term research agenda or program. A second way of doing design research as a PhD student or postdoc is that candidates apply for predefined projects for which there is funding, say from a national research council or foundation. In that case, supervisors can select suitable candidates for the topic. A third route is for candidates, mostly teachers in my experience, to write a proposal, often with the help of a supervisor, and find funding for it. In some countries, there are special bursaries and programs for teachers that want to get a PhD and thus help to bring educational practice and theory closer together (e.g., Bakx, Bakker, Koopman, & Beijaard, 2016). The dual promotion program in Bremen combines a master's and PhD program in which candidates simultaneously gain their teaching degree (MA) and a PhD in education. It goes without saying that each of these ways of engaging in research may need its own type of supervision.

In my interview study about design research, I have asked experts from various countries about their experiences with supervising researchers. Where I put no year to a name, I refer to an interviewee rather than a publication. In this chapter, I combine their answers with my own experiences, ordered per research phase from choice of candidate to the defense of a dissertation.

Before the project

Helping to write a proposal

Most educational and funding programs require candidates to write a proposal. Given the open nature of design research, this is not always so easy (Kelly, 2006; Phillips, 2006). Yet some guidelines can be followed (Edelson, 2006; Herrington, McKenney, Reeves, & Oliver, 2007). In Chapter 7, I also provide general writing guidelines. One tip to get external funding is to promise design research for developing a quality intervention, but also plan solid evaluation or even an experiment. Without the latter, it is often harder to get the money.

Required expertise

Design research in education requires a double expertise: design and research. Actually, experience in teaching a particular topic may be a third required expertise. There are very few candidates that already have such hybrid or triple expertise at the start of their project. In some countries, such as the Netherlands and Germany, there are more and more opportunities for in-service teachers and even pre-service teachers to combine teaching with research. Such teachers typically have a strong background in their own discipline (English, geography, history, music, etc.) and in teaching it, but not necessarily in social scientific research. For most of them, this transition to the social sciences is quite a challenge. For this reason, I often advise teachers who are interested in a PhD project to enroll in research methods courses and take plenty of time alongside such courses to write their proposal. This may take a year or more, but it gives them a head start and it increases their chances of getting funding. Combining teaching and research can be quite a challenge, because it requires boundary crossing between different worlds (Bakx et al., 2016). This shuttling between the practices of school and university, however, also has learning potential to develop new expertise.

Selection of candidates

For the selection of candidates (or reflecting on whether you consider yourself suitable for a PhD project in design research), it is worth thinking through the qualities required. The experts I interviewed stressed that design research is challenging, and that candidates, therefore, need to be good at the regular things one would expect of a PhD student or postdoc, plus:

- have expertise in and passion for the area of the design (emphasized by many interviewees);
- have good communication skills because they typically have to collaborate with heads of school, teachers, students, or perhaps trainers (McKenney & Brand-Gruwel, 2015);
- have the ability to handle insecurity;
- have good writing skills (or the ability to develop them), because the design researcher cannot follow fixed writing formats as are common in reporting quantitative studies. Rather, narratives need to be convincing (cf. Easley, 1977);
- have the ability to work in a larger team that works on a longer-term project.

The last point was made by scholars in the US, where such big projects are more common than elsewhere. The advantage is that individual students can focus on a very specific aspect of the larger project, an aspect they find interesting. The division of labor also implies that a student does not have to be good at everything in the whole process. However, the design researchers I have met or supervised in the Netherlands and Germany typically have their own project. Supervisors mostly advise but do not co-design, collect data, or co-analyze. They typically give feedback on all aspects and act as co-authors. In the US and UK, I have seen very different practices, where principal investigators are really taking part in the research from writing the proposal, via co-designing, to collecting data and writing publications.

I know young researchers who need clarity and control, and even want to be positivists in their thinking – something that does not go very well with design research. For such people, design research may not be a suitable approach, unless they are hoping to become more flexible.

During the project

Allow the candidate to gain broader expertise

If the student is not familiar with a field of expertise or a tool on which the design research focuses, a first step would be to stimulate them to become an expert in the domain at stake. For example, much design research focuses on the potential of new technology. Any student intending to make the most of such technology needs to become deeply familiar with it so as to think through how it could be used or adapted in powerful ways.

During my PhD project I was lucky to be part of the *TinkerPlots* project – a software design project funded by the US National Science Foundation, directed by a leading statistics educator, Cliff Konold (Konold & Miller, 2005). One lesson I learned is that so much practical knowledge is easily and freely shared in teams (and during conferences) that never ends up in a scientific publication. Getting in touch and working with experienced people, during conferences or otherwise, is therefore very stimulating for early career researchers.

More generally, McKenney and Brand-Gruwel (2015) distinguish three roles: researcher, developer (designer), and facilitator. In these roles, they argue, four competences are required: empathy, orchestration, flexibility, and social competence. Empathy includes what I would refer to as the ability to take the perspectives of others. Orchestration includes organizational qualities of arranging everything. Flexibility is required because as a design researcher one does not have much control: co-design, emerging insights, and creativity all imply potential change. Last, social competence is needed to collaborate with all involved to keep things going. More recently, Kali, Eylon, McKenney, and Kidron (in press) mention another important competence: boundary-crossing competence, which Walker and Nocon (2007) define as "the ability to function competently in multiple contexts" (p. 178).

Design first, research second

In his design research course, Dor Abrahamson says to his starting students: "Don't worry about the research, first focus on the design." This applies to students with expertise in the field for which they design, but without expertise in social scientific research. "You have to build the context of design before the questions emerge," he adds. To help his students, he gives them a template discussed in Chapter 9. In the first sessions of his course on design research, Abrahamson talks about design only. Gradually he stimulates the participants to talk about their designs in more general terms (artifact, function, learning ecology) and look for commonalities between different design ideas that the participants work on. Over time, by reading scientific literature attuned to their own design, they come to think more theoretically about their own and others' designs and start worrying about methodology. Typically this transition emerges quite naturally, Abrahamson says.

It is for this reason that the typical master's or PhD student who does not have a background in a social science, such as educational science or psychology, may best postpone the reading about methodological issues until s/he feels ready (Chapter 5). In practice, this may have to be quite soon, for example, if a formal requirement of the funder is that a detailed research proposal has to be written at an early stage of the project.

In line with the previous point, several experts agreed that the research question should not be fixed too soon in the process. Of course, a design problem (what do you want to achieve with your design?) needs to be defined rather early in the process, but it takes time to identify an interesting phenomenon that is both new enough from a scientific perspective and fascinating enough for the candidate to clutch onto for the coming years. It sometimes takes two-thirds of the project to get the research questions in definitive form. Lehrer added that cultivating patience in students is an important task of the supervisor.

In Cobb's experience, students tend to tell what they want to do, but not why. So his first endeavors are to help them make explicit what they want to figure out and why: "I'm not asking for a very tight statement of a research question, but I am asking for what can eventually be *developed* into a research question, because I think that drives the whole thing." As mentioned in Chapter 3, the hypothetical learning trajectories he uses focus on the big ideas and thus do not contain many details.

In my experience, criteria for research questions should not be given to students too early because the many norms in research practice can be paralyzing. First ensure that water flows through the river before you start redirecting or damming it, as one of my music teachers used to say.

Think big, start small

It is advised to pilot ideas early on – whether an initial idea, doodling on a napkin in a bar, or testing an activity on one or two kids. Some researchers prefer the ecologically valid context of a classroom to do design research, but several design researchers take the – in my opinion – more realistic stance that starting small is wise, by filtering out obvious problems in small settings (Collins, 1992; Tessmer, 1993), even within design based implementation research (Fishman, Penuel, Allen, Cheng, & Sabelli, 2013).

Whatever the pilot or initial study is about, it needs to be framed as a case of something more general (Chapter 9), a theoretical idea that you try to embody in your design (Sandoval, 2014). Otherwise, no theoretical generalization is possible (Yin, 1994). After all, the researcher is designing a possible future, and this future has to be characterized in some way beyond the concrete design. One way in which a supervisor can stimulate such theoretical thinking is by discussing the design of artifacts from daily life (e.g., nutcrackers) in terms of design characteristics and function (cf. Chapter 9). I have used Abrahamson's metaphor successfully in workshops: The intended outcome or function of a nutcracker is to crack nuts (duh!). The mechanism or mediating process deployed is typically the physical law of the lever (see Figure 8.1). If F1 is the force used on one side at a distance of d1 from the fulcrum, then the resulting force F2 on the other side at shorter distance d2 can be much higher, because $F1 \times d1 = F2 \times d2$. To achieve this, the design of the nutcracker needs to have a particular characteristic: the distance from the fulcrum to the force-using hand needs to be bigger than the distance from the fulcrum to the nut.

Something similar, though not as deterministic, holds for the working of a design: A characteristic is embodied in a design, and is expected to lead to particular mechanisms that lead to the intended outcome (Sandoval, 2014). Helping students frame their design in more general, theoretical terms can thus

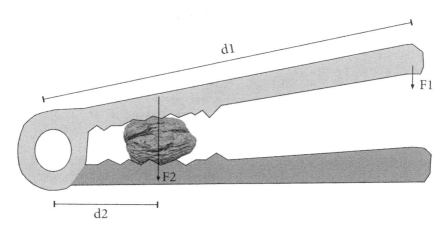

Figure 8.1 Lever mechanism of a nutcracker

help to ensure they focus on big issues rather than what Papert (2004) calls *Sunday-Monday issues* – small changes one can make to an instructional tool or activity overnight.

Helping to cut up the elephant

A design research project can become huge. Because of design researchers' preference for authentic settings, holistic views, and studying larger ecologies, the number of relevant issues can be overwhelming. An important task for any supervisor is thus to help students break the project down into smaller and more manageable studies. One of my colleagues, Albert Pilot, calls this "cutting up the elephant." In Chapters 4 and 6 I discuss the smaller studies that can be conducted within a design research project (e.g., problem analysis, design, implementation, evaluation, redesign). There are several generic models for design research that can help one think through a good structure for the overall project (Dowse & Howie, 2013; McKenney & Reeves, 2012; Wademan, 2005). It is also worth looking at examples of design research projects by PhD students to see how they have managed to conduct them (e.g., Prins, 2010).

Another metaphor to make a design research project less overwhelming is by framing it as an unfolding journey rather than a destination (Van den Boer, 2003). In my interview with Brenda Bannan (personal communication, December 19, 2016), she characterized this journey as "an inquiry process, where you're trying to build something in your learning by building that thing and testing it out in the real world and seeing what happens and using those insights to then re-design."

Textbox 8.1

Question: How can one keep a design research project **manageable** for one MA or PhD student?

Response: This depends on the situation. When the student's design study is part of a larger project, perhaps a large grant, you can define one smaller aspect that is worth studying in and of itself from a particular theoretical lens (e.g., student interest, engagement, tool use, nature of interaction). If the student is a teacher researcher with a lot of experience in a particular domain and a supportive school environment that really wants to implement an innovation anyway, then you even may consider design based implementation research (DBIR), as proposed by Fishman, Penuel and colleagues (Fishman, Penuel, Allen, Cheng, & Sabelli, 2013). However, when working with a master's student, keeping whatever is designed small (one or two lessons or learning activities) seems necessary. An alternative is for the student to redesign something that has already been studied but still has some flaws. Then there is already a design and a research base on which to build. Another option that may work if several students are interested in the same project is to define complementary studies such as a problem analysis, a needs analysis, an expert study on learning goals, a textbook analysis of these learning goals, a study of students' prior knowledge of this topic, or a literature review on this topic (see also Chapters 4 and 6). In later phases of the project you can think of judging various aspects of implementation to develop and validate assessment instruments.

In any case, one should bear in mind the student's academic trajectories and programmatic requirements as well as their interest and apparent capacity. Doctoral students need evidence in their projects that they have become an autonomous researcher. A master's student should not put on their plate more than they can chew given their constrained time. A preservice teacher in a graduate program might be obligated to abide with some departmental protocol stipulating that their project is arguably on phenomena pertaining to classroom practice and of relevance to the collaborating school.

Part II of this book includes two-pagers from undergraduate and graduate students who took a design research course as well as two full papers from graduate students. These examples give a sense of what is possible within a limited time frame of one semester.

Prepare students during their education

Brenda Bannan suggested that students can already be prepared for a PhD project in their master's program. In the doctoral program of learning technology design research,[1] students already do micro-cycles of design research at an early stage, which then becomes pilot work for their dissertation. In this way, students sometimes already have two or three years' experience with a particular topic before they do their PhD research on it. Chapters 10–17 are examples of student work during another graduate program. Some of this work grew into a PhD project (as explained in Chapter 9).

Form a research team or collaboration with schools

For the aforementioned "elephant-related" reasons, almost all interviewees stressed that design research is ideally done by a bigger team. This only works if resources for such teams are available. Most PhD projects using design research that I am aware of in Europe are solo projects. Yet funders may stimulate PhD candidates to form interlinked research projects focusing on a single setting and design from multiple perspectives. This would make the design efforts and part of the literature review underlying it more efficient and more productive. Moreover, different students can bring in different qualities and types of expertise.

Tom Reeves argued for establishing long-term relationships with schools in the area so that there is a common understanding of the problems that schools and researchers jointly want to tackle. Different students can then work on different aspects of these problems within a pre-existing infrastructure. Students could, for example, evaluate initiatives started by others (teachers, schools, researchers, or combinations) without having to set up everything themselves.

Design researchers who work in authentic learning environments or even involve different stakeholders in a joint project, such as in DBIR, typically interact with people from multiple practices. This implies less control than some researchers would like to have on the design, learning goals, and procedures (Penuel, 2014; Penuel & Gallagher, 2017). In the interview with Penuel, he stressed the delicate balance between the authority of the scientific literature and of participants with their own constraints, views, and goals. Penuel emphasized that DBIR projects are typically too large for PhD students to conduct. Rather, PhD students learn "how to negotiate the focus of a project with an external partner." For this he uses an apprenticeship model, where students first see how a senior researcher does such negotiation with stakeholders in the project. This again implies that design researchers need to acquire particular skills that may be less relevant to other types of research projects (McKenney & Reeves, 2012). More generally, design researchers typically need boundary-crossing competences – to interact with people from different practices with different goals, tools, norms, rules knowledge, and histories (Akkerman, Bronk-horst, & Zitter, 2013). It is only in recent years that more insight into the work by educational design teams has been uncovered (Kali, 2016).

Changing research questions

The aforementioned point of having patience with arriving at proper research questions also implies that students often need some reassurance about chang-ing their research questions. As with much (other) qualitative research, it is fine to hone the question along the way. As described in Chapter 4, students need to become aware of the difference between their own research questions and proper research questions. To decide whether a question really counts as a research question often requires reading additional literature.

However, several interviewees also warned for an opposite problem. It some-times happens that early career researchers use the label of design research to mask that they do not really know what they want to know. The advice not to worry about the final research question is then used as an excuse for not having provisional research questions. Of course, such students need nudging to work with clearer aims and questions.

Keep asking: What is this a case of?

What helps in staying on track is to ask: What is what you study a case of? How can you frame this theoretically (Chapter 9)? Once deeply into the design and testing phases, students are often bogged down in all kinds of very concrete decisions and observations. Taking a moment to reflect on what building this research was all about may then be good to see the details within the bigger picture, and thus help to distinguish what matters from a research perspective from what matters in terms of keeping the practical things going.

This may be especially important for students whose initial drive is to make the best possible design for their topic. If they have not been trained in edu-cational sciences, their inclination may be research-based design, rather than design based research. Such early career researchers may need regular remind-ing of the knowledge yield of their project. What may help, also to keep in mind what the design and observed phenomena are a case of, is to stimulate students to keep reading the relevant literature. This also prevents them from reinventing the wheel.

What is the function of this part of the study?

One question I often ask during workshops with PhD students is which research function the particular study has in the bigger project (Chapter 4). For the rigor of the analysis of data, it makes a big difference whether students are improving their designs (research-based design) or are evaluating their designs (design based research). When doing quick iterations, it does not make sense to make verbatim transcriptions of interviews, let alone to do interrater reliability checks on analysis procedures. However, if a particular analysis seems worth publishing as interesting in its own right, then transcribing, making a coding book, and computing a measure of agreement (e.g., Cohen's kappa, Krippendorff's alpha, intraclass correlation) become serious options. Some social scientists are skeptical about reliability checks (Thomas, 2013). Yet in practice, reviewers often ask for reliability measures. A good alternative or addition can be member checking (at least with adults) – a validation of your interpretation (say of an interview done with a teacher).

I also often ask early career researchers whether they are after a proof of principle (is this possible?) or whether they want to change practice. As pointed out in Chapter 6, such choices imply very different argumentative grammars. If a proof of principle is sufficient, showing that an educational idea or new tool can work is enough. However, if the ambition is to change practice in a sustainable way beyond the involvement of the researcher, very different approaches are required (Cole & Distributive Literacy Consortium, 2006; Penuel & Gallagher, 2017).

Textbox 8.2

Question: Should each design cycle be analyzed in the same way?
Response: Not necessarily. Early cycles typically have a formative function to improve the design, or hone the research question. As Plomp (2013) writes, it makes sense to test a design first on relevance and consistency before evaluating its practicality and effectiveness. Later cycles can have a more summative function, for example to assess if educational goals have been achieved.

   However, if the intention is to make claims about the improvement of, for example, design principles across cycles – as done by Kali (2008), then comparison is only possible if the same analysis is applied to each cycle. See also Chapter 6 to decide which argumentative grammar is at stake.

Staying open-minded

Most students I know and hear about in the interviews have a rather linear view of doing research. This does not only apply to research questions, but also to using hypothetical learning trajectories (HLTs) or conjecture maps. Though powerful in focusing students on what they want to achieve and observe, such research instruments can also narrow their minds on predefined objects of study. If the comparison of HLTs or conjecture maps with the collected data seems too narrow, then additional more open coding can be worth considering. I have found the constant comparative method from grounded theory (Boeije, 2002, 2010; Glaser, 1976) to be a powerful technique for such broader analysis. In my experience, however, students often try to stick too close to guidelines of how to perform such analyses, and it is often necessary to define an analysis approach slightly different from the original resources, for example as proposed by Cobb and Whitenack (1996).

Several interviewees emphasized the importance of staying open-minded. An ecological view of learning implies that many more things may matter than initially theorized. When making field notes or analyzing videos, it is worth making notes of all potentially interesting or relevant factors, even those outside the predefined variables or objects of study. Some design researchers like keeping a diary of all kinds of thoughts they had during their research. If something interesting pops up in retrospective analysis, they at least have a record of their considerations. Design researchers can thus learn from ethnographers (Burgess, 1981).

It is commonly necessary to change the learning goals because the initial formulations were too ambitious or too broad, or to change the initial unit of analysis. More frequently, students have to broaden the unit of analysis because the collective is more important than their initial focus on individuals. Perhaps students note that classroom norms have a much bigger impact than they had initially expected (e.g., Yackel & Cobb, 1996).

Learning from failure

Many educational researchers are hesitant to report failure, despite its importance for scientific progress (Firestein, 2015). Andy diSessa told me that his audiences often respond surprised if he first talks about things that went wrong in his design research (e.g., diSessa, 2008). This is not so surprising in cultures where success matters. However, many design researchers I talked to emphasize the importance of lessons from what went wrong. O'Neill (2012) uses the history of aeronautics to argue for publicly sharing failures to move the field forward. This way of thinking seems more common in engineering than in education.

One common failure is that teachers do not implement designs as intended. Should we be surprised? How many of us like being told what to do and when? There can be many reasons why teachers do not act according to the researcher's plan. Chapter 20 (Konrad) provides an example of how one can shift from teachers-as-implementer to teacher-as-active-agent or even co-designer. More generally, students are often worried if they do not reach the stage of evaluation or comparison that they wanted to reach. Often, my advice is to make the obstacles the new object of research. So rather than continuing to see teachers or others as the hurdle in the enactment of design researchers' ideas, shift the attention to understanding teachers in the newly created settings. A challenge, which one of my PhD students has also encountered, is that such a shift requires much additional reading and sometimes even the involvement of an additional supervisor who is more expert in the new topic of research (e.g., teacher professional development).

Failure can actually have nice rhetorical power too, because it justifies the design researcher talking about at least two cycles of design (e.g., Simon, Kara, Norton, Placa, in press) or of the need to change to a different theoretical construct to improve analysis (e.g., Kapon & diSessa, 2012).

There is no need to avoid experiments

Design researchers often defend their work against the dominance of randomized controlled trials. They point to the limitations of experiments and thinking in terms of a limited set of independent and dependent variables. However, as several interviewees emphasized, there is a place for experiments in design research as well. Once a student knows the context and the working of a design so well that he or she is confident about the variables that matter, there is nothing wrong with testing a hypothesis experimentally. Moreover, as pointed out in the first intermezzo: If numbers of participants are big enough, such as is sometimes the case with MOOCs, experiments are possible within design research projects to guide important design decisions.

Publish or perish

One of the challenging tasks for design researchers is to publish their studies in journal articles. In the Netherlands and several other countries, the expectation is more and more that a PhD dissertation includes about four journal articles, of which at least one has to be accepted before the defense can be done. This can be difficult for several reasons. One is that design research, like much qualitative scientific enterprise, often asks for *thick descriptions* (Geertz, 1973). Where quantitative studies often can be reported in a few thousand words, design studies typically require more space. The article by Cobb, McClain, and Gravemeijer (2003) is 78 pages long! Only few journals accept such long papers.

A second reason is that many reviewers are still not very familiar with the methodological framework of design research. Recently I received reviews for a manuscript submitted to a journal that deliberately strives to be progressive. The two reviewers both asked for a control group, whereas we had made explicit that we aimed for different learning goals than in regular education, so a control group would not make sense. Yet these reviewers were so conditioned (in our view) that they could not imagine the value of a description for how particular learning could be fostered and what the learning gain could be from pre- to posttest. The manuscript was finally published in another journal (Smit, Bakker, Van Eerde, & Kuijpers, 2016).

A third reason is that design research tends to be holistic. A learning ecology has many facets, and it is not so easy to identify the key issues. It is rare that a few variables can be singled out for manipulation or description. Many reviewers are not so interested in the identification of learning goals, the design, or implementation if not accompanied by a report of the learning effects. However, reporting all four aspects in one journal article rarely succeeds. Hence design researchers need to be creative in focusing on cases of something more general.

When working on an article, Susan McKenney asks the student to come to the meeting with a few "inspiration articles" from the intended journal that are conceptually or methodologically close to what they intend to write. They deconstruct these articles together to see how they can make their own writing work for that journal.

One trick I have often seen, perhaps too often, is to write about design research as a methodological enterprise. As long as design research has not yet matured, this is inevitable, but I agree with several interviewees that what the field most needs is high-quality examples of design research (e.g., Barab, Thomas, Dodge, Carteaux, & Tuzun, 2005; Cobb et al., 2003; Edelson, 2001).

When not to call it design research

As many interviewees emphasized, design research is an orientation, not a strict methodology or a distinct research approach. The orientation includes a serious attempt to design something that improves an educational setting. This typically requires several iterations. However, there may be several reasons not to do design research after all, or not to call it design research in scientific publications.

One obvious reason to decide not to do design research is if the primary focus is research-based design, or if another research strategy is a better fit with the research question. One tendency I have observed is that students start with an ideal to improve a situation. They have an idea of how a particular teaching approach could benefit learners in some respect. Many of them initially think of doing an experiment to test if their idea works, but they gradually realize that getting to the stage of doing a proper experiment mostly is a steep path. It requires designing something that works well enough to count as an embodiment of the theoretical idea and thinking through what mechanisms are at stake to achieve the intended outcomes. Mostly students discover that their initial thinking in terms of a few variables does not do justice to the complexity of the situation. Some of them then opt for design research. However, as pointed out several times, it is very well possible that in starting with a design orientation they stumble upon relevant problems or phenomena that are worth investigating and publishing as interesting in their own right.

Several interviewees (e.g., Susan McKenney) emphasized they do a lot of "front-end work," referring to understanding the problem better, identifying students' prior knowledge or teachers' current practices, unraveling the target expertise, studying the literature on potential ways of achieving something, or formulating design criteria (e.g., Boschman, McKenney, Pieters, & Voogt, 2016; Boschman, McKenney, & Voogt, 2015; Raval, McKenney, & Pieters, 2012; Vanderhoven, Schellens, & Valcke, 2013; Vanderhoven, Schellens, Valcke, Raes, 2014).

Another reason for some people not to call their work design research is if they have managed to complete only one design cycle. Even though one does not always need all cross-cutting characteristics of design research to call it such (Cobb et al., 2003), most scholars are still hesitant to use the term when having done just one cycle of design, testing, and analysis.

It happens quite often that design researchers, when publishing part of their work, do not even mention the term design research. A pragmatic reason could be that what they present is better understood by the audience of the journal as something else, say a case study or an intervention study. I know several colleagues who present only the last cycle of their design research project as an intervention study, and thus save words needed to explain the larger design study.

A related reason could be that it does not add much to the story to tell the reader that the study was part of a design research project. I have co-authored several articles that were conducted in the broader setting of a design research project involving design and redesign of tablet applications but were in themselves not design studies. For example, when using newly designed embodied tasks for proportional reasoning, the newly created settings facilitated the study of new phenomena, such as the emergence of so-called attentional anchors (Abrahamson, Shayan, Bakker, & Van der Schaaf, 2016; Duijzer, Shayan, Bakker, Van der Schaaf, & Abrahamson, 2017). Similarly, data generated from an earlier design research project on statistics education allowed us to critique fundamental and theoretical issues in semiotics (Bakker, 2007; Bakker & Hoffmann, 2005); and rich data from another design research project highlighted aspects of whole-class scaffolding that would not have easily come to light in descriptive studies (Bakker & Smit, 2017; Smit, Van Eerde, & Bakker, 2013).

End phase

Book or papers?

Nobody said that publishing studies from a design research project is easy (Reeves, McKenney, & Herrington, 2011), so it requires creativity and high-quality writing to get it done. As supervisors, together with our students we need to set the standards and be clear about the criteria. One question to ask is whether it is better to write a book or papers.

In some institutes there is no question: PhD students have to write a particular number of papers (mostly three or four) of which perhaps one or two have to be accepted before the defense can take place. But in other research groups, there is a choice, with pros and cons on both sides. Advantages of writing a book (monograph) include:

(a) Design research is often hard to cut up in paper-sized chunks. By writing a book, you avoid repetition of theoretical backgrounds typically seen in collections of papers.
(b) In a book, you can report on initial design cycles including the failures that are sometimes hard to sell in paper form. A book allows for thick descriptions (Geertz, 1973) and rich, complex stories (Reeves et al., 2011).
(c) The PhD candidate is the sole author, which makes it easier to judge the candidate's contribution. In multi-author papers, this is difficult to see. The degree of support or even co-writing varies considerably across supervisors.

However, there are also benefits to writing papers:

(a) By starting to write early, you learn to write in an early phase. Paper-sized publications are less intimidating than a whole book, and putting papers together with an introduction and a discussion chapter is more manageable than writing a whole monograph in the last year.
(b) In terms of a future career in academia, it is essential in many countries to have a few good journal articles.
(c) There will be less time between conducting a study and its publication than when writing a complete dissertation.
(d) Dissertations in several countries often remain unpublished.
(e) For supervisors, papers are attractive because their supervision time pays out in co-authored publications.
(f) Journal articles are typically more accessible and more easily found than books.

Of course, those with ambition can do both: Write a monograph and write as many articles as is feasible.

Selection of committee members

When it comes to a defense of a dissertation, selecting committee members is something that requires some consideration. Given that design research is still relatively new and takes place in a different commissive space from that of the majority of educational researchers, the selection of committee members to judge the quality of a dissertation is important. This does not mean that mild people have to be approached but those who can judge the quality of the design research project in its own right. Over the past years, this seems to have become easier (Brenda Bannan, personal communication, December 19, 2016). It may be necessary to make explicit criteria against which design researchers would like their work to be judged. For example, one early career researcher

I interviewed was somewhat disappointed that supervisors or committee members only judged the quality of the research without paying attention to the qualities of what was co-designed. As Plomp (2013) points out, various criteria can be applied to designs in the different phases of development (relevance, consistency, practicality, effectiveness).

Stay upbeat

Some colleagues say that design research is the hardest and most ambitious among the research approaches (cf. Phillips & Dolle, 2006). In some of the interviews, I indeed sensed this ambitious take on design research: Big teams and long-term engagement are required; design researchers need many different types of expertise; design research should not only lead to high-quality products, but also ontological innovation (diSessa & Cobb, 2004). It is not surprising that an upcoming research approach has to safeguard itself against sloppy examples. However, I think too-high norms can also paralyze students.

In my interviews, I was thus pleasantly surprised by optimistic views. For example, Larike Bronkhorst considered formative and design research as "the nicest; it's one of the nicest types of educational research, because you come into contact with the humans that are going to use it and you get to be creative." Practitioners enriched her ideas, and their feedback was rewarding. She also emphasized that the fact that design research has not yet matured as a methodology (cf. Cobb, Jackson, & Dunlap, 2017) implies that she as an early career researcher had to think through many fundamental methodological issues – something that she would not have done if they had used a fully matured methodology.

Qiyun Wang, a graduate of the University of Twente, considered design research a very "safe" approach. By this he meant that one can always learn something interesting that is worth reporting. His view on experimental studies was that they were a lot of work given the required sample sizes and that they often led to no or small effects (cf. Russel, 2001). In such a case, there seems to be very little to report.

I would like to end on a personal note. Although I sometimes wonder why educational sciences have made so little progress – think back to Dewey's (1900) and Glaser's (1976) plea for a linking science – I also find it very stimulating that I can contribute to the further development of a methodological approach that aims to bring together fundamental, theoretical insights and educational practice. The work to be done is really substantial, so early career researchers can make huge contributions to the field.

Note

1 https://learntech.gmu.edu/design-research

References

Abrahamson, D., Shayan, S., Bakker, A., & Van der Schaaf, M. (2016). Eye-tracking Piaget: Capturing the emergence of attentional anchors in the coordination of proportional motor action. *Human Development, 58*(4–5), 218–244.

Akkerman, S. F., Bronkhorst, L. H., & Zitter, I. (2013). The complexity of educational design research. *Quality & Quantity, 47*(1), 421–439.

Bakker, A. (2007). Diagrammatic reasoning and hypostatic abstraction in statistics education. *Semiotica, 164*, 9–29.

Bakker, A., & Hoffmann, M. H. G. (2005). Diagrammatic reasoning as the basis for developing concepts: A semiotic analysis of students' learning about statistical distribution. *Educational Studies in Mathematics, 60*(3), 333–358.

Bakker, A., & Smit, J. (2017). Theory development in design based research: An example about scaffolding mathematical language. In S. Doff & R. Komoss (Eds.), *Making change happen* (pp. 111–126). Wiesbaden, Germany: Springer.

Bakx, A., Bakker, A., Koopman, M., & Beijaard, D. (2016). Boundary crossing by science teacher researchers in a PhD program. *Teaching and Teacher Education, 60*, 76–87.

Barab, S., Thomas, M., Dodge, T., Carteaux, R., & Tuzun, H. (2005). Making learning fun: Quest Atlantis, a game without guns. *Educational Technology Research and Development, 53*(1), 86–107.

Boeije, H. (2002). A purposeful approach to the constant comparative method in the analysis of qualitative interviews. *Quality & Quantity, 36*(4), 391–409.

Boeije, H. (2010). *Analysis in qualitative research.* London, UK: Sage.

Boschman, F., McKenney, S., Pieters, J., & Voogt, J. (2016). Exploring the role of content knowledge in teacher design conversations. *Journal of Computer Assisted Learning, 32*(2), 157–169.

Boschman, F., McKenney, S., & Voogt, J. (2015). Exploring teachers' use of TPACK in design talk: The collaborative design of technology-rich early literacy activities. *Computers & Education, 82*(Supplement C), 250–262. doi:10.1016/j.compedu.2014.11.010

Burgess, R. G. (1981). Keeping a research diary. *Cambridge Journal of Education, 11*(1), 75–83. doi:10.1080/0305764810110106

Cobb, P., Jackson, K., & Dunlap, C. (2017). Conducting design studies to investigate and support mathematics students' and teachers' learning. In J. Cai (Ed.), *First compendium for research in mathematics education* (pp. 208–233). Reston, VA: National Council of Teachers of Mathematics.

Cobb, P., McClain, K., & Gravemeijer, K. P. E. (2003). Learning about statistical covariation. *Cognition and Instruction, 21*(1), 1–78.

Cobb, P., & Whitenack, J. W. (1996). A method for conducting longitudinal analyses of classroom videorecordings and transcripts. *Educational Studies in Mathematics, 30*(3), 213–228.

Cole, M., & Distributive Literacy Consortium. (2006). *The fifth dimension: An after-school program built on diversity.* New York, NY: Russell Sage Foundation.

Collins, A. (1992). Toward a design science of education. In E. Scanlon & T. O'Shea (Eds.), *New directions in educational technology* (pp. 15–22). New York, NY: Springer.

Dewey, J. (1900). Psychology and social practice. *Psychological Review, 7*(2), 105–124.

diSessa, A. A. (2008). Can students re-invent fundamental scientific principles? Evaluating the promise of new-media literacies. In T. Willoughby & E. Wood (Eds.), *Children's learning in a digital world* (pp. 218–248). Oxford, UK: Blackwell.

diSessa, A. A., & Cobb, P. (2004). Ontological innovation and the role of theory in design experiments. *Journal of the Learning Sciences, 13*(1), 77–103.

Dowse, C., & Howie, S. (2013). Promoting academic research writing with South African master's students in the field of education. In T. Plomp & N. Nieveen (Eds.), *Educational design research – Part B: Illustrative cases* (pp. 851–879). Enschede, the Netherlands: SLO.

Duijzer, A. C. G., Shayan, S., Bakker, A., Van der Schaaf, M. F., & Abrahamson, D. (2017). Touchscreen tablets: Coordinating action and perception for mathematical cognition. *Frontiers in Psychology, 8*(144). doi:10.3389/fpsyg.2017.00144

Easley, J. A. (1977). *On clinical studies in mathematics education.* Columbus, OH: Ohio State University.

Edelson, D. C. (2001). Learning-for-use: A framework for the design of technology-supported inquiry activities. *Journal of Research in Science Teaching, 38*(3), 355–385.

Edelson, D. C. (2006). Balancing innovation and risk: Assessing design research proposals. In J. van den Akker, K. P. E. Gravemeijer, S. McKenney, & N. Nieveen (Eds.), *Educational Design Research* (pp. 100–106). London, UK: Routledge.

Firestein, S. (2015). *Failure: Why science is so successful.* Oxford, UK: Oxford University Press.

Fishman, B. J., Penuel, W. R., Allen, A. R., Cheng, B. H., & Sabelli, N. O. R. A. (2013). Design based implementation research: An emerging model for transforming the relationship of research and practice. *National Society for the Study of Education, 112*(2), 136–156.

Geertz, C. (1973). Thick description: Toward an interpretive theory of culture. In C. Geertz (Ed.), *The interpretation of cultures: Selected essays* (pp. 3–30). New York, NY: Basic Books.

Glaser, R. (1976). Components of a psychology of instruction: Toward a science of design. *Review of Educational Research, 46*(1), 1–24.

Herrington, J., McKenney, S., Reeves, T., & Oliver, R. (2007). Design based research and doctoral students: Guidelines for preparing a dissertation proposal. *Paper Presented at the Proceedings of World Conference on Educational Multimedia, Hypermedia and Telecommunications 2007*, Chesapeake, VA.

Kali, Y. (2008). The design principles database as means for promoting design based research. In A. E. Kelly, R. A. Lesh, & J. Y. Baek (Eds.), *Handbook of design research methods in education: Innovations in science, technology, engineering, and mathematics learning and teaching* (pp. 423–438). Mahwah, NJ: Lawrence Erlbaum Associates.

Kali, Y. (2016). Transformative learning in design research: The story behind the scenes. *Keynote Presentation at ICLS 2016*, Singapore. Retrieved from www.isls.org/icls/2016/docs/Keynote2-Yael_Kali-ICLS2016-keynote-FINAL(condenced).pdf.

Kali, Y., Eylon, B. S., McKenney, S., & Kidron, A. (in press). Design-centric research-practice partnerships: Three key lenses for building productive bridges between theory and practice. In J. M. Spector, B. B. Lockee, & M. D. Childress (Eds.), *Learning, design, and technology: An international compendium of theory, research, practice, and policy.* London, UK: Springer.

Kapon, S., & diSessa, A. A. (2012). Reasoning through instructional analogies. *Cognition and Instruction, 30*(3), 261–310.

Kelly, A. E. (2006). Quality criteria for design research. In J. van den Akker, K. P. E. Gravemeijer, S. McKenney, & N. Nieveen (Eds.), *Educational design research* (pp. 107–118). London, UK: Routledge.

Konold, C., & Miller, C. D. (2005). *TinkerPlots: Dynamic data exploration [Computer software].* Emeryville, CA: Key Curriculum Press.

McKenney, S., & Brand-Gruwel, S. (2015). Design researcher learning through and for collaboration with practitioners. *Paper Presented at the Bi-annual Meeting of the European Association for Research on Learning and Instruction (EARLI).* August 25–29, Cyprus.

McKenney, S., & Reeves, T. C. (2012). *Conducting educational design research.* London, UK: Routledge.

O'Neill, D. K. (2012). Designs that fly: What the history of aeronautics tells us about the future of design based research in education. *International Journal of Research & Method in Education, 35*(2), 119–140.

Papert, S. (2004). Keynote speech. *Paper Presented at the i3 1 to 1 Notebook Conference*, Sydney, Australia. May 31–June 2004. Retrieved from http://vimeo.com/9092144

Penuel, W. R. (2014). Emerging forms of formative intervention research in education. *Mind, Culture, and Activity, 21*(2), 97–117.

Penuel, W. R., & Gallagher, D. J. (2017). *Creating research practice partnerships in education.* Boston, MA: Harvard Education Press.

Phillips, D. (2006). Assessing the quality of design research proposals. In J. Van den Akker, K. P. E. Gravemeijer, S. McKenney, & N. Nieveen (Eds.), *Educational design research* (pp. 93–99). London, UK: Routledge.

Phillips, D. C., & Dolle, J. R. (2006). From Plato to Brown and beyond: Theory, practice, and the promise of design experiments. In L. Verschaffel, F. Dochy, M. Boekaerts, & S. Vosniadou (Eds.), *Instructional psychology: Past, present and future trends. Sixteen essays in honour of Erik De Corte* (pp. 277–292). Oxford, UK: Elsevier.

Plomp, T. (2013). Educational design research: An introduction. In T. Plomp & N. Nieveen (Eds.), *Educational design research: Part A: An introduction* (pp. 10–51). Enschede, the Netherlands: SLO.

Prins, G. T. (2010). *Teaching and learning of modelling in chemistry education: Authentic practices as contexts for learning.* Utrecht, the Netherlands: CD-Beta Press.

Raval, H., McKenney, S., & Pieters, J. (2012). Contextual factors that foster or inhibit para-teacher professional development: The case of an Indian, non-governmental organization. *International Journal of Training and Development, 16*(1), 23–38.

Reeves, T. C., McKenney, S., & Herrington, J. (2011). Publishing and perishing: The critical importance of educational design research. *Australasian Journal of Educational Technology, 27*(1), 55–65.

Russel, T. L. (2001). *The no significant difference phenomenon: A comparative research annotated bibliography on technology for distance education* (5th ed.). Chicago, IL: The International Distance Education Certification Center.

Sandoval, W. A. (2014). Conjecture mapping: An approach to systematic educational design research. *Journal of the Learning Sciences, 23*(1), 18–36.

Simon, M. A., Kara, M., Norton, A., & Placa, N. (in press). Fostering construction of a meaning for multiplication that subsumes whole-number and fraction multiplication: A study of the Learning Through Activity research program. *Journal of Mathematical Behavior.*

Smit, J., Bakker, A., Van Eerde, D., & Kuijpers, M. (2016). Using genre pedagogy to promote student proficiency in the language required for interpreting line graphs. *Mathematics Education Research Journal, 28*(3), 457–478.

Smit, J., Van Eerde, H. A. A., & Bakker, A. (2013). A conceptualisation of whole-class scaffolding. *British Educational Research Journal, 39*(5), 817–834.

Tessmer, M. (1993). *Planning and conducting formative evaluations: Improving the quality of education and training.* Abingdon, UK: Routledge.

Thomas, G. (2013). *How to do your research project: A guide for students in education and applied social sciences* (2nd ed.). London, UK: Sage.

Van den Boer, C. (2003). *Als je begrijpt wat ik bedoel: Een zoektocht voor verklaringen voor achterblijvende prestaties van allochtone leerlingen in het wiskundeonderwijs [If you know what I mean: A journey to explain lagging achievements of immigrant students in mathematics education].* Utrecht, the Netherlands: Utrecht: CD-Beta Press.

Vanderhoven, E., Schellens, T., & Valcke, M. (2013). Exploring the usefulness of school education about risks on social network sites: A survey study. *Journal of Media Literacy Education*, *5*(1), 285–294.

Vanderhoven, E., Schellens, T., Valcke, M., & Raes, A. (2014). How safe do teenagers behave on Facebook? An observational study. *PLoS ONE*, *9*(8), e104036.

Wademan, M. R. (2005). *Utilizing development research to guide people-capability maturity model adoption considerations*. (Doctoral dissertation). Syracuse, NY: Syracuse University. Dissertation Abstracts International, 67–01A, 434. (UMI No. 3205587)

Walker, D., & Nocon, H. (2007). Boundary-crossing competence: Theoretical considerations and educational design. *Mind, Culture, and Activity*, *14*(3), 178–195.

Yackel, E., & Cobb, P. (1996). Sociomathematical norms, argumentation, and autonomy in mathematics. *Journal for Research in Mathematics Education*, *27*(4), 458–477. doi:10.2307/749877

Yin, R. (1994). *Case study research: Design and methods*. Thousand Oaks, CA: Sage.

Part II

Examples

In this part, concrete examples are provided of design research projects (design studies) in different phases of development. Part II starts with a discussion of Dor Abrahamson's design research course at the University of California, Berkeley (Chapter 9). In this course students have to do a design study and report on it in a one-pager and a full paper, all in one semester. To show what undergraduate and graduate students are capable of, a variety of such one-pagers (here published on more pages) and full papers are published here as much as possible in their original presentation (Chapters 10–17). Then two chapters from the first year of PhD project highlight several aspects of writing a research proposal and formulating design principles, conjectures maps, or hypothetical learning trajectories (Chapters 18 and 19). Chapter 20 reflects on the role that a teacher played in a design study. The last example is meant to show what often remains hidden in the kitchen of the design researcher: working with hypothetical learning trajectories and struggling with succinct publication of what has been learned (Chapter 21). The book ends with a chapter in which I reflect on the mission of this book and formulate a wish list for the future of design research.

Chapter 9

Teaching design research as a case of cultivating a community of professional practice

Dor Abrahamson

Summary

In this chapter, Dor Abrahamson reflects on his course "Design Based Research Forum." Essentially a practicum on the development and evaluation of pedagogical artifacts and activities, the course offers students from a wide range of disciplines an introduction to the learning sciences theory and methods. Within a single semester, students who are often conducting their very first research study are guided to progress from product ideation and literature research through prototyping, usability piloting, micro-analysis of empirical data, iteration, and write-up. The chapter, which surveys and exemplifies key course activities, coheres thematically around the notion that students become design researchers through adopting discursive routines for conceptualizing mundane artifacts as situated in evolved cultural-historical practice and conceptualizing behaviors with these artifacts as cases of theoretical constructs from educational research literature.

Foreword

Walking down the corridors of my department the other day, I was surprised yet heartened to overhear a graduate student comment, "Yes, but as Dor would say, what is this *a case of*?" It struck me that the student had taken my design research course the year before. Reflecting on my surprise, I realized I had never considered what long-term residual effects the course might have on its participants. And I was heartened to realize that this residual effect might be in the form of epistemic practices, in particular new ways of thinking and communicating about matters of educational research.

The reader might wonder why an instructor of a design research course might wish to conceptualize its longitudinal impact in terms of the general forms of reasoning it fosters rather than, perhaps, specific forms of competence. After all, why not evaluate the impact of a design research course in terms of students' capacity to enact what might be presumed as the core skills of the trade, that is, developing pedagogical materials? Indeed, these materials – their production, implementation, and dissemination – are what initially motivate students to take the course. In fact my only firm prerequisite for taking this course is that students must already have some incipient idea of what they would like to develop; and then the ultimate building, testing, and improving of these materials is what incentivizes, focalizes, rationalizes, and organizes students' efforts throughout the course, crystalizing all the course activities into a single coherent goal-oriented experience. Notwithstanding, the objective of this chapter is to argue for an alternative view of design research courses as being about much more than materials per se. Developing effective pedagogical materials is predicated on appropriating and mobilizing a host of professional dispositions, resources, and skills, including a wide range both of theories of learning and research methods. A design researcher is primarily a researcher – an educational researcher informed by theory and contributing to theory, yet driven by passion for and commitment to improving content instruction. As such, design research courses may constitute an initiation into the academic practice of the learning sciences. To contextualize my thesis, I will discuss my own course.

This is not a research paper, for the simple reason that I have never conducted formal studies of my instruction in this course nor of my students' learning therein. As such, the validity of my assertions on how the course offers students formative experiences as apprenticing learning scientists – or even my implicit assertion that the course does indeed offer students formative experiences – is a priori structurally delimited and should be regarded as no more than my own reflections on my practice as a course instructor and, more generally, as a design researcher who is a member of the community of learning scientists. The utility and reach of this chapter would rise only where colleagues find the ideas compelling in shaping their thoughts on their own practice and perhaps in planning to teach a similar course.

As the title suggests, I regard the teaching of my design research course as a case of cultivating a community of professional practice, where participants' social enactment of the cultural practice in question – developing and critiquing pedagogical materials – creates opportunities for individuals to become acculturated into the praxis of design research. In the remainder of this chapter I will first present an overview of the course and then elaborate on my argument that it constitutes an acculturation forum. Next, I will attempt to support this view by describing and exemplifying my course activities, anecdotally characterizing each activity as an opportunity for individuals to engage collectively in the guided cultivation of design research dispositions and epistemic practices.

Overview of the design research course

"Design Based Research Forum" is an intensive curriculum-development practicum for graduate students in training to become educational researchers. The course has historically drawn graduate as well as undergraduate students from across the Graduate School of Education (GSE) programs as well as from other UC Berkeley departments, such as architecture, engineering, and computer science, and MDs from the University of California San Francisco (UCSF) School of Medicine taking their master's-equivalent in the GSE. The course introduces the design based approach to educational research and, more broadly, themes, theories, methods, and lore of the learning sciences field.

Following several introductory weeks that set the scene for things to come, students begin developing their individual design research projects. These projects each take on a specific pedagogical challenge and are implemented in diverse contexts and media, such as innovating slide presentation techniques for oncologists learning to diagnose hematological pathologies in microscopic images of blood samples; middle school students learning to include warrants as well as explanations in using evidence to structure their scientific argumentation; environmental engineers developing methodology for enhancing participatory co-design of agricultural facilities with Native American populations; or mathematics teachers developing principles for creating group activities that enhance student collaboration.

Every week thereafter, students are each assigned personally customized readings from the canons of the field, which they present in a subsequent meeting. Once the prototypes are ready, the students each pilot their activities on study participants. They then analyze audio-video footage and artifacts collected during these sessions, improve on their designs, implement again, and write all this up in a research paper. The lion's share of our weekly three-hour meetings is a supportive group critique of these individual projects under development as well as a variety of exercises, lectures, and reflections. By virtue of learning to speak coherently *across* projects, the students develop fluency with central theoretical constructs as well as practice constructive peer-to-peer mentoring. As the weeks go by, the students typically become increasingly engaged in the group discussion and increasingly adept in design discourse. It is gratifying to see them draw on the literature in comparing and contrasting the projects. At the end of the semester, students submit a full-fledged final paper (see Appendix 9.A for a template) as well as a single-page executive summary (see examples in Part II where they have become two-pagers because of the book format). Students often develop course projects into larger studies, such as by carrying over empirical data from the design research course project into a qualitative-analysis methods course in the subsequent semester; expanding the term paper into a milestone programmatic requirement (a "position paper"); submitting a conference or journal paper; developing a grant proposal; or even developing a doctoral thesis.

The course as currently structured, with one instructor and no teaching assistants, has two drawbacks: (1) capacity – the course ideally hosts five students and is capped at six students, because of the intense attention each project needs at each meeting; and (2) instructor effort – the individualized style of the course demands inordinate attention to the needs of each student, such as through office hours and extended communications. Given greater financial support from the university, one could foresee a course structure in which two or three advanced graduate students, who have taken the course in the past, then serve as course teaching assistants. These assistants would themselves each take on up to five course participants, whom they meet during office hours. The course meetings would then consist of far briefer check-in rotations. Course instructors would periodically meet the teaching assistants to help resolve any mentoring issues that may arise. This course structure would create for the advanced graduate students vital professional-development opportunities both to practice mentoring students and, specifically, to teach this course, which they could then add to their own portfolio. Doing so would be instrumental in disseminating the course, once these students are hired elsewhere.

The design research course as a disciplinary initiation context

I am a design researcher of mathematics cognition and instruction. As a professor, I have now been teaching design research for over a dozen years. Early on, my colleagues and I, members of faculty in the Education in Mathematics, Science, and Technology doctoral program at UC Berkeley's Graduate School of Education, designated this course as one of several options for doctoral students to fulfill the program's "Curriculum" course requirement. Yet only recently did it dawn on me that I think of this course as about far more than only curriculum. It is a context – and pretext – for introducing students to educational research writ large. Students taking this course are often in their first or second year of our program. Granted, they are attracted to the course because the syllabus states they will be trained in a methodology for pursuing a hunch (idea, high-level conjecture) about the pedagogical potential of some instructional object or technique to improve people's learning of particular content. Yet once in the course they soon find out that this methodology comes with disciplinary baggage – that doing design research entails learning to think as an educational researcher. Thus, whereas the students do indeed develop their experimental artifacts and activities, evaluate them empirically, and write up a research report – all this over the course of a single academic semester – the enduring mark of this course on these budding researchers emerges not so much from the product they build but rather through the process; the process of envisioning, articulating, theorizing, debating, and critiquing technical details of their own designs as well as those of their peers. The designs themselves may fall by the wayside of their careers, but the experience of engaging in design research forges new epistemic dispositions, such as asking what an observed phenomenon is a case of.

Scholars of the learning sciences have portrayed design research as the discipline's idiosyncratic praxis, even its ethos and mores. Granted, this team-spirit sentiment harbored by learning scientists may be no more than a convenient standard to bear; emancipatory bravado rhetoric of a budding field . . . Yet regardless of its cohesive function as an emerging community's flagship, doing design research for the first time does indeed demand adopting far more than a set of perfunctory how-to protocols for product engineering or usability testing.

Design research is a proactive approach to educational inquiry, in which problems germane to the learning sciences emerge in the context of debating and evaluating best solutions for enduring problems of instructional practice. Its tenacious empirical orientation pits researchers against the limitations of their driving theory, which the designed artifacts concretize, motivating them to challenge and improve on the theory. Design research could be viewed as a constructionist approach to educational inquiry, in the sense that the practitioner's core design and development efforts create opportunities for more significant conceptual growth emanating from deeper insights informing each iterated decision (Abrahamson, 2015b). For this growth to occur, design researchers must constantly step back from the trees to see the forest; they must characterize their creations' unique features as well as their data's exclusive events as examples of more general phenomena – as cases of. Not only does doing so invite theoretical discourse about canonical literature, but it also fosters the epistemic habit so vital to the social sciences of conceptualizing theory as a cognitive lens on observed phenomena. The project-based character of the Design Based Research Forum necessarily requires students to develop an intellectual versatility whereby they warrant their peer-critique by appealing to theoretical stances emerging from course readings and prior conversations. In facilitating these conversations, I attempt to cultivate the discursive norm of couching technical details of specific artifacts in language that transcends the particular and thus bridges across projects, offering portable observations, genuinely useful take-home messages that accrue as our organizational know-how.

Course activities designed to cultivate a community of practice

Weekly meetings are composed of some mixture of the following activities:

- *Artifact of the day*: collaborative object analysis exercise
- *Check in*: students each present their progress, other students critique
- *Readings*: students report on the paper they have read, explaining what they learned from it and how it is relevant to their own and others' projects
- *Design exercises*: creative, goal-oriented work with media

- *Theory game*: experiential challenges to ground a new construct
- *Project case study lecture*: the instructor presents a design research study
- *Data analysis exercise*: the instructor screens a short video clip and students analyze it
- *Films*: the instructor screens a lecture or documentary and all discuss.

Below I explain these activities, exemplifying them from the course history.

Artifact of the day

Every course meeting begins with the *Artifact of the Day* activity, in which we spend anywhere from 50 minutes (early in the semester) to 10 minutes or less (later in the semester) analyzing an object (see Figure 9.1). Here are examples of objects that have served us well as artifacts of the day: wood vs. metal nut crackers; cork–screw bottle openers without vs. with levers; a variety of cheese graters; forks vs. chopsticks; a used ballet shoe; a dialysis filter; a glue gun; hair scissors; an Allen wrench tool kit; a miniature music organ; a swinging drinking

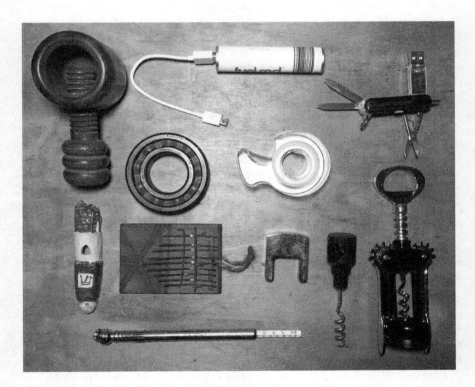

Figure 9.1 Examples of artifacts discussed in the course

bird; a remedial aspirator device; special book formats, such as a recursive book, pop-up book, interactive crafts book, and a book in the form of a map; and a pack of standard cards. This exercise creates a space, time, and license to dwell in a particular form of reasoning and discourse, in which we think about multiple aspects of a concrete artifact, including its evolution, geopolitical and cultural history, design, forms of use, ergonomics, and subjective connotations. The instructor facilitates this activity to model design discourse, including a particular vocabulary echelon, figures of speech, analytic orientation toward the mundane, and sustained revaluing of the artifactual ecology. Is this object a case of the QWERTY effect (cf. Jasmin & Casasanto, 2012), of skeuomorphism, or a colonial mannerism? An anachronism expressing retrograde assumptions about cognition, technology, race, gender, or culture? The activity is designed to serve students in the future as a model or precedent for how they should orient toward the artifact they will develop for this course. During the first several weeks the instructor brings the artifacts, but thereafter students rotate in bringing artifacts (e.g., a nephrologist brought a stethoscope to demonstrate heart diagnostic techniques, a cognitive linguist brought her rubber ducky to discuss buoyancy). Toward the end of the semester this activity fades out, to optimize time allocation to the research projects that include students' designed artifacts. Appendix 9.B summarizes a 30-minute artifact-of-the-day conversation about a corkscrew.

Check in

Students each present for peer-critique their progress to date. They introduce their project, state their objectives, display their work – including materials, protocols, and any empirical data gathered – and specify their challenges and dilemmas moving forward. Peers offer observations, and the instructor re-voices each observation from the theory of learning perspective, introducing constructs and citing authors, which s/he writes on the board. Thus the design feature is presented as a case of a broader phenomenon discussed in educational research literature, and the student is encouraged to read a particular paper so as to focalize their investigative orientation. As such, the product development effort becomes framed as an opportunity to evaluate theoretical positions. As the conversation moves on to the next course participant, the instructor encourages the cohort to keep referring to the constructs now written on the board as potentially productive lenses for making sense of the educational products.

Readings

During the first several weeks, the instructor assigns "classical" readings on design research (e.g., Collins, 1992; Confrey, 2005; Edelson, 2002). These readings can be challenging, because the students are still fledgling design researchers who orient to their work far more as doing design than doing design research, which they do not yet understand. The instructor supports the readings through presenting their own case projects; through surveying a set of one-page executive summaries of term projects created by students in previous years; and by using key phrases from the papers during the check-in rotation. The readings serve in part to populate the still-vague idea of design research in the form of a social milieu, replete with its provenance, leaders, identity, and character, to offer course participants a collective intellectual identity. By doing design research, the students become a team of design researchers, and by becoming a team of design researchers they will all do better design research (cf. Heath, 1991). Once students begin developing their own projects, they are each assigned their own readings, which often occur to the instructor during the check-in activity. Each student will then report on their readings in the subsequent week, and they are tagged as the go-to resident expert on the ideas and methods expressed in their reading, thus encouraging interactions among students seeking each other's expertise. As students reach the empirical stage of their project, we read about methods, such as how to conduct a clinical interview (e.g., Ginsburg, 1997).

Design exercise

In the early weeks of the semester, before the students have built their own artifacts, the instructor facilitates a group activity, in which a specific design problem is presented, such as elementary students' difficulty with fractions or adults' confusion over the rationale of daylight savings time; a very large array of modeling media are offered, ranging from plastic construction sets through to play-dough and rubber bands; and students are asked to work individually or in pairs to devise a design solution and argue for its potential viability. The cohort and instructor then listen intently to each presentation, and the instructor models a form of questioning that spurs the designer to articulate their rationale in ways that dig into the cognitive and sociocultural underpinnings of the learning challenge as well as to formulate focused empirical questions about the potential implementation of these objects in light of theoretical positions that emerge from the conversation. In passing, the group discusses and critiques the interactive affordances and tradeoffs of the various media. For example, play-dough is solid but opaque; rubber bands are elastic, but their continuous extension would require a discrete frame of reference so as to measure their length; the layout of diagrams should be sensitive to cultural characteristics, such as adapting to literacy practices of reading from right to left. As such, everything is problematized, everything is a case of.

Theory game

The course instructor creates and facilitates a participatory activity, in which student pairs engage in problem-solving tasks designed to exemplify and foreground an idea from the learning sciences. For example, to introduce the construct of professional vision from cognitive anthropology (Goodwin, 1994), the instructor hands out booklets where each page presents a collection of images from some professional discipline as well as a focused question requiring particular expertise. One page may include a collection of excerpts from musical scores from the Renaissance through to the twenty-first century, and the question is to determine which is the earliest score. Another page shows different stitching techniques, and activity participants are asked which is the most difficult and why. The instructor includes pages personally tailored to individual students in the class, such as a map of one student's small hometown in Oregon, where the question is about shortest driving routes during rush hour; a poem in Serbo-Croatian lamenting the woes of war, where only one student in the group could possibly point out subtle uses of ambiguity; or bouldering sketches where only the resident expert climber could assess the danger of specific moves. As students present their solutions, the instructor models for the group how to interview the student so as to understand what they know. The instructor then assigns (some of the students) a relevant paper as a reading for the subsequent week. In the following course meetings, the instructor keeps the new theoretical ideas alive in the group discussion by evoking key phrases from the readings. For example, when a student presents her work during the check-in rotation, the instructor might use Goodwin's phrases to ask her, "What should we highlight and code for this child in the visual display?"

Project case study lecture

Being a design researcher, the instructor has a host of ready-made presentations on their various previous and ongoing projects (e.g., Abrahamson, 2012; Abrahamson, Shayan, Bakker, & Van der Schaaf, 2016; Fuson & Abrahamson, 2005). These are invaluable resources to model an expert's narrative of design research studies, from problem definition through rationale and heuristic frameworks to solutions, implementations, iterations, insights, and inferences for theories of learning (Abrahamson, 2009, 2014, 2017; Abrahamson & Lindgren, 2014). These presentations include the display of selected empirical results, such as copies of children's work or excerpts from video recordings of task-based, semi-structured clinical interviews, which in turn enable the instructor to comment on research methodology. These lectures usually take up to one hour, and are followed by discussion. In subsequent course meetings, the instructor may refer back to those projects to demonstrate a disposition, technique, or idea. In course evaluations, students have mentioned that as much as these presentations are informative per se, they model a passion for the practice of design research.

Data-analysis exercise

Just as students learn to see artifacts in a new way, they need to learn to see people-working-with-artifacts in a new way. I have found that the best case studies are those that do not require much context. That is, rather than lecture on a design research project that implemented a complex rationale, I bring my students brief home videos of kids doing stuff with things. On the very first course meeting I screen a 75-second video that shows my then-10-month-old daughter playing with a plastic contraption. The toy is designed for toddlers to hammer a ball into a narrow hole and watch it roll down a crisscross diagonal inner conduit until it pops out at the bottom. Instead, she places the ball directly into the egress, to the confused delight of the onlookers. I distribute the video online so the students can watch it repeatedly, and I ask them to work in pairs and come up with comments on anything that they found interesting. As in other activities, I re-voice students' comments, alluding to the data as a case of a more general idea from the learning sciences. Students are moderately alarmed to behold how much we can talk about some baby messing with stuff. I tell them that my lab once spent half a year analyzing three seconds of data (Abrahamson, 2007).

Films

Some course content is best presented through watching source filmography. Two such films on hand, both available online, are *Piaget on Piaget* (Piaget, 1977) and Seymour Papert's 2004 Sydney lecture (Papert, 2004). Granted, one could easily assign these films as homework assignments, and at times I may choose to do so. However, watching the films together appears to bear benefits in terms of fostering group cohesion, focusing the discussion immediately after the screening, and enabling us to refer back to particular moments or even stop the screening for clarifying questions.

Closing comments

During the penultimate lesson of the semester, I tell my students that my criteria for the success of this seminar are the quality of the projects, the level of discussion, depth of engagement, frequency of spontaneous insights, degree of sharing across projects, and ultimately each student's learning. I also reveal to the students that the course was a pretext to introduce them to the learning sciences. We summarize and list the design heuristics that emerged through our work together, survey the theory we read and methods we employed, and we discuss possible directions for future development. For the last course meeting I invite colleagues and students from the department to a formal presentation from the course participants. In the following semester, the cohort presents their individual projects at the departmental research day, where they exhibit and explain their artifacts and findings in a structured poster session, using their one-page executive summary printed out in large format.

As a mentor, my greatest challenge has always been to facilitate design research students' transition from focusing on products per se to asking bigger questions.

As compared to educational designers, even those who are well informed by theories of learning yet are ultimately focused on generating (and marketing) products, design researchers are servants of two masters – product and theory, with theory being the more powerful master. My industry colleagues have been shocked and appalled to learn that my laboratory might suspend its production of an artifact for a year as we obsess over the meaning of some 10-year-old child's gesture. Indeed design research students arrive with much gumption to build but little orientation to what we might learn about learning through building and testing products. The objective of the design research course is to celebrate and stoke students' design motivation even as we cultivate their increasing curiosity in theory. To these ends, the students should both experience the insight that theory can offer, and identify with elders of the field as role models they would aspire to emulate. The students should become comfortable in joining the nerdy ranks of those who gaze at a toothpick and ask what it might be a case of.

I have found that articulating a research question (RQ) is the pivotal axis of a successful design research project. Once I have agreed with a student on an RQ, I heave a sigh of relief, because we now know what literature on which to draw, what methods to apply, and where this study might ultimately be published. I trust that an RQ will emerge for every single project, but I do not know when that will happen. Students might begin the course with a question, but for the most part they need to develop one during the course. What is most difficult for the students, and especially those coming from the exact sciences, is to enter empirical tryouts without yet having an RQ. "How could we possibly conduct an experiment when we don't even have an RQ?" they ask me in frustration. "Don't worry," I respond. "Spend some hours looking at your data over and over, then come back and show me something interesting you saw there." This notion of "something interesting" is intriguing, because we find "interesting" that which is coherent enough to present itself as a "thing," yet unusual enough to attract our attention – it is new yet inexplicable, it sparks our curiosity. What would Piaget say about this thing? What would Vygotsky say? Almost invariably, that interesting thing becomes the focus of analysis and blooms into an RQ that ultimately will hone the design problem for the next cycle. Of course, we must first determine what that thing is a case of.

When I mentioned that design researchers create and publish about products and theory, I omitted that we also create reflections on our own process. These might be in the form of articulating heuristic design frameworks for other researchers to conduct research projects in which they build educational materials (Abrahamson, 2014, 2015a; Easterday, Rees Lewis, & Gerber, 2016; Edelson, 2002; Pratt & Noss, 2010; Yerushalmy, 2013), descriptions of our own development as design researchers (Abrahamson, 2015b), or analyses of our own design process, where the social process becomes our data (Abrahamson & Chase, 2015a; Flood, Neff, & Abrahamson, 2015). The current chapter is perhaps a case of something else – it is about teaching design research.

Throughout this chapter I have foregrounded professional practices, and in particular epistemic dispositions to artifacts and learning, as the ultimate focus and outcome of this design research, and in so doing I have backgrounded the design products themselves as mere contexts for serving these more general orientations and skills. That said, quite often these specific artifacts – and more broadly the design research of these artifacts – carries students far beyond the seminar. For example, graduate student Leah Rosenbaum published elements of her Fall 2015 course project (Chapter 13), in which she evaluated a mechanical device supporting calculus learning, as a conference proceedings paper (Rosenbaum & Abrahamson, 2016). She then developed her paper into a manuscript that she submitted first as partial fulfillment of her doctoral requirements (a "position paper") and now as a manuscript she is about to submit to the journal *Qualitative Research*. Another graduate student, Becca Shareff, also from Fall 2015, developed a multi-agent, interactive computer-based modeling-and-simulation environment in the NetLogo software (Wilensky, 1999) for middle school students to combine science and gardening lessons (Chapter 10). Becca presented her project at a national conference (Shareff, 2016) and then further developed the paper with her academic advisor into a journal submission (Shareff & Wilkerson, in review). Becca is now developing this work into her doctoral dissertation proposal.

Kiera Chase took the design research course in Fall 2012, then again in Spring 2013 (see Chapter 11). She created Giant Steps for Algebra (GS4A), a design in which pre-algebra students discover the foundations of algebra by using available media to model an engaging narrative about a giant who hides treasure on a remote island. Through the two semesters, she moved from concrete to virtual modeling media. The project created an empirical context for developing an original activity architecture for discovery learning in interactive environments (*reverse scaffolding*) as well as a construct depicting pre-conceptual emerging mathematical knowledge (*situated intermediary learning objective*, or *SILO*). Then over summer 2013 we included in the project two interns from India with expertise in educational technology, who both subsequently became graduate students at elite US universities, while Kiera expanded her project into her dissertation thesis, which she has successfully defended. The GS4A project resulted in several conference and journal papers (Abrahamson & Chase, 2015a, 2015b; Abrahamson, Chase, Kumar, & Jain, 2014; Chase & Abrahamson, 2013, 2015a, 2015b, 2016, 2018). Each of these students is a living case of what we learn when we engage in design research.

Author note

As the chapter may have suggested, this course uses numerous multi-media resources, which would be difficult to share with colleagues. Also, some of the resources, such as heuristics, readings, videography, and lore are very much idiosyncratic to my own research history (an MA in cognitive psychology; a

PhD in the learning sciences), domain expertise (mathematics, in particular rational numbers, probability, and algebra), media expertise (e.g., programming complexity-inquiry modeling-and-simulation environments in NetLogo; remote-sensing embodied-interaction devices; artificial intelligence), age focus (9–12 years), intellectual preferences (focus on cognitive, sociocultural, and embodiment theory), personal hobbies (music, martial arts, reading), and so on. However, I would be glad to make these resources publicly available. Pending my students' consent, I would also share their course work. For inquiries, kindly write directly to me. My email address is located within the contributor biography section at the front of the book.

Appendix 9.A

Template used in the design research course

Structure of a Design Based Research Paper Reporting on a Design Project

Abstract (up to 150 words, with emphasis on findings and conclusions)

INTRODUCTION (Design Rationale)

- **Design problem** (background and objectives)
  - What is the general context of the study, for example, what is something that children need to know? Specify age, content, and concepts. Use formal definitions and notation. Explain why the hiring body (e.g., NSF) wants students to know this.
  - What is the evidence for this design problem? Research, national scores, etc.
  - What is the specific problem you are addressing with your design; for example, what are children not learning as well as they should?
  - Present some gripping example that helps your audience, who may be informed on the subject, to re-experience the content as non-trivial (problematized content).
- **Previous solutions** and their problems (critical, design oriented curriculum review)
  - What is the range of solutions out there for this particular design problem; for example, what materials and activities do teachers commonly use to teach fractions? Home onto one or two focal properties of previous solutions that will become thematic to your cognitive domain analysis, conjecture, and solution below.
- **Cognitive domain analysis** that draws on a specified philosophy/theory of learning. In this section, you offer an innovative interpretation of the problem. (Either launch from previous solutions to critique and modify them, or begin by offering your re-structuration of the domain and only later use this to critique the previous solution.)
  - What is the reason for this design problem; for example, why are children not learning fractions as well as they should? Could the materials be different?

- What are previous solutions missing, e.g., what latent/dormant resource are they not using? In other words, you are looking for a misfit between cognitive architecture (student) and information structure (representations).
- This section is usually the heart of your intellectual innovation. If possible, though, this should fall short of offering the implication, which begins below.

- **Conjecture** (Implementing theory to practice)

  - Here you should speak with confidence, coming from the earlier treatment, to take us through to a general specification of your hunch (the "If only . . ." statement).
  - The conjecture is the "design kernel." It emanates from asking, "How do I myself experience this content? The design phenomenalizes this (tacit) visualization – the design creates opportunities to enact and mediate your way of seeing the content.

- **Design solution** (the creative innovation)

  - What is your solution for the design problem, and particularly, what is the thing you hope to design that will solve the problem in a new way?
  - Specify materials, activities, and facilitation emphases.

- **Research Question** (Note: Of course, we want to evaluate whether the design is effective, and so an obvious RQ is whether the design "worked." But RQ in DBR should rise above topical context – it should be about more than "Does it work?" It should see the implementation as a case study of something more general. Yet often we find out these more general questions only after we've begun developing and trying out the design, so don't worry if you don't yet have this big question early on in writing the paper – just focus on your domain analyses, conjectures, and solutions, and keep yourself open to the literature that might inform this iterative process.)

METHODS

- Participants
- Materials
- Procedure
- Data Gathered
- Data Analysis

RESULTS

CONCLUSIONS (+ limitations, future work)

REFLECTION

(this is for course papers, not for publications – this is where you step back and think about your personal process through working on the project)

REFERENCES (Works Cited)

APPENDIX

- Materials used: Interview Protocol, etc.

Structure of a conversation on an artifact of the day, in this case a cork-screw bottle opener

- Background, context
  - What is this object?
    - It is an artifact that serves a larger activity structure or cultural practice, that of preservation or conservation, suspending consumption of liquids for later need (e.g., winter, college, camping, war, travel, transportation, under water, extreme conditions, sterilization). It is used to access the contents of a sealed vessel.
  - When do we use it?
    - To discontinue this preservation; to extract preserved goods.
  - What is unique, thematic, or interesting about this practice?
    - Preservation works by means of isolating a substance kept in a vessel from exterior elements, such as keeping wine from oxygen.
  - Personal angle: Where'd you get this? Why did you choose it? Do you have a relevant anecdote?
    - I love the sound of wine pouring out of a bottle. I'm never sure whether to put the cork in the organic refuse bin or in the landfill. I think cork is grown in Portugal. There once was a shortage of cork, and they made them from rubber. We have a corkscrew at home that looks like a person with two arms as levers. We call it "Chayim!"
- Expanding the conversation
  - **History**: How did this evolve? Was it always around? What are milestones in developing this design solution? Have the considerations changed (the case of QWERTY)? Are there priors/variants/alternatives that fill the same function, i.e., solve the same problem of practice (e.g., other types of bottle openers – pressure)? Who uses this object, where, and why? Is this related to available elements/knowledge/skill/technology (e.g., iron; tools for extracting iron; tools for shaping iron)? How did the invention of this object in any way change the course of history? (export)
  - **Manufacture, use, standardization**: How come the tool works so widely, for any bottle anywhere? What historical process/considerations brought that about? Any tradeoffs to that? Where is this made? By whom? Since when?

- **Ergonomics**: How do you use it? How can it be that most anyone can use this? Who cannot? Would some change to this object make it more widely useable? Would we want that? (e.g., limit youngsters' access to substance)
- **Structure, mechanism**: What are the features of this object? *Make a sketch*, highlighting its features, and then explain the function of these features as well as the ultimate purpose of these functions (e.g., how this particular function interacts with other functions ultimately so as to make the object work as it should and get its work done).
- **Learning**: *Create a manual*. How do people learn to use this? How did you? Are there degrees of expertise associated with using it? (bartender)
- **Creative use**: What non-standard uses might this object be put to? (re-instrumentalizing the artifact, such as using a cork-screw bottle opener to extract wax from a candlestick, as weapon, as puppet)

- **Education**: Can you think of any curricular content (e.g., STEM) that this object could help someone understand? In what context? How might this happen? Is that the best way to learn this content? Sketch out an activity to support learning.

  - Physics of a lever, distributing work over distance, gears; for pump opener, air pressure wields force
  - Engineering principles
  - Chemistry and biology of wine oxidization

References

Abrahamson, D. (2007). Handling problems: Embodied reasoning in situated mathematics. In T. Lamberg & L. Wiest (Eds.). *Proceedings of the Twenty Ninth Annual Meeting of the North American Chapter of the International Group for the Psychology of Mathematics Education* (pp. 219–226). Stateline (Lake Tahoe), NV: University of Nevada, Reno.

Abrahamson, D. (2009). Embodied design: Constructing means for constructing meaning. *Educational Studies in Mathematics, 70*(1), 27–47. [Electronic supplementary material at https://edrl.berkeley.edu/content/seeing-chance].

Abrahamson, D. (2012). Seeing chance: Perceptual reasoning as an epistemic resource for grounding compound event spaces. *ZDM Mathematics Education, 44*(7), 869–881. doi:10.1007/s11858-012-0454-6

Abrahamson, D. (2014). Building educational activities for understanding: An elaboration on the embodied-design framework and its epistemic grounds. *International Journal of Child-Computer Interaction, 2*(1), 1–16. doi:10.1016/j.ijcci.2014.07.002

Abrahamson, D. (2015a). The monster in the machine, or why educational technology needs embodied design. In V. R. Lee (Ed.), *Learning technologies and the body: Integration and implementation* (pp. 21–38). New York: Routledge.

Abrahamson, D. (2015b). Reinventing learning: A design research odyssey. In S. Prediger, K. Gravemeijer, & J. Confrey (Eds.), Design research with a focus on learning processes [Special issue]. *ZDM Mathematics Education, 47*(6), 1013–1026. doi:10.1007/s11858-014-0646-3

Abrahamson, D. (2017). Embodiment and mathematical learning. In K. Peppler (Ed.), *The SAGE encyclopedia of out-of-school learning* (pp. 247–252). New York: SAGE.

Abrahamson, D., & Chase, K. (2015a). Interfacing practices: Domain theory emerges via collaborative reflection. *Reflective Practice, 16*(3), 372–389. doi:10.1080/14623943.2015.1052384

Abrahamson, D., & Chase, K. (2015b). Leveling algebra transparency: Giant steps towards a new approach to learning? *Paper Presented at the Annual Meeting of the American Educational Research Association,* Chicago, April 16–20.

Abrahamson, D., Chase, K., Kumar, V., & Jain, R. (2014). Leveling transparency via situated, intermediary learning objectives. In J. L. Polman, E. A. Kyza, D. K. O'Neill, I. Tabak, W. R. Penuel, A. S. Jurow, K. O'Connor, T. Lee, & L. D'Amico (Eds.), *Learning and becoming in practice – Proceedings of "Learning and Becoming in Practice," the 11th International Conference of the Learning Sciences (ICLS) 2014* (Vol. 1, pp. 23–30). Boulder, CO: International Society of the Learning Sciences.

Abrahamson, D., & Lindgren, R. (2014). Embodiment and embodied design. In R. K. Sawyer (Ed.), *The Cambridge handbook of the learning* sciences (2nd ed.) (pp. 358–376). Cambridge, UK: Cambridge University Press.

Abrahamson, D., Shayan, S., Bakker, A., & Van der Schaaf, M. F. (2016). Eye-tracking Piaget: Capturing the emergence of attentional anchors in the coordination of proportional motor action. *Human Development, 58*(4–5), 218–244.

Chase, K., & Abrahamson, D. (2013). Rethinking transparency: Constructing meaning in a physical and digital design for algebra. In J. P. Hourcade, E. A. Miller, & A. Egeland (Eds.), *Proceedings of the 12th Annual Interaction Design and Children Conference (IDC 2013)* (Vol. "Short Papers," pp. 475–478). The New School & Sesame Workshop, New York: ACM.

Chase, K., & Abrahamson, D. (2015a). Reverse scaffolding: A constructivist design architecture for mathematics learning with educational technology. In B. Shapiro, C. Quintana, S. Gilutz, & M. Skov (Eds.), *Proceedings of the 14th Annual Conference of ACM SIGCHI Interaction Design & Children (IDC 2015)* (Vol. "Full papers," pp. 189–198). Tufts University, Boston: ACM.

Chase, K., & Abrahamson, D. (2015b). Reverse-scaffolding algebra: Empirical evaluation of design architecture. In A. Bakker, J. Smit, & R. Wegerif (Eds.), Scaffolding and dialogic teaching in mathematics education [Special issue]. *ZDM Mathematics Education, 47*(7), 1195–1209. doi:10.1007/s11858-015-0710-7

Chase, K., & Abrahamson, D. (2016). Searching for buried treasure: Uncovering the discovery in discovery-based learning. *Paper Presented at the Annual Meeting of the American Educational Research Association,* Washington, DC, April 8–12.

Chase, K., & Abrahamson, D. (2018). Searching for buried treasure: Uncovering discovery in discovery-based learning. In D. Abrahamson & M. Kapur (Eds.), Practicing discovery-based learning: Evaluating new horizons [Special issue]. *Instructional Science, 46*(1), 11–33.

Collins, A. (1992). Towards a design science of education. In E. Scanlon & T. O'Shea (Eds.), *New directions in educational technology* (pp. 15–22). Berlin: Springer.

Confrey, J. (2005). The evolution of design studies as methodology. In R. K. Sawyer (Ed.), *The Cambridge handbook of the learning sciences* (pp. 135–151). New York, NY: Cambridge University Press.

Easterday, M. W., Rees Lewis, D. G., & Gerber, E. M. (2016). The logic of the theoretical and practical products of design research. *Australasian Journal of Educational Technology, 32*(4), 125–144.

Edelson, D. C. (2002). Design research: What we learn when we engage in design. *Journal of the Learning Sciences, 11*(1), 105–121.

Flood,V. J., Neff, M., & Abrahamson, D. (2015). Boundary interactions: Resolving interdisciplinary collaboration challenges using digitized embodied performances. In O. Lindwall, P. Häkkinen,T. Koschmann, P.Tchounikine, & S. Ludvigsen (Eds.), *Exploring the material conditions of learning: opportunities and challenges for CSCL*, the *Proceedings of the Computer Supported Collaborative Learning (CSCL) Conference* (Vol. 1, pp. 94–101). Gothenburg, Sweden: ISLS.

Fuson, K. C., & Abrahamson, D. (2005). Understanding ratio and proportion as an example of the apprehending zone and conceptual-phase problem-solving models. In J. I. D. Campbell (Ed.), *Handbook of mathematical cognition* (pp. 213–234). New York: Psychology Press.

Ginsburg, H. P. (1997). *Entering the child's mind.* New York: Cambridge University Press.

Goodwin, C. (1994). Professional vision. *American Anthropologist, 96*(3), 603–633.

Heath, S. B. (1991). "It's about winning:" The language of knowledge in baseball. In L. B. Resnick, J. M. Levine, & S. D. Teasley (Eds.), *Perspectives on socially shared cognition* (pp. 101–124). Washington, DC: American Psychological Association.

Jasmin, K., & Casasanto, D. (2012). The QWERTY effect: How typing shapes the meanings of words. *Psychonomic Bulletin & Review, 19*(3), 499–504.

Packer, M. J., & Maddox, C. (2016). Mapping the territory of the Learning Sciences. In M. A. Evans, M. J. Packer, & R. K. Sawyer (Eds.), *Reflections on the Learning Sciences* (pp. 126–154). Cambridge, UK: Cambridge University Press.

Papert, S. (2004). *Keynote speech.* Paper presented at the i3 1 to 1 Notebook Conference, Sydney, Australia. May 31–June 2004. http://vimeo.com/9092144

Piaget, J. (1977). Piaget on Piaget: The epistemology of Jean Piaget. New Haven: Yale University Media Design Studio.

Pratt, D., & Noss, R. (2010). Designing for mathematical abstraction. *International Journal of Computers for Mathematical Learning, 15*(2), 81–97.

Rosenbaum, L. F., & Abrahamson, D. (2016). Back to the drawing board: On studying interaction with mechanical design. In M. B. Wood, E. E. Turner, M. Civil, & J. A. Eli (Eds.), *Sin fronteras: Questioning borders with(in) mathematics education – Proceedings of the 38th annual meeting of the North-American Chapter of the International Group for the Psychology of Mathematics Education (PME-NA)* (Vol. 13, Theory and research methods, pp. 1612–1615). Tucson: University of Arizona.

Shareff, R. (2016). *Bringing outside in: Transplanting experiential garden knowledge in computational models.* Poster presented at the 13th Annual Research Symposium of the North American Association for Environmental Education, Madison, WI.

Shareff, R., & Wilkerson, M. H. (in review). *Grounding science: Participatory design as learning in an ecological modeling environment.*

Wilensky, U. (1999). *NetLogo.* Northwestern University, Evanston, IL: The Center for Connected Learning and Computer-Based Modeling http://ccl.northwestern.edu/netlogo/

Yerushalmy, M. (2013). Designing for inquiry curriculum in school mathematics. *Educational Designer, 2*(6), Retrieved June 1, 2013, from http://www.educationaldesigner.org/ed/volume2012/issue2016/article2022/index.htm

Chapter 10

"Harvesting" ecosystem dynamics through a computational model of a garden

Rebecca Shareff

Objective: link experiential learning to classroom content via accessible technological tool

Rationales for hands-on learning experiences, particularly in extra-curricular environments, abound. Given suitable tools and technology, discoveries made in real-life settings can be built upon and revisited in the classroom. In particular, this project aims to connect student observations of garden ecosystems to the scientific practices of developing and testing models.

Background: challenges of outdoor education and the affordances of agent-based models

Whereas school gardens have been adopted by many as offering valuable out-door learning experiences, classroom curriculum is not geared to incorporate the rich academic opportunities that these experiences could potentially offer (Williams & Dixon, 2013). Despite the gardens' numerous psycho-social and nutritional benefits (Ozer, 2007), construction and maintenance of gardens requires dedicated attention, funds, and curriculum – hence teachers and principals hesitate to invest in gardening programs (Graham, Beall, Lussier, McLaughlin, & Zidenberg-Cherr, 2005). With the unveiling of Next Generation Science Standards, teachers are tasked with creating new models of instruction and assessment, yet few structures exist connecting these standards to the outdoor environment.

This project attempts to solve issues both of gardening-based academics and science standards by supplementing these with a third curricular element, computational literacy practices. In particular, agent-based modeling enables students to investigate and reason about complex scientific phenomena, such as garden ecosystems. Used to enrich instruction in many scientific domains, modeling-and-simulation environments such as *NetLogo* (Wilensky, 1999) allow users to manipulate a system's behavioral rules so as to understand how macro-scale phenomena emerge from micro-scale interactions. As a classroom resource, NetLogo models minimize time and space constraints, increase episte-mological pluralism, allow for variety in data-driven inferences, and encourage

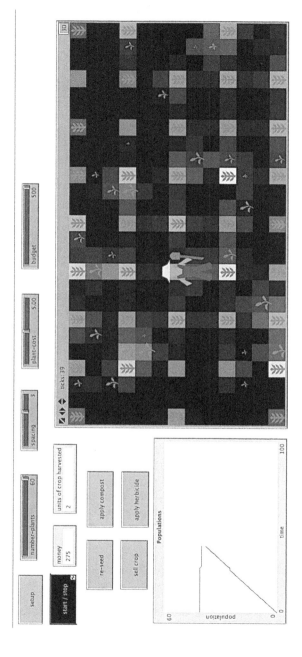

Figure 10.1 Computational model of a garden made in NetLogo

mathematical and computational thinking; these practices are highly aligned with K–12 Next Generation Science Standards (NGSS Lead States, 2013). The models are accessible to a wide range of ages and skill levels and have been shown to deepen and enrich student comprehension of the content they dynamically animate (Wilensky & Reisman, 2006).

Design: instructional sequence incorporating a NetLogo model of a garden ecosystem

For this project, I designed and constructed a model of a garden ecosystem as well as a variety of tasks (see Figure 10.1). Through iterated cycles of proto-typing, strategic planning meetings, and debugging sessions, the virtual garden came to life and ultimately became a space to examine soil quality, budgeting, weed growth, and the effects of plant spacing, all real concerns of the actual school-garden environment where this tool is soon to be piloted. Toward designing a middle school gardening unit, I conducted four pilot interviews with Grades 6 and 8 students. They were each shown the model, asked to run it a few times under different parameters, and make predictions about the utility of particular functions. They also explored many features and offered their own perceived connections to math and science content. Data analysis revealed students' various strategies for orienting to this virtual environment, as well as the intelligibility of interface features. Ultimately, the model should represent the actual school garden and enable students to simulate its authentic problems through modeling-based inquiry. Ongoing analyses, interface design, and debugging will allow for the continued development of a series of tasks by which students can progress in their knowledge of gardens, science, and computer-based modeling.

Conclusions

Technological tools are important resources for students to avail themselves of learning opportunities inherent to experiential education, while satisfying current academic standards. In designing these resources and their corresponding instructional sequences, the interests and abilities of students and teachers must be simultaneously taken into consideration to promote optimal results.

References

Graham, H., Beall, D. L., Lussier, M., McLaughlin, P., & Zidenberg-Cherr, S. (2005). Use of school gardens in academic instruction. *Journal of Nutrition Education and Behavior, 37*(3), 147–151.

NGSS Lead States (2013). *Next generation science standards: For states, by states.* Washington, DC: The National Academies Press.

Ozer, E. J. (2007). The effects of school gardens on students and schools: Conceptualization and considerations for maximizing healthy development. *Health Education & Behavior, 34*(6), 846–863.

Wilensky, U. (1999). *NetLogo*. Center for Connected Learning and Computer-Based Modeling (CCL), Northwestern University, Evanston, IL.

Wilensky, U., & Reisman, K. (2006). Thinking like a wolf, a sheep, or a firefly. *Cognition and Instruction, 24*(2), 171–209.

Williams, D. R., & Dixon, P. S. (2013). Impact of garden-based learning on academic outcomes in schools: Synthesis of research between 1990 and 2010. *Review of Educational Research, 83*(2), 211–235.

Chapter 11

Giant Steps for Algebra

Kiera Chase

Two-pager written as a master's student for the design based research course described in Chapter 9

Objectives: algebra metaphors and learning

This design based research project investigated alternative cognitive foundations for algebraic reasoning. The initial impetus for the design was a conjecture associating students' poor understanding of algebra content with the pervasive metaphor underlying their conceptualization of algebraic equations (Vlassis, 2002). Building on Dickinson and Eade (2004), the design instantiated algebraic expressions (e.g., $2x + 1 = 3x - 2$), which are traditionally visualized as two distinct sets of discrete quantities balanced across a scale, as two distinct journeys an agent takes to traverse a single continuous linear interval.

Design problem and process

In arithmetic thinking the equals sign is conceptualized operationally (Carpenter, Franke, & Levi, 2003). This conceptualization of the equals sign is absent of a relational sense (Jones, Inglis, Gilmore, & Dowens, 2012) — a sense that is pivotal for conventional treatment of algebraic equations. Using a story metaphor to ground concepts, the design seeks to offer a more nuanced and relational interpretation of the sign.

The physical design consists of a sand tray with small marbles buried in the sand. There were six stories that described the process by which the "treasures" were buried. The relationship between two different trips revealed the length of the variable (giant steps) in inches and thus the location of the treasure. There were three conditions based on the different problem-solving tools provided (paper and pencil, pushpins and corkboard, elastic ruler and fixed inch markers).

Design discoveries

The researcher engaged in micro-ethnographic qualitative analysis. The analyses focused on the three experimental conditions and the extent to which the

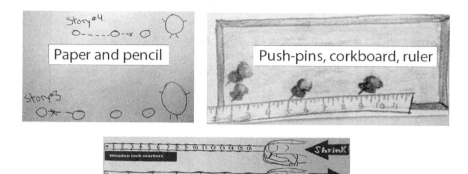

Figure 11.1 Each set of material resources represents an experimental condition

tools obfuscated or illuminated the phenomena. Transparency emerged as a pivotal construct highlighting this design's opportunities and challenges and how aspects of the design enabled participants to "see" phenomena through their models. The analyses revealed the importance of spatially aligning the two journeys such that the relationship between the variable and integer could be identified. This critical coordination was facilitated by the participants' use of their models as a method for visualizing the two separate journeys as overlaid, almost as if these occurred simultaneously (see Figure 11.1 with provided materials and the participant generated model). Through this action participants were able to see the two sides of the equation as co-indexical of the equations' identity, and the location of the treasure.

Conclusions

The construct of transparency illuminated the relations between learner, task, artifact, and content. We argue that the design restructured the solution of unknown-value problems as centered on manual coordination of situated quantities. And yet participants' accomplishment of such conceptually critical coordinations was predicated on the subjective transparency of relevant perceptual elements within the media. We thus corroborate and expand on constructivist critiques of modeling: What you do not build, you may not see.

Technology-based redesign

As we consider improvements to the *Giant Steps for Algebra* design, we have begun to develop a technology-based interface analogous to the concrete

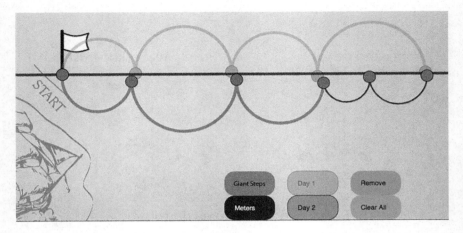

Figure 11.2 A screenshot of the Giant Steps interface in manual mode

instantiations. Considerations for development include previous research indicating "computer manipulatives can help students build on their physical experiences, tying them tightly to symbolic representations" (Clements & Sarama, 2009, p. 148). Digital media afford programmable display elements that could include stretch/shrink equipartitioned rulers, for example. However, our findings suggest that automatized transformation might remain opaque to the learner. As we continue to develop the computer-based version of *Giant Steps for Algebra* (see Figure 11.2), we will carefully determine criteria for assessing whether the learner is ready to shift gears from manual to automatic with respect to each programmable element. For example, once the learner has demonstrated proficiency in building journeys with equal steps, the interaction mode will change to enable scaling with uniform units.

References

Carpenter, T. P., Franke, M. L., & Levi, L. (2003). *Thinking mathematically*. Portsmouth, NH: Heinemann.

Clements, D., & Sarama, J. (2009). "Concrete" computer manipulatives in mathematics education. *Child Development Perspectives*, *3*(3), 145–150.

Dickinson, P., & Eade, F. (2004) Using the number-line to investigate the solving of linear equations. *For the Learning of Mathematics*, *24*(2), 41–47.

Jones, I., Inglis, M., Gilmore, C., & Dowens, M. (2012). Substitution and sameness: Two components of a relational conception of the equals sign. *Journal of Experimental Child Psychology*, *113*, 166–176.

Vlassis, J. (2002). The balance model: Hindrance or support for the solving of linear equations with one unknown. *Educational Studies in Mathematics*, *49*(3), 341–359.

Chapter 12

Explicit oral and written reasoning during science argumentation

M. Lisette Lopez

Two-pager written as a master's student for the Design Based Research Forum described in Chapter 9

Objective: create material object to serve as an analogy supporting scientific argumentation

The purpose of this design project was to develop and evaluate an assembleable material structure that forms and mobilizes student reasoning during science inquiry by way of constituting an interactive analogy of goal argumentation mechanics.

Background: reasoning and science argumentation

Learning to support a claim with evidence is fundamental to appropriating scientific practice (Erduran & Jiménez-Aleixandre, 2008). Science educators and national standards have thus called to enhance the practice of science argumentation throughout K–12 (National Research Council, 1996; National Governors Association, 2011. Research on argumentation suggests that students are challenged in particular to explain how or why their evidence supports their claim (McNeill, Lizotte, Krajcik, and Marx, 2006), albeit they are quite persuasive and adept at making arguments about personally relevant issues (McNeill & Krajcik, 2011). How might we enable students to use their everyday resources to sustain complex reasoning during scientific argumentation?

Design: a material anchor for a conceptual blend to support argumentation

Inspired by the theoretical construct of a *material anchor for a conceptual blend* (Hutchins, 2005), I sought an accessible, common, concrete, cultural analogy for students to encode structural components of their scientific argumentation while they reason about specific content. In a material anchor, "a mental space is blended with a material structure that is sufficiently immutable to

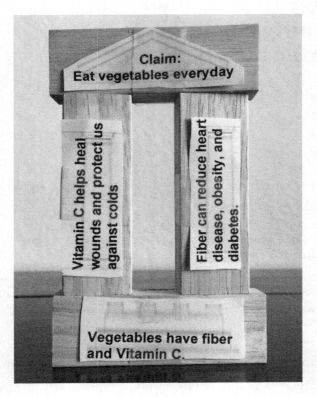

Figure 12.1 Build an Argument material anchor depicting the reasoning process that articulates how evidence supports a claim

hold the conceptual relationships fixed while other operations are performed" (Hutchins, 2005, p. 1562). I created the *Build an Argument* material anchor (Figure 12.1), a culturally familiar physical block structure that needs to support a top block, and blended it with an epistemic notion of abstract scientific arguments needing ideas to connect evidence to claims. "Part of the cognitive power of metaphor derives from the fact that it is possible to reason effectively about unfamiliar concepts, which would otherwise be unstable, if they can first be blended with stable familiar concepts" (Hutchins, 2005, p. 1573). Here, base equals evidence, supporting columns equals connecting ideas or reasoning, and roof equals a claim that must be supported. In the blended space, the blocks are experienced as parts of an argument, cuing students to seek ideas (columns) to hold together the overall structure (the argument). In determining the parts of an argument, I borrowed from the seminal work of Toulmin (1958), respecting claims, evidence, and warrants.

Findings: appropriating the *Build an Argument* mechanics to offer explicit reasoning

A pair of 12-year-old female students participated in a pilot trial of the activity. Assigned with scientific inquiry problems, the participants were prompted to sort available evidence according to how it could potentially support claims. Next, they used the *Build an Argument* kit to explain how the evidence connects to the claim. Finally, they wrote down their reasoning. The session was audio- and video-taped for subsequent study. I performed microgenetic qualitative analysis of the recording as well as student artifacts in an attempt to reveal implicit reasoning processes. The first finding was that the material anchor was understood and appropriated by the participants to enhance their argumentation. This was reflected in the participants' facile and creative uses of the kit that made evident their utilization of its embedded epistemic criteria. One participant explicitly stated that the kit was helpful. Secondly, the activities with *Build an Argument* supported student reasoning, as evidenced by the students offering more explicit reasoning *during* and *after* this supported activity as compared to *before* it.

Conclusions

Materials anchors for conceptual blends, such as the *Build an Argument* assembly kit, may be effective means of supporting student scientific reasoning, by way of deploying complex reasoning structures into familiar mechanics of concrete objects.

References

Erduran, S., & Jiménez-Aleixandre, M. P. (Eds.) (2008). *Argumentation in science education.* New York, NY: Springer.

Hutchins, E. (2005). Material anchors for conceptual blends. *Journal of Pragmatics, 37*(10), 1555–1577.

McNeill, K. L., & Krajcik, J. S. (2011). *Supporting grade 5–8 Students in constructing explanations in science: The claim, evidence, and reasoning.* New York, NY: Pearson Allyn & Bacon.

McNeill, K. L., Lizotte, D. J., Krajcik, J., & Marx, R. W. (2006). Supporting students' construction of scientific explanations by fading scaffolds in instructional materials. *Journal of the Learning Sciences, 15*(2), 153–191.

National Governors Association Center for Best Practices, Council of Chief State School Officers. (2011). *Common core state standards.* Washington, DC: National Governors Association Center for Best Practices, Council of Chief State School Officers.

National Research Council (U.S.). (1996). *National science education standards: Observe, interact, change, learn.* Washington, DC: National Academy Press.

Toulmin, S. (1958). *The uses of argument.* Cambridge, UK: Cambridge University Press.

Chapter 13

An embodied approach to derivatives

Leah Rosenbaum

Two-pager written as a doctoral student for the Design Based Research Forum described in Chapter 9.

Objective: increasing access to calculus

Calculus is traditionally a gatekeeper to higher education, particularly in STEM fields. An accessible approach to calculus could make the course and the educational and career opportunities it carries available to a broader range of students.

Background: an embodied approach to a traditionally symbolic and graphical problem

Students tend to conceptualize functions as strings of symbols (Thompson, 1994), overlooking the functional characteristics that those symbols represent. In particular, students may recite the formula for the limit definition of derivative (Figure 13.1) while simultaneously failing to recognize that a rotating secant line approximates a tangent line (Figure 13.2), where this relationship forms the graphical basis for the former definition (Orton, 1983).

Embodied design aims to create physically situated challenges such that the action-perception behaviors toward solving these challenges become cognitive resources (Abrahamson, 2014). Faced with a physical problem, students first experience secants and tangents at a hands-/body-on level where their movements can be motivated and constrained by a field of promoted action, a physical setting that guides students toward specific movements (Abrahamson & Trninic, 2015). Once moving in mathematical ways, students encounter domain-specific tools and symbols with which to formalize their physical strategies, translating their movements into mathematical terms. Resulting formal

$$f'(x_0) = \lim_{h \to 0} \frac{f(x_0 + h) - f(x_0)}{h}$$

Figure 13.1 The limit definition of derivative.

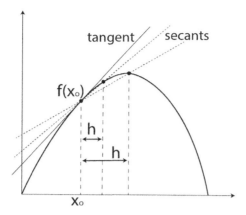

Figure 13.2 Rotating secant lines approximate the tangent

expressions carry the target concept as well as students' personal, physical experiences (Abrahamson, 2014).

Design: the calcmachine – an artifact for embodying derivatives

I sought to develop a physical environment in which students' intuitive bodily actions contribute to their making sense of the limit definition of derivative. The physical model contains a metal curve approximating a parabola and a drawing bar that travels along the curve, attached by two points (Figure 13.3, top). Students trace against the bar to draw, moving in ways that are perceptually and physically guided and constrained by the environment. Suggested configurations of lines (Figure 13.3, bottom) are designed to promote movement relevant to reasoning about secant and tangent lines. Prompting students to reflect on the strengths and limitations of their movement schemes, the activity aims to orient students to the relationships between the curve, their movements, and the configurations they can produce.

This environment is intended as a field of promoted action relevant to reasoning about secant and tangent lines, the basis of the limit definition of derivatives. Mathematical tools such as grid paper or labels for the points could prompt students to express and generalize their physical experiences using normative mathematical forms.

Findings

Participants in a pilot study spent significant time orienting themselves on the model's operation and use as a drawing tool. This work offered insight into

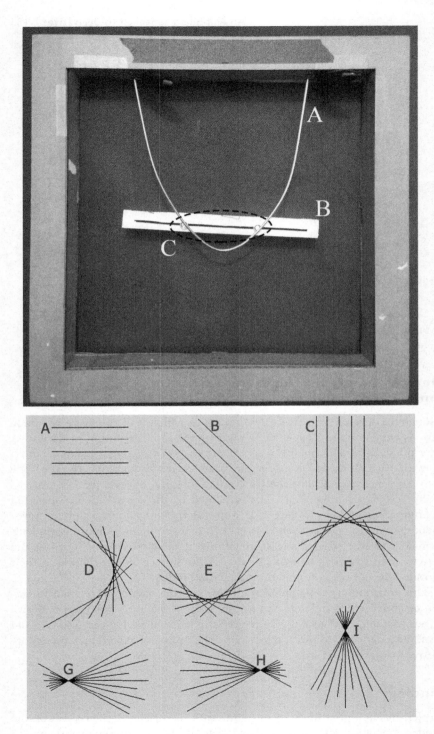

Figure 13.3 (top) The physical model includes (A) a parabolic curve, (B) a drawing bar, and (C) connection points. (bottom) Suggested configurations.

participants' learning about the model, but did not indicate significant mathematics learning. Future work will focus on connecting bodily actions to the mathematics. Centering such physical action as an academic resource holds promise for meaningful learning that is rooted in students' own experiences.

References

Abrahamson, D. (2014). Building educational activities for understanding: An elaboration on the embodied-design framework and its epistemic grounds. *International Journal of Child-Computer Interaction, 2*(1), 1–16.

Abrahamson, D., & Trninic, D. (2015). Bringing forth mathematical concepts: Signifying sensorimotor enactment in fields of promoted action. *ZDM Mathematics Education, 47*(2), 295–306.

Orton, A. (1983). Students' understanding of differentiation. *Educational Studies in Mathematics, 14*(3), 235–250.

Thompson, P. W. (1994). Images of rate and operational understanding of the fundamental theorem of calculus. In P. Cobb (Ed.), *Learning mathematics* (pp. 125–170). Dordrecht, the Netherlands: Springer.

Chapter 14

Building bridges
Uniting students, researchers, and teachers to improve a course

Anna Weltman

Two-pager written as a doctoral student for the Design Based Research Forum described in Chapter 9

Objective: build a more meaningful pre-service teacher classroom placement experience

This project builds bridges between three groups of stakeholders involved in preparing high school mathematics teachers: pre-service teachers (PST); practicing teachers who mentor them; and teacher educators/researchers. The study is grounded in an undergraduate level teacher-education course for prospective secondary mathematics and science teachers at a large research university. The research will evaluate an innovative intervention, in which PST and their mentor teachers collaborate on an inquiry project focused on some problem of classroom practice of their own choice.

Background

"Pitfalls" in learning to teach from experience

Researchers recognize that PST struggle with the conflict between their experiences in classroom placements and in coursework (Ronfeldt & Grossman, 2008). The challenges PST face negotiating that conflict can inhibit their learning and lead them to selectively interpret theories and practices to fit the realities they experience (Feiman-Nemser & Buchmann, 1983; McDonald, Kazemi, & Kavanagh, 2013).

Conflict can be productive

Ward, Nolen, and Horn's (2011) research shows that if appropriate supports exist, the conflicts that student teachers experience can be productive. They identify the notion of "productive friction" and describe how PST identity develops in between figured worlds (Horn, Nolen, Ward, & Campbell, 2008). I extend their idea of "productive friction" from student teachers to all PST, and hypothesize that some conflict can be leveraged to support PST learning by reimagining the interaction between novice and expert during the placement experience

Design: the collaborative inquiry project

Rather than leave the work of negotiation between research and practice to the PST alone, this project situates it in an inquiry project conducted collaboratively by PST, practicing teachers, and researchers. The three stakeholders bring different types of resources, and the study aims to investigate negotiations among them as they all work to value, understand, and integrate their resources productively. Initial work involves five local high school math teachers, nine students enrolled in a course (coded Learning in Math and Science, or LMS), and two course instructors. To date:

- High school teachers and course instructors met to choose two aspirational goals for their teaching and several projects that support those goals and are manageable for PST.
- The students met with their mentor teachers to select a project. They also developed initial questions to guide observations in classrooms and reading in LMS that accompany the project. This was supported by an adaptation of the TRU Math Conversation Guide (Baldinger & Louie, 2015).

Initial findings show that the high school teachers see a need for reimagining the role of PST in their classrooms. One teacher described feeling that PST "parachute" into her classroom when they teach a lesson, a metaphor that captures a common impression that PST from the LMS course do not get to know the classrooms they visit and sometimes interact with students in ways that run against the teachers' norms and goals. All five expressed desires for more time to talk with their PST to explain their teaching practices and provide guidance for what to do and look for in the classroom. Furthermore, it appears that mentor teachers and PST could engage in productive discussions about classrooms grounded in evidence while focused on a shared project and supported by an observation framework like TRU.

Conclusions

It is still too early to draw conclusions. However, work done to date suggests promise in helping PST focus their interactions and observations in classrooms and use materials from coursework in planning and reflecting on a lesson. The project has also acquainted the high school teachers with the content of the course and the goals of the LMS course instructors, and vice versa. The development of these two "bridges" so early in the project demonstrates potential for future work.

References

Baldinger, E., & Louie, N. (2015). *TRU Math conversation guide: A tool for teacher learning and growth*. Berkeley, CA & E. Lansing, MI: Graduate School of Education, University of California, Berkeley & College of Education, Michigan State University. Retrieved from http://ats.berkeley.edu/tools.html.

Feiman-Nemser, S., & Buchmann, M. (1983). *Pitfalls of experience in teacher preparation*. Michigan: The Institute for Research on Teaching.

Horn, I. S., Nolen, S. B., Ward, C., & Campbell, S. S. (2008). Developing practices in multiple worlds: The role of identity in learning to teach. *Teacher Education Quarterly, 35*(3), 61–72.

McDonald, M., Kazemi, E., & Kavanagh, S. S. (2013). Core practices and pedagogies of teacher education: A call for a common language and collective activity. *Journal of Teacher Education, 64*(5), 378–386.

Ronfeldt, M., & Grossman, P. (2008). Becoming a professional: Experimenting with possible selves in professional preparation. *Teacher Education Quarterly, 35*(3), 41–60.

Ward, C. J., Nolen, S. B., & Horn, I. S. (2011). Productive friction: How conflict in student teaching creates opportunities for learning at the boundary. *International Journal of Educational Research, 50*(1), 14–20.

Chapter 15

Easy equilibrium

Discovery in an introductory chemistry course

Nadir Bilici

Two-pager written as a neurobiology undergraduate student for the Design Based Research Forum described in Chapter 9

Objective: creating an evolution of thought

This design focuses on easy equilibrium's (EE) design effectiveness at addressing difficulties in understanding equilibrium for students in UC Berkeley's introductory chemistry course, Chem1A. Equilibrium is a fundamental topic in chemistry, and just as algebra is the gateway to understanding complex mathematics, equilibrium is the gateway to understanding many processes in the natural sciences. The design presents itself as an alternative method to teach the concept in a more efficient manner by exposing students to many modalities in a progressive format that fosters a phenomenological evolution of thought.

Background: "teaching science is the process of telling smaller and smaller lies"

The problem in understanding equilibrium is that students have a formalistic curriculum about a complex phenomenon – as bidirectional, dynamic, and simultaneous processes. During my fall 2010 semester in Chem1A lab, a theoretical chemist graduate student instructor commented, "Teaching science is the process of telling smaller and smaller lies." Throughout basic chemistry education, students are repetitively taught that reactions proceed in one direction, but equilibrium defies this logic. Upon learning about equilibrium, many students have difficulties breaking down the formalisms that they have been taught, as the concept is only as real and adaptable to them as numbers are on a paper; as a result, they are unable to make the logical leap to understand the reversibility of chemical equations. According to Nathan (2012), "formalisms are confined to specialized representational forms that use heavily regulated notational systems with no inherent meaning except those that are established by convention to convey concepts and relations with a high degree of specificity" (p. 125). The Chem1A curriculum as it stands does not afford novice chemists to explore chemistry in multiple modalities, and without dialogue or a qualitative foundation for understanding equilibrium, students have difficulties in developing a representational understanding for the analytical problems with which they are first presented.

Design: progressive bridging analogies

The goal of EE is for students first to develop an understanding, beyond ratios on paper – that is honest to the equilibrium phenomenon – before they progress toward more difficult concepts. Becvar, Hollan, and Hutchins (2005) maintain that representations "operate as instantiations of essential spatiodynamic features that are not efficiently conveyed in other modalities . . . and as such, are vital resources for shaping theoretical understandings in collaborative, face-to-face scientific activity" (p. 122). The dynamicism of EE is designed to introduce the complexity underlying equilibrium. Using *NetLogo* (Wilensky, 1999), I built two simulations of equilibrium (Figure 15.1). I also built a physical model with water and dye (Figure 15.2) as a *bridging analogy* into the Net-Logo model (Clement, 1993). This physical–virtual design was further inspired by the *bifocal modeling* design framework (Blikstein & Wilensky, 2007).

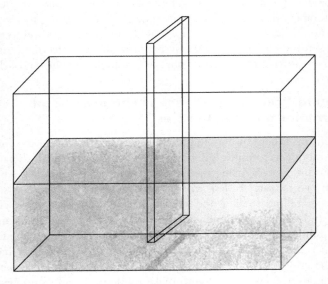

Figure 15.1 A physical model demonstrating equilibrium: A plastic divider separates two compartments of water in a clear box. As the divider is raised, red dye inserted into the left side slowly moves to the clear right side until both sides show an equal level of redness, demonstrating that equilibrium is achieved.

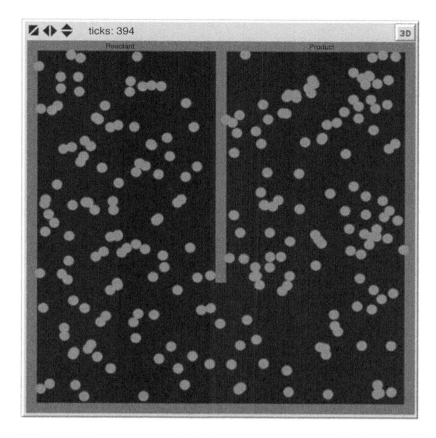

Figure 15.2 NetLogo program depicting a one-to-one equilibrium achieved. Leading up to this point, all of the particles were instantiated on the left side and were left to move freely, allowing the user to see that the system would eventually equilibrate to have an equal number of particles on each side.

Findings

As students progressed through the three models, they evolved a sophisticated understanding of equilibrium. The juxtaposition of the three models brought forth understanding about Brownian motion of particles when a reaction is said to be at equilibrium. Students' view of a naïve, homeostatic equilibrium was perturbed as the virtual models of quantitative movement gave a more precise understanding of concentration gradients and reaction rates. The virtual models provided a simplified, mediated view that students trusted after experiencing the honesty of the physical model. The easy equilibrium design illustrated the dynamics of equilibrium by allowing users to visualize the qualitative, quantitative, and quintessential meaning of the ratios K and Q.

References

Becvar, L.A., Hollan, J., & Hutchins, E. (2005). Hands as molecules: Representational gestures used for developing theory in a scientific laboratory. *Semiotica, 156*(4), 89–112.

Blikstein, P., & Wilensky, U. (2007). Bifocal modeling: A framework for combining computer modeling, robotics and real-world sensing. *Paper Presented at the Annual Meeting of the American Educational Research Association*, Chicago, IL, April 9–13.

Clement, J. (1993). Using bridging analogies and anchoring institutions to deal with students' preconceptions in physics. *Journal of Research in Science Teaching, 30*(10), 1241–1257.

Nathan, J. (2012). Rethinking formalisms in formal education. *Educational Psychologist, 47*(2), 125–148.

Wilensky, U. (1999). *NetLogo*. Evanston, IL: The Center for Connected Learning and Computer-Based Modeling, Northwestern University. Retrieved from http://ccl.north western.edu/netlogo/.

Chapter 16

Rearview mirrors for the "expert blind spot"

Using design to access surgeons' tacit knowledge and create shared referents for teaching

Emily Huang

Paper written as a master's student for the Design Based Research Forum course described in Chapter 9

How are skills learned? An integration of constructivism and embodied cognition

A surgical resident operates across the table from her attending. With a fluid motion, he demonstrates how to use his fingers to bluntly dissect the spermatic cord from surrounding tissue in the inguinal canal, and then separate the structures with a Penrose drain snapped to the surgical field drape. During the next case, the resident is given her turn, and with much greater effort, is able to accomplish the same task for the first time in her training.

What is actually happening when one learns how to do something new with one's hands? Who is in charge: brain or body? In the fields of cognitive psychology and philosophy, opinion has swung between two schools of thought: cognitive constructivism, influenced by the theories of Piaget; and embodied cognition, exemplified by the writings of the Dreyfus brothers.

Drawing from Piaget's explanations of childhood cognitive development through its various stages, cognitive constructivism suggests that mature learning is a result of abstract reflection, the "traditional cognitive (Cartesian) method in which skills are acquired and deployed through analytical thought and symbolic representation without investigating the significance of the body's reactions to situations" (Åsvoll, 2012, p. 791). This type of formal and abstract learning is theorized to be the climax of cognitive development through more primitive stages of concrete, reflexive reaction (Piaget, 1953).

The logical conclusion of the cognitive constructivist point of view is that the best way to learn a skill is through deconstruction: understanding the constitutive steps and being able to reproduce them faithfully each time. Repetition of the skill, through *deliberate practice* (Ericsson et al., 1993; Ericsson, 2004), focuses attention on specific aspects of the skill in order to improve it in a desired way, while immediate and specific feedback directs changes toward performance goals.

The practice of *reflection* is also a natural extension of cognitivism: It involves deep thinking about problems and a practice of mapping new problems onto known, solved ones (Schön, 1983; Barley, 2012). In contexts where the relevant information is available to cognition, reflective thinking is extremely valuable, serving as the driving force for development of increased expertise via meta-cognition, or "thinking about thinking" (Barley, 2012; Ertmer & Newby, 1996). Surgeons may not recognize it, but cognitive constructivist thinking is predom-inant in medical education, from surgical textbooks that describe dissections as a sequence of steps to dictated operative reports containing blow-by-blow accounts of a procedure. Likewise, some approaches to the enhancement (and transmission) of perceptual surgical expertise are firmly rooted in reflection: for example, the use of videotaped surgical procedures to assess intraoperative judgment (Dominguez et al., 1996). Without access to adequate conceptual representation, this type of reflection would be impossible.

Unfortunately, cognitive representation sometimes falls short of skill. To use a well-worn example, no one learns to ride a bicycle by studying diagrams and listening to lectures. As with all physical skills, you have to just get out there and *do* it, at least once, to truly know how to do it. And once you have done it, it is impossible to represent to another how it is done. Surgeons intuitively understand this dilemma: If pressed to describe exactly how they perform a certain dissection, they will invariably conclude with "I could describe it to you *ad infinitum*, but you really have to just get in there and *do* it; then you'll see." Training to become a surgeon has always been an apprenticeship for a reason: Surgery is a skill you must learn with your whole body.

To those who approach the world from a perspective of embodied cogni-tion, this is not surprising. The French phenomenological philosopher Maurice Merleau-Ponty (1908–1961) expressed this perspective eloquently, writing that "the body is our general medium of having a world" (Merleau-Ponty, quoted in Dreyfus & Dreyfus, 1999). To discuss the idea of "intelligence without repre-sentation," Hubert and Stuart Dreyfus elaborated on two concepts introduced by Merleau-Ponty: *intentional arc* and *maximal grip*.

> The intentional arc names the tight connection between the agent and the world, viz. that, as the agent acquires skills, those skills are "stored," not as representations in the mind, but as dispositions to respond to the solicita-tions of situations in the world. Maximal grip names the body's tendency to respond to these solicitations in such a way as to bring the current situ-ation closer to the agent's sense of an optimal gestalt.
>
> (Dreyfus & Dreyfus, 1999; Dreyfus, 2002, p. 367)

In contrast to cognitive constructivism, embodied cognition posits that learning arises from the ground up; that is, skills are responses of the body to situations that are detected in the world. Skills grow iteratively more refined as responses to the infinite variety of situations that may arise to require them; the process of refinement is driven by the body's natural desire to feel that it has performed optimally.

A constructivist might imagine that he could create a surgical robot, programming into it the correct steps and the correct responses to a number of different situations it might face during the course of a procedure. But as he began to consider the mounting complexities of what might occur in the operating room, he would feel overwhelmed, and despair that his robot could never account for them all. Luckily, the surgeon is not limited by rules and abstract analysis, and has a body with an exponential (although not limitless) number of degrees of freedom. Each complexity she may have to deal with in the operating room is matched by the degree of flexibility she can bring to bear on it using her own body. A constructed surgical robot might damage structures during dissection of a heavily scarred operative field, but the fingers of a skilled surgeon deftly separate scar from delicate vessels without a second thought. At the end of the day, the surgeon will report that she knows how to perform this action, but that she has difficulty describing exactly how she does it. Her cognition is embodied, and her knowledge is tacit.

This transition from construction to embodied cognition is mirrored in the stages of skill acquisition. Ideally, a learner progresses from applying rule-based behaviors in a context-free environment to coping with an increasing multitude of situations; in this way, he gradually replaces deliberate reasoning with intuitive behavior (Dreyfus & Dreyfus, 1980; Bransford, 1999). In the process, his relationship to the world is transformed through the lens of his new skill; situations in which he can use the new skill suddenly become more attractive, and each new situation elicits some modification of the skill to cope with details, producing sometimes intense concentration, sometimes frustration, and sometimes pure joy. This is not just *deliberate practice* (Ericsson et al., 1993; Ericsson, 2004) but something beyond repetition of a specific motor pattern; it is "repetition without repetition" that reorganizes the body's movements to solve a motor problem better and better each time (Bernstein, 1996). By the time he becomes an expert, our learner has achieved an intuitive state where "what must be done, simply is done" (Dreyfus & Dreyfus, 1999). For example, when asked about his secret for hitting home runs during the World Series, San Francisco Giants infielder Pablo Sandoval famously replied, matter-of-factly, "swing the bat."

As it turns out, acquisition of skills via this powerful tool, the body, is not even limited to practice of skills directly *requiring* interaction with the world. A rising volume of literature describes the effects of embodied cognition in more and more abstract realms, including mathematics (Abrahamson & Trninic, 2011; Schoenfeld, 1998) and imaginary inferences (Schwartz & Black, 1999). In addition, the idea of embodiment takes on a cultural significance, as learners strive to embody experts in their practice of skills, a concept that has been explored extensively from an ethnographic standpoint (Becvar Weddle & Holland, 2010; Cassell, 1998). These revelations entail additional layers of power (for example, extending the body's ways of understanding, in Schwartz & Black, 1999) and problems (e.g., resolving conceptions of the body as gendered vs. professional, in Cassell, 1998) for learners, which, while not the focus of this discussion, are important to recognize as part of the greater jungle that learners must navigate.

A child who has learned to open jars by unscrewing their lids might reasonably be expected to apply her embodied understanding of a screw-top to a bottle of water, but there are still many situations in which even the very basics of a new skill are beyond an intuitive grasp and require explicit instruction. For example, one would never expect a new learner to just "figure out" how to play the violin, or even how to drive a car. In a sense, this is precisely the flip side of the coin of nearly infinitely flexible dexterity: "We see now how important it is for pedagogical practitioners to be able to analyze correctly a movement and to define which levels of construction it belongs to" (Bernstein, 1996). Likewise, Dreyfus and Dreyfus emphasize that the development of intuitive expertise begins with an explicit, rule-based approach to problems: "Normally the instruction process begins with the instructor decomposing the task environment into context-free features which the beginner can recognize without previous experience in the task domain" (Dreyfus & Dreyfus, 1999). The paradox is that "deconstruction," in this context, actually makes the concept more abstract, aligning it to general rules rather than a context-specific instruction.

The tension between the formal abstraction of constructivism and the intuition of embodied cognition is thus best described as an argument about whether experts are truly abstract or concrete:

> Briefly, it can be suggested that the constructivism that Piaget and Vygotsky pioneered emphasises a development and learning that proceeds from the concrete (sensomotoric, reflexes) to the abstract (formal-logical thought, higher mental functions), whilst the Dreyfus brothers believed that the practice of skills begins with the abstract (non–context-sensitive rules at the beginner stage) and move towards the concrete (intuitive situation-sensitive reactions at the expert stage).
>
> (Åsvoll, 2012, p. 796)

The frustratingly untidy answer to this argument is that experts are at once capable of *both* abstract thought and intuitive action. The expert surgeon sees exactly what needs to be done in order to dissect the spermatic cord out from surrounding tissue and simply does it; his mental energy is left free to think about other abstractions, such as what type of mesh he plans to use for the repair of the patient's hernia. The expert violinist intuitively places his fingers on the instrument to produce tones, but consciously gives the music dynamic phrasing. "Higher" mental functions and the intuition of the body must work together to produce expert performance.

How to promote skill acquisition (i.e., how to be a good teacher)

If learning a skill which requires manual dexterity is like learning to solve a class of problems with your body, then teachers can influence the process in several important ways: (1) they can define the bounds of the problems; (2) they can provide tools and strategies for solving the problems; and (3) they can provide feedback to improve performance. I will next address each of these issues for surgical teachers, as well as a potential pitfall, the *expert blind spot*.

Boundaries

All theories of learning describe some variation on placing the learner in a position to experience new problems in a supported way. Vygotsky wrote of the Zone of Proximal Development as "the distance between the actual developmental level as determined by independent problem solving and the level of potential development as determined through problem solving under adult guidance, or in collaboration with more capable peers" (Vygotsky, 1978), emphasizing the importance of social and cultural interaction in creating that zone for children. Scaffolding, a technique in which the teacher initially performs most of the functions of a skill and gradually allows the student to assume them, is a technique frequently used in the operating room to promote growth in the zone of proximal development; take, for example, this quoted description a surgeon gives of teaching a medical student how to use a drill:

> Did you notice what we did with you? I mean you were probably so conscious of what you were doing, but both [the resident] and I were right on you. It's almost like learning to ride a bike. I was guiding your hand. [The resident] was over there. We were giving you all this silent feedback, like giving you the counter-pressure and stuff, so you wouldn't fail. So that's the part where it's that baby step and then you slowly withdraw the support.
>
> (Prentice, 2007, p. 544)

While the student develops his skill using the drill, the surgeon performs some of the functions (for example, providing counter-pressure). Interestingly, the surgeon uses the metaphor of learning to ride a bike, stating that her role in teaching was not only to guide the learner's hand, but also to prevent failure. This intimates at a very relevant concern in the field of surgery: failure in a real operating room can have severe consequences, regardless of how the boundaries of the motor problems were defined. Controlled environments (simulation labs), like training wheels, are a logical way to reduce risk while presenting surgeon trainees with motor problems of gradually increasing complexity. When the training wheels are eventually removed, a quantum leap must still occur in skill development as the learner performs in the real arena for the first time.

A related way of defining boundaries to the class of problems solved by learners is the idea of a field of promoted action (Reed & Bril, 1996), in which culture plays a key role in defining the types of motor problems to which learners are exposed, particularly when they are developing. This influences the types of action patterns developed and preferred by individuals from different cultural backgrounds, by exposure to "selected opportunities for experience and action" (Reed & Bril, 1996). Strategies for establishing the field of promoted action are abundant in the operating room, but those with the most prominent influence on skill learning are guidance via molding or directing (physically or verbally positioning the hands optimally for performance of the skill), and effective demonstration of a concept via gesture (Becvar Weddle & Holland, 2010).

An interesting example of the effects of field of promoted action in the operating room is promotion of dissection with electrocautery vs. blunt dissectors during laparoscopic cholecystectomy. Since different institutions have culturally based preferences for one type of dissection over the other, surgeons who train at different programs often end up developing very different action patterns for solving the motor problem of dissecting gallbladders.

Tools and strategies

For surgeons (and many other skilled performers, such as violinists), the process of skill acquisition is complicated by the necessity of learning to use "tools of the trade," or *instruments*. While a violin is clearly an instrument, the term should be specifically defined ". . . as an extension of the body, a functional organ made up of an artifact component (an artifact, or the part of an artifact mobilized in the activity) and a psychological component" (Trouche, 2004). The aforementioned psychological component is an intention, and an ability, to use the artifact for a purpose.

Conversely, "*instrumentation* is precisely this process by which the artifact *prints its mark* on the subject, i.e., allows him/her to develop an activity within some boundaries (the constraints of the artifact). One might say, for example, that the scalpel *instruments* a surgeon" (Trouche, 2004). In the motor learning that occurs during surgical training, instrumentation entails not only "know how" about tool use, but also strategy development for approaching surgical problems in patients' bodies. After all, it can be argued that not only scalpels, but also the patient's body, define the boundaries of a surgeon's activities, effectively instrumenting the surgeon (Prentice, 2005).

Teachers play a key role in the orientation of surgical learners to the instruments and strategies they can use to solve motor problems. These can be taught explicitly (like suture manipulation for knot tying), discovered with guidance within the zone of proximal development (like the proper amount of pressure to apply to a drill while the teacher provides counter-pressure described above;

Prentice, 2007), or even just observed without guidance. Orientation can be extremely powerful, even if it is cursory; for example, teaching novices specific techniques for handling suture significantly improves their performance of tying surgical knots (Chern et al., 2011), and asking older adults to attend to an external focus improves performance of a balance task (Chiviacowsky, Wulf, & Wally, 2010). The body of evidence on attentional strategies in sports science suggests that not only can orienting a learner's attention in a certain way improve performance of a skill (such as swimming; Stoate & Wulf, 2011), but it must also be tailored to a learner's level of skill (Perkins-Ceccato, Passmore, & Lee, 2003).

Feedback

During the course of skill acquisition, students gradually become competent at monitoring and self-regulating important aspects of their own performance. Teachers can help develop this competency by performing "other-monitoring," utilizing many modes of feedback and gradually decreasing their involvement in the function as the student progresses and is able to take on those functions himself. Many of the same techniques useful for proscribing boundaries to the motor problem and demonstrating strategies for solving it are also useful for providing feedback either verbally, via physical touch and maneuvering, or by demonstration via gesture (Becvar Weddle & Holland, 2010). New technology has also provided a number of exciting opportunities to enhance feedback modes. For example, sports and music coaches have long used video as an adjunct for self-assessment; now surgeons are beginning to use video for assessment in simulations as well (Jamshidi, LaMasters, Eisenberg, Duh, & Curet, 2009). Eventually, "postgame" video self-assessment of performance in the operating room will also be possible.

Regardless of available avenues and adjuncts, the main challenge remains that in order to provide useful feedback, teachers must be aware of the necessary monitoring functions, have access to the right information for other-monitoring, and be able to communicate the feedback in an effective manner.

Expert blind spot: the final challenge

All of the foregoing analysis of skill learning and skill teaching leads to this point: that not only do teachers need to understand the content they are teaching (in this case, the skill), but they also must understand how best to teach it.

One of the many challenges confronting teachers of any technical skill is that of deconstructing, or parsing, the skill for the novice to follow. In any domain, be it surgery, tennis, or playing an instrument, teachers are usually experts who have long ago consolidated a tight intentional arc, so much so that in any given situation, "what must be done, simply is done" (Dreyfus & Dreyfus, 1999). These teachers easily fall victim to the phenomenon of the "expert blind spot": misconceptions about, or omissions from, what is important for learners to attend to in the initial stages of skill acquisition (Ball, 2000; Nathan, Koedinger, & Alibali, 2001).

Some experts are able to see into their blind spots and draw out the important and relevant skill aspects for their lucky students; these experts deserve also to be called expert teachers. Expert teachers parse time and space to educate the attention of the novice (Byrne, 2006; Churchill, 2011), create points of reference for reflective practice, and dynamically monitor student performance, all while giving feedback in effective ways. When aspects of strategies for performing the skill are obscured, the expert teacher becomes aware of the problem and creates ways to address it. A well-detailed example in the literature is Churchill's example of an expert pottery teacher who, understanding that his hands are obscured while demonstrating inside his vessel on the potter's wheel, reenacts his motions above the wheel where his student is able to see them (Churchill, 2011). It is not unreasonable to imagine that we might turn more experts into expert teachers by showing them ways to become aware of, then overcome, the expert blind spot.

Design of a novel apparatus to improve teaching and learning of vascular dissection

The skill of vascular dissection exemplifies all of the challenges described above for teachers and students. The typical description of the skill by experts, as "you get around it with the clamp," is too quick and obscured for the novice to parse, and provides no specific reference to the fine motor movements involved in spreading the jaws of the clamp, the feel of the connective tissue as it stretches against the clamp during dissection, the proprioception of the tip of the clamp being just under the edge of the vessel without puncturing it, etc. Interestingly, surgeons even have a colloquialism for this skill, "noogering," which experts find very difficult to define! Part of the problem is lack of "pedagogical knowledge" (Nathan, 2001) despite content knowledge, on the teacher's part. But another substantial part of the problem is also that key sensory information about the skill is actually physically inaccessible to both the learner and the teacher. For example, as a surgeon demonstrates vascular dissection, the portion of the dissection taking place behind the vessel is visually inaccessible to the learner. In the final performance of the skill, proprioceptive and haptic sensory modes take over when vision is unavailable, but those too are unavailable to the learner unless the teacher is able to verbalize them (and we know that sensory modes are among the most difficult things to express).

I felt that these challenges could be overcome with thoughtful design, so I created an artifact that allows surgeons to demonstrate to learners what is underneath or behind a vascular dissection. When used simultaneously by a teacher and a student, the design affords additional modes of sensory perception about the task (vision) while expanding on the physical field of promoted action, extending it to explicitly include the back wall of the vascular dissection. The design also gives teacher and student new shared referents for discourse around the instruction, whether that may be questions about the skill from the student, or feedback about performance from the teacher.

Initial design of the artifact involved a glass dish supported on an unobtrusive stand, allowing for visualization of the process of dissection from below via a mirror. A pork splenic vein dissection was used for simulation of vascular dissection.

Figure 16.1 Vascular dissection apparatus, first iteration

In demonstrating the first iteration of the design to informants, we discovered several unexpected affordances about the artifact, including that an instructor could physically demonstrate or point to an area of the dissection from behind. The second design iteration thus replaced the hard glass with a soft vinyl tray to provide an opportunity for tactile feedback from below, giving instructors and students an additional mode of interaction. A second issue of design involved directionality of the mirror, which could be directed to face the person performing the dissection or away from that person. After experimentation, I chose to align the mirror to face the surgeon, limiting surgeon and student to standing on the same side of the dissection. During the demonstration, informants discussed the possibility of using video technology to expand the angles of view from below; however, a certain "honesty" of visual perception was preserved with the mirror. As described below, this became an important design limitation.

I tested the second design iteration in the Surgical Skills Center at UCSF with an expert-teacher and novices (medical students). The students were an ideal test group in many ways (completely unexposed to this class of problem previously, unlike even the lowest training-level residents), and fairly enthusiastic about the opportunity to engage in a high-fidelity "simulated surgery." On the other hand, the students, as less focused learners than residents, were easily distracted to playing with the materials instead of adhering to the defined boundaries of the presented problem.

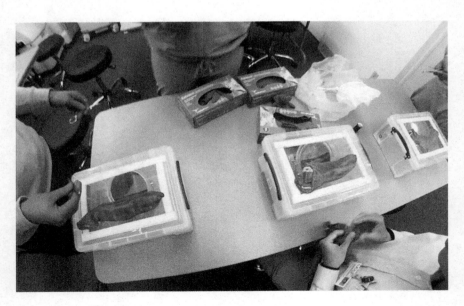

Figure 16.2 Vascular dissection apparatus, second iteration

During the two-hour session, I filmed interactions between the students and instructor, later analyzing their utterances and actions as they used the artifact. Key observations were: (1) Instructor and students alike required time to discover the affordances of the artifact; (2) some learners more readily adopted the available affordances than others; and (3) it was important to strictly define the boundaries of the task (to dissect around the vessel multiple times in multiple places vs. around the vessel in one place and then along the sides) for the students, in order to prevent unproductive activity. It was interesting to note that those learners who most enthusiastically adopted the affordances of the apparatus itself were also the most fluent in describing their experiences while performing the dissection (one student is quoted below).

Additionally, two observations about the design itself became clear. First, surgical procedures are typically performed with an assistant across the operating table, and so expecting teacher and student to stand side by side (as potters are able to do) was somewhat naïve. In reality, the directionality of the mirror gave only one person in each pair (the person operating) access to the new visual information, thereby partially defeating the intended purpose of shared referents. It became clear that sacrificing the honesty of a mirror would be necessary to make the information more broadly available through video rebroadcasting. Second, while the vinyl tray was designed to serve as an additional avenue for tactile feedback between teacher and student, the sturdier supports in the second iteration of the design were obtrusive enough to discourage any of the trainees or the teacher from using it; again, redesign in another iteration would have to account for this.

Future directions

A third iteration of the design is in the works, but the more important theoretical lessons to learn from this design endeavor have already been revealed in in the process, and may be applied easily to future instructional interactions. For example, in understanding that shared referents are important for instruction, we can make surgical instructors aware of the need to look for and use them in all the situations in which they are available. If reflection is not available in the moment, then we can use video to make the moment available later (a project we will be undertaking in the Skills Center in the near future).

It appears that the most important positive effect of this design was that its very presence promoted reflection by the expert on what expert blind spots might exist in the course of this type of instruction. Simply by presenting a new artifact to the field of promoted action, the apparatus encouraged discussion between teacher and students about available modes of perception and how to attend to them. In exploring the new artifact, attempting to discover its affordances, teachers and students were forced to consider what modes of perception were available – and important – to them. While designed to remove a barrier that normally forces surgeons to proceed based on proprioceptive and haptic feedback only, use of the artifact actually resulted in increased discussion of all types of feedback (visual, proprioceptive, and haptic). For example, when asked what she thought of the design itself, one student stated:

> I feel like I used it at the beginning to figure out where I was going to put my incision, kind of like an ultrasound … I don't know that I used it much when I was dissecting unless I wasn't sure that I was behind it, but I also felt that … less than I needed to see [pointing at mirror w instrument] what I was doing, I needed to learn clearly [E interjects "learn to feel"] yeah [making scooping motion of getting behind vessel in air], and know what it was that was on the end of my right angle [rubs tip of right angle with other finger] and if it was something I could cut or what.

I would argue, that for mature learners, simply making them aware of the various potential pitfalls in teaching and learning physical skills can give them the ammunition they need to overcome many of them.

———————

Note: For a video of the design, see www.youtube.com/watch?v=PB8pt9s4x9s.

References

Abrahamson, D., & Trninic, D. (2011). Toward an embodied-interaction design framework for mathematical concepts. In P. Blikstein & P. Marshall (Eds.), *Proceedings of the 10th Annual Interaction Design and Children Conference* (IDC 2011), Ann Arbor, MI, June 20–23 (Vol. Full papers, pp. 1–10). IDC.

Åsvoll, H. (2012). Perspectives on reflection and intuition in teacher practice: A comparison and possible integration of the cognitive constructivist and the Dreyfusian intuitive perspectives. *Reflective Practice: International and Multidisciplinary Perspectives, 13*(6), 789–804.

Ball, D. L. (2000). Bridging practices: Intertwining content and pedagogy in teaching and learning to teach. *Journal of Teacher Education, 51*(3), 241–247.

Barley, M. (2012). Learning from reflective practice and metacognition – An anaesthetist's perspective. *Reflective Practice: International and Multidisciplinary Perspectives, 13*(2), 271–280.

Becvar Weddle, L. A., & Holland, J. D. (2010). Professional perception and expert action: Scaffolding embodied practices and professional education. *Mind, Culture, and Activity, 17*, 119–148.

Bernstein, N. A. (1996). On dexterity and its development. In M. L. Latash & M. T. Turvey (Eds.), *Dexterity and its development* (pp. 3–224). Mahwah, NJ: Lawrence Erlbaum Associates.

Bransford, J. D., Brown, A. L., & Cocking, R. R. (1999). How experts differ from novices. In J. D. Bransford, A. L. Cocking, & R. R. Cocking (Eds.), *How people learn* (pp. 19–38). Washington, DC: National Academies Press.

Byrne, R. W. (2006). Parsing behavior: A mundane origin for an extraordinary ability? In N. J. Enfield & S. C. Levinson (Eds.), *Roots of human sociality* (pp. 478–505). Oxford, UK: Berg.

Cassell, J. (1998). *The woman in the surgeon's body*. Cambridge, MA: Harvard University Press.

Chern, H., Presser, N., O'Sullivan, P., Utley, B., Reilly, L., & Kim, E. (2011). *Teaching two-handed knot tying: Can we do better?* Poster Presentation, AAMC Western Regional Conference. Stanford, CA.

Chiviacowsky, S., Wulf, G., & Wally, R. (2010). An external focus of attention enhances balance learning in older adults. *Gait & Posture, 32*(4), 572–575.

Churchill, E. (2011). Skill learning, parsing, and narrated enactments: Decomposing and blending action at the potter's wheel. Manuscript in preparation.

Dominguez, C. O., Flach, J. M., McKellar, D. P., & Dunn, M. (1996). Using videotaped cases to elicit perceptual expertise in laparoscopic surgery. In *Proceedings of the Third Annual Symposium on Human Interaction with Complex Systems* (pp. 116–123). Los Alamitos, CA: IEEE Computer Society Press.

Dreyfus, H. L. (2002). Intelligence without representation – Merleau-Ponty's critique of mental representation. *Phenomenology and the Cognitive Sciences, 1*, 367–383.

Dreyfus, H. L., & Dreyfus, S. E. (1999). The challenge of Merleau-Ponty's phenomenology of embodiment for cognitive science. In G. Weiss & H. F. Haber (Eds.), *Perspectives on embodiment: The intersections of nature and culture* (pp. 103–120). New York, NY: Routledge.

Dreyfus, S. E., & Dreyfus, H. L. (1980). *A five-stage model of the mental activities involved in directed skill acquisition* (No. ORC-80-2). Berkeley, CA: University of California Berkeley Operations Research Center.

Ericsson, K. A. (2004). Deliberate practice and the acquisition and maintenance of expert performance in medicine and related domains. *Academic Medicine, 79*(10), S70–S81.

Ericsson, K. A., Krampe, R. T., & Tesch-Römer, C. (1993). The role of deliberate practice in the acquisition of expert performance. *Psychological Review, 100*(3), 363.

Ertmer, P. A., & Newby, T. J. (1996). The expert learner: Strategic, self-regulated, and reflective. *Instructional Science, 24*, 1–24.

Jamshidi, R., LaMasters, T., Eisenberg, D., Duh, Q. Y., & Curet, M. (2009). Video self-assessment augments development of videoscopic suturing skill. *Journal of the American College of Surgeons, 209*(5), 622–625.

Nathan, M., Koedinger, K. R., & Alibali, M. (2001). Expert blind spot: When content knowledge eclipses pedagogical content knowledge. In L. Chen & Y. Zhuo (Eds.), *Proceedings of the Third International Conference on Cognitive Science*. Beijing: Press of the University of Science and Technology of China.

Perkins-Ceccato, N., Passmore, S. R., & Lee, T. (2003). Effects of focus of attention depend on golfers' skill. *Journal of Sports Sciences, 21*(8), 593–600.

Piaget, J. (1953). *The origin of intelligence in the child*. London: Routledge & Kegan & Paul.

Prentice, R. (2005). The anatomy of a surgical simulation: The mutual articulation of bodies in and through the machine. *social Studies of Science, 35*(6), 837–866.

Prentice, R. (2007). Drilling surgeons: The social lessons of embodied surgical learning. *Science, Technology & Human Values, 32*(5), 534–553.

Reed, E. S., & Bril, B. (1996). The primacy of action in development. In M. L. Latash & M. T. Turvey (Eds.), *Dexterity and its development* (pp. 431–451). Mahwah, NJ: Lawrence Erlbaum Associates.

Schön, D. A. (1983). *The reflective practitioner: How professionals think in action*. Aldershot: Ashgate.

Schoenfeld, A. H. (1998). Making pasta and making mathematics: From cookbook procedures to really cooking. In J. G. Greeno & S. V. Goldman (Eds.), *Thinking practice in mathematics and science learning* (pp. 299–319). Mahwah, NJ: Lawrence Erlbaum Associates.

Schwartz, D. L., & Black, T. (1999). Inferences through imagined actions: Knowing by simulated doing. *Journal of Experimental Psychology, 25*(1), 116–136.

Stoate, I., & Wulf, G. (2011). Does the attentional focus adopted by swimmers affect their performance? *International Journal of Sports Science and Coaching, 6*(1), 99–108.

Trouche, L. (2004). Managing the complexity of human/machine interactions in computerized learning environments: Guiding students' command process through instrumental orchestrations. *International Journal of Computers for Mathematical Learning, 9*(3), 281–307.

Vygotsky, L. S. (1978). *Mind in society: The development of higher psychological processes.* Cambridge, MA: Harvard University Press.

Chapter 17

Children's reasoning about animal lifecycles

Tradeoffs across four different designs

Kathryn Lanouette

Paper written as a master's student for the design research course described in Chapter 9

Preface

In this chapter, Kathryn Lanouette, a doctoral candidate at UC Berkeley in the Graduate School of Education, shares a course paper from her first semester in a design based research course taught by Dor Abrahamson in fall 2012. Lanouette draws upon two central ideas to organize her argumentation and empirical work. First, children's ways of seeing the world should be productive resources for science learning. Second, children's use of representational forms in elementary school science contexts should be designed to engage children's own intuitions about the living world around them and support children's rigorous engagement with scientific ideas. Working with these ideas, Lanouette first describes several challenges elementary students encounter when learning about animal lifecycles, including making one-to-one comparisons, coordinating different temporal scales, navigating scientific vocabulary, and interpreting schematic depictions of organisms' lifecycles. She then motivates and describes four designs she developed to address these challenges to meet the course requirements. Each design privileges different materials and modalities yet attempts to support children using their intuitions to make comparisons between and within different species' lifecycles.

Five years have passed since Lanouette wrote the course paper; in her ongoing doctoral dissertation research, Lanouette builds upon her early ideas. She uses design based research to advance our understanding of elementary students' emerging capabilities to create, share, and contest explanations of local ecosystems. Of special interest is students' use of digital participatory maps to reason about complex ecological relationships and the ways in which children use their daily experiences in the surrounding neighborhood to make sense of digital as well as other ways of representing ecosystems. Her dissertation research is funded by an award from the National Academy of Education/ Spencer Dissertation Fellowship program (2017–2018).

Design problem

In many elementary school science curricula, students study animal lifecycles by raising and observing a variety of living insects (e.g., monarch butterflies, silkworm moths, milkweed insects) and amphibians (e.g., frogs, salamanders) in their classrooms. Drawing from their everyday experiences with animals and their own experiences growing and changing, children bring an intuitive sense about these organisms' developmental stages, the sequence of these developmental stages, and temporal duration of these stages and sequences. But children have difficulty expressing and building on their intuitions as they compare and contrast different organisms' developmental processes because existing lifecycle representations often distort and omit key information about these developmental processes.

In this design based study, four designs were devised to more clearly delineate developmental stages, sequence of stages, and temporal durations of stages to support elementary school age children making comparisons between and within different species' lifecycles. In the sections that follow, I first describe previous solutions to this problem and provide an analysis that highlights potential disconnects between children's ways of thinking and the representational forms commonly used in classroom contexts. I then provide a rationale for and share four design solutions, each reflecting different design choices. Lastly, I share my methods and reflections on the design process, informed by Bamberger and Schön's (1983) conceptualization of learning as an ongoing reflective process of building and rebuilding with materials.

Problems with previous design solutions

The diagrammatic representations in texts commonly used to support instruction in elementary school science do little to engage children with the higher order thinking of which they are capable. In part, the representational/design problem stems from an underestimation of young children's cognitive capabilities (Brown, Campione, Metz, & Ash, 1997). The limited support for higher order thinking in textual representations is also rooted in many educators' limited attention to children's intuitive ways of reasoning about biological life, using what Inagaki and Hatano (2002) refer to as "personification." Indeed, intuitive resources like personification could support children's comparative analysis of animal species' developmental stages, stage sequences, and the way temporal durations of stages and sequences vary. To compound matters, for purposes of simplification, many diagrammatic representations of insect or amphibian lifecycles distort the developmental stage durations and the absolute duration of the species' life. Further, due to controversies surrounding the discussion of procreation and birth with young children, many representations often intentionally omit key developmental stages and the sequencing of stages, stymieing children's intuitive understandings of and curiosity about organisms' developmental stages, sequences, and temporal durations of development (see Appendix A for examples of different lifecycle representations).

Cognitive domain analysis

In this section, I describe several conceptual challenges children encounter as they attempt to relate other organisms' developmental stages, the sequence of these developmental stages, and temporal duration of these stages and sequences with their own human lifecycle.

Challenges include making one-to-one comparisons between themselves and other organisms, coordinating varying temporal scales, navigating scientific vocabulary, and interpreting diagrammatic representations of lifecycles.

Making one-to-one comparisons

Drawing from their own experiences, children often attempt to make one-to-one comparisons between themselves and the different stages of other organisms' development. By personifying the organism, children seek to align their own developmental processes of birth, infancy, and childhood with these different organisms' processes. This proves challenging because insect and amphibian metamorphoses do not easily align with the developmental stages that mammals undergo. For example, comparing a human to a frog or butterfly, there are striking differences in gestation, birth processes, and development that complicate children's one-to-one comparisons.

Coordinating different temporal scales

Due to varying units of measurement (e.g., days, weeks, months, years), it is challenging for children to compare the temporal scale of other species' lifecycles due to the constant conversion between units. This becomes problematic for several reasons. First, it is possible that this unit conversion prevents children's natural calculations of time, interfering with children's intuitive sense of these temporal relationships. Second, these constant conversions strain young children's rational-numerical fluency, limiting children's expression of an embodied sense of proportion (Abrahamson, 2012). Last, when children compare themselves to another species, they are making comparisons both between and among species' lifecycles. These inter-lifecycle and intra-lifecycle comparisons demand additional working memory load to reason about both the proportional scaling of developmental stages and the absolute duration of the species' lives.

Navigating scientific vocabulary

As children make stage and sequence comparisons, scientific vocabulary adds another layer of complexity. When young children attempt to relate these new words to commonly used terms for human developmental stages and sequencing (e.g., baby, child, teenager, adult), children must attend to the subtleties inherent in scientific language. For example, even though the silkworm moth and monarch butterfly are both insects that undergo metamorphosis, the structure constructed by the pupa is differently named (e.g., cocoon vs. chrysalis). In addition, establishing a temporal "starting line" for the lifecycle proves challenging due to developmental variations following conception. On top of these challenges, due to the contested nature of discussing reproduction and birth in school settings, especially with young children, adults often obfuscate key developmental stage- and sequence-related terminology.

Interpreting instructional materials

Instructional materials, such as diagrammatical representations and trade books, further compound children's challenges making one-to-one comparisons further by distorting stage proportions, sequencing, and temporal duration. Diagrammatic depictions frequently blur proportional scaling of stages with the absolute duration of the species's life. Many representations employ a clock schema to show the sequencing of temporal events but the proportional relationship between stages is distorted. For example, in a common lifecycle diagram, the adult silkworm moth is placed between the nine o'clock and twelve o'clock position, suggesting that the adult stage lasts 25% of the moth's life when in fact that stage represents less than 8% of the moth's total life (see Appendix A for common examples).

Design rationale

To address these challenges, I created four instructional designs (see Appendix B, Tables 17.1 and 17.2) for more detail), each informed by a set of overarching design principles. These design principles include:

- Demarcating developmental stages and sequence to support comparison between and within species;
- Aligning different organisms' lifecycle stages in close proximity to facilitate direct scaled comparisons;
- Maintaining a fixed unit of time to support temporal scale comparisons; and
- Using text sparingly by color coding developmental stages to support comparisons between and within species

Due to the added complexity of developmental variations following conception, the egg/in utero stage was omitted across all four designs. Throughout all four designs, emphasis was placed on supporting, rather than ignoring or redirecting, children's naïve approaches (e.g., Abrahamson, 2012; Clement, 1993) to thinking about the living world.

Design solutions

Working with a variety of materials, I created four different designs: Lifecycle Timeline, Lifecycle Spinner, Lifecycle Gears, and Lifecycle Rolling Stamp. Across all designs, I maintained the following color-coding to convey the different developmental stages (e.g., orange showing the larval stage, blue showing the pupa stage, green showing the adult stage, and a black line showing the beginning and end of lifecycle). Additionally, in all designs, children control the tempo at which time passes through their physical movement of the materials.

In the Lifecycle Timelines, I aligned four species' repeating lifecycles (cat, silkworm moth, black widow spider, and frog) in parallel progression on a canvas board. Using a clear plastic cylindrical rod, children were encouraged to move or roll the rod slowly down the board, enabling them to simultaneously compare the stage, sequence, and temporal duration of the different organisms' lifecycles (see Figure 17.1, a).

In the Lifecycle Spinner, I nested three circles together, with the innermost circle depicting a cat lifecycle, the second circle depicting frog lifecycles, and the outermost circle depicting a silkworm moth (see Figure 17.1, b). Affixed to

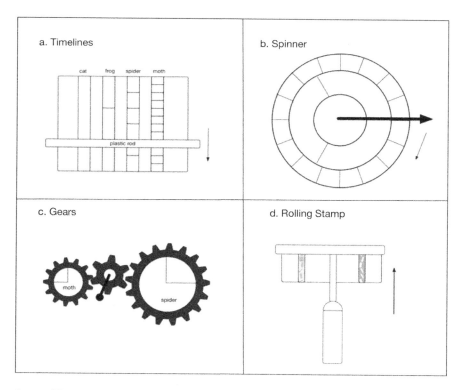

Figure 17.1 Four designs

the center was a metal spinner that children were encouraged to move slowly around the circular board.

In the Lifecycle Gears, I used three plastic gears to depict a silkworm lifecycle (the small circle on left), "time" (the middle circle with a hand crank), and a black widow spider (large circle on the right). As children turned the center "time" crank, a sound was generated as each passing gear cog ticked against a small paper tab (see Figure 17.1, c).

In the Lifecycle Rolling Stamp, I wrapped two hand-scored rubber bands around a silkscreen print roller, with one rubber band depicting a silkworm moth lifecycle and the other rubber band depicting a black widow spider lifecycle. As children inked the rolling stamp, they were encouraged to use an inkpad with two separate colors so as to further distinguish the two species' lifecycles (see Figure 17.1, d).

Methods and reflection

These four designs are a first step in articulating insights into the complexity of learning and instruction about animal lifecycles. In addition to my semi-structured interview with one child (age 6.2 years), many of my insights came from my own direct interactions with the materials. As Bamberger and Schön (1983) noted, a "reflective conversation" occurs "between makers and their materials in the course of shaping meaning and coherence" (p. 69). Indeed, it was through the process of designing and building that I came to better understand many of the challenges and opportunities children might encounter with this scientific content and related representational forms.

In this section, I first describe insights that emerged from my direct work building and rebuilding with the materials. I then share insights that emerged from the semi-structured interview. In three of the designs, I used colored pencils to show the different developmental stages. In working with these materials, I noticed the abrupt transition between stages each time I physically switched colored pencils. By representing the stages as colors – not text – I became increasingly aware of both the static and fluid quality of these temporal representations. For example, while these sharp vertical lines highlighted the stage boundaries (supporting children's intra- and inter-species comparisons), organisms' gradual developmental changes were obscured.

Building a gear-based design generated different insights. In my conversations with a young child working with the Lifecycle Gears, we discussed adding additional circular gears to represent other species' lifecycles. With excitement, the child suggested different species we might add but paused abruptly and explained that the new animals would have to "fit." (Child: "You could put a goat here [*gesturing to the left side of the gear mounts*] and a rabbit here [*pointing to the right side of the gear mounts*] but . . . oh . . . they would have to fit!") "Fit" was a fascinating word – both for its physical implications (number of cogs on each gear) and its implication of a proportional relationship between different animal species' lifecycles. In that moment, I was reminded how children's expression of proportional understandings is dramatically shaped by the materials at hand and the questions asked.

Across these four designs, questioning proved telling at capturing shifts in children's reasoning as they worked with the different designs. For example, when I asked at the beginning of the interview involving the Lifecycle Timeline "Which animal would you prefer to be and why?" the child quickly responded: "I would be a cat!" When asked why, the child responded, "They live the longest." After working with both the Lifecycle Timeline and the Lifecycle Spinner, the same question was met with a different answer: "I would be a silkworm because they are a kid the longest." From this shift in answers, it seems the child was able to observe that the silkworm moth had a proportionally longer "childhood" than the cat or frog, making them a "kid" the longest. By interacting with the different designs, the child seemed to be indicating she was proportionally comparing species within lifecycles. She also appeared to be able to synchronize both comparisons together to reason about the relative value of being a kid or grown up.

Throughout the interview, the child often connected her own experiences eating food with her family, playing with a sibling, and growing taller with the other animals' lifecycles. For example, toward the end of the interview after the child had worked with the four different designs, she spontaneously offered her thinking about why some animals might spend more time in certain developmental stages compared to other animals. The child offered, "Maybe the silkworm is having to spend more time looking for food . . . That's why it is a baby the longest!" At other times, she used the terms "baby" and "grown up" to talk about insects' and arachnids' larval and adult phases as well as other personifying terms ("sleepy," "hard work"). From this initial design work and conversations with a child, it seems there are generative possibilities for further developing both the interview protocol and the designed materials to better solicit children's thinking about these proportional relationships.

Limitations and future work

While these four designs generated many insights, there were several design decisions that created substantive problems. One problematic decision was omitting the gestational phase of the organisms' lifecycles. Due to variation in where the embryo develops (e.g., egg vs. in utero) and how "birth" is defined in different organisms, I had decided not include this initial stage in any of the four designs. Yet omitting this key developmental stage became problematic for two reasons. First, by "starting" the lifecycle at the larval stage, an important developmental stage was omitted, distorting intra- and inter-proportional relationships. Second, by skipping this stage, my design contributed to children's confusion about conception and birth. In future work, adding an egg/in utero stage would be crucial to establishing a more accurate proportional relationship between and among species' lifecycles and to support children's more authentic understanding of organisms' developmental stages.

A second problematic decision involved lining up lifecycles back to back. In emphasizing the stages, sequence, and scale aspects of different species' lifecycles, the cyclic aspects of the cycle became lost. Even when using concentric designs as in the Lifecycle Spinner, each species' reproduction, death, and birth phases were unclear. Lifecycles simply stopped and then instantly started, all within the same black line. Yet conceptually, this is problematic for children because a key step in an organism's lifecycle, the transfer of genetic material, is obscured (Lehrer & Schauble, 2012).

Through the design process, several future directions for research also emerged, including focusing on designs that encourage an embodiment of the full cyclic process. For example, a large rolling stamp, designed for both individual and partnered operation, might support a deeper understanding of the cycle by establishing congruence between the perceptuomotor schema and the target cognitive form (Abrahamson & Trninic, 2011; Johnsone-Glenberg et al., 2009). By rolling the stamp, a child seems capable of both physically embodying the process of the temporal cycle (through the stamp's forward-rolling motion through space) and simultaneously recording the process (by imprinting the motion as a static, linear form on paper).

In addition, it also seems promising to further explore design features that highlight the dynamic processes of organisms' lifecycles. Within all four designs, as I reflected on the tension between static and fluid notations of time (Bamberger, 2010), I became curious about how future designs might highlight these dynamic proportional temporal relationships. Using a combination of auditory feedback and kinesthetic movement, how might the two be interwoven to foster awareness of time unfolding (a fluid process) while physically representing the passage of time (a static product)? It seems that rhythm, both expressed through sound and a child's physical movement, might generate deeper connections about both the proportional scaling of developmental stages and the absolute duration of the species' lifecycle.

Appendix A

Common visual diagrams used in elementary school science.

Monarch butterfly image example

The first image represents more common depictions of insect lifecycles (see Figure 17.2). In this image, the reproduction phase is completely omitted, leaving a gap between the end of the adult butterfly's life and the beginning of future generations. Additionally, the clock schema distorts the proportional duration of each development stage. For example, it takes the monarch butterfly approximately one month to change from an egg to an adult butterfly, yet the remaining adult stages can last anywhere from one month to nine months depending on migration patterns. In this image, the adult phase appears to account for only 25% of the organism's lifecycle.

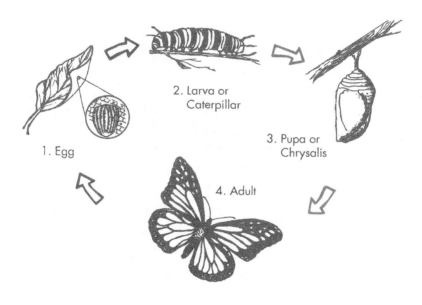

LIFE CYCLE OF THE MONARCH BUTTERFLY

Figure 17.2 Monarch butterfly lifecycle.

Credit: USDA Forest Service.

Silkworm moth lifecycle example

In this second image (see Figure 17.3), a sharp contrast to most available images, several phases of development are clearly featured, including reproduction and the time span between the eggs being laid and hatching. Yet because the illustrator employs a clock schema to show the sequencing of temporal events, the proportional relationship between stages is still distorted. For example, in this image the adult silkworm moth is placed in the nine o'clock position, suggesting that the adult stage lasts 25% of the moth's life when in fact that stage represents less than 8% of the moth's total life.

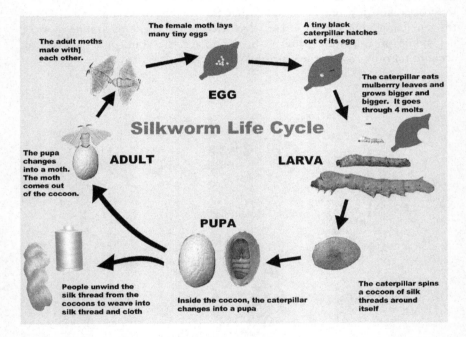

Figure 17.3 Silkworm moth lifecycle.

Credit: Sue Kayton.

Appendix B

In this section, I include two planning documents used in the design process. In this first table, I identify several of the current design problems, provide a cognitive domain analysis, and consider potential design solutions that I use in the four designs.

Table 17.1 Design problem table: Problems, cognitive domain analysis, and design solutions

Design problem	Cognitive domain analysis	Design solutions
Children's inclination to make direct comparisons between themselves and other species' lifecycles not well supported by representational forms	**Stage & Sequence:** * Challenging to match up developmental stages and sequence of stages with human lifecycle * Differences in developmental stages and sequences complicate anthropocentric inclinations	**Stage & Sequence:** * Visually break apart developmental stages and sequence
	Intra- & Inter- comparisons: * Challenging to compare between and within other species' lifecycles * Hard to keep track of "where" you are * Significant working memory load to manipulate stage vocabulary and sequence	**Intra- & Inter- comparisons:** * Use parallel and concentric alignment of stages to facilitate direct scaled comparisons * Use wand, spinner, and cog ticker to establish fixed location in relation to all other species
	Scale: * Challenging to match up temporal scale of other species' lifecycles due to varying units of measurement (days, weeks, months, years) * Structure possibly interferes with children's intuitive sense of these temporal relationships * Developing rational-numerical fluency limits children's expression of an embodied sense of proportion	**Scale:** * Maintain fixed unit of time in all designs to support temporal scale comparisons

(Continued)

Table 17.1 (Continued)

Design problem	Cognitive domain analysis	Design solutions
Complex scientific vocabulary used to describe developmental stages and sequence	**Sequence:** * Skewed alignment of scientific vocabulary with human developmental stages due to different sequencing of stages and alternation between scientific/everyday vocabulary requires significant working memory load	**Sequence:** * Replace stage-related scientific vocabulary with color coding system to support visual comparison
	Stage & Sequence: * Starting point (birth) of species poorly defined, complicating establishment of an equal temporal starting point * Reproduction of species poorly defined, complicating sequence progression * Controversial area of dialogue with children and within society, causing vague wording and intentional absence of key cyclic stages	**Stage & Sequence:** * Omit egg/in utero developmental stage
Instructional materials further complicate stage, sequence, and scale comparisons	**Stage, Sequence, & Scale:** * Diagrams distort stage proportions, sequencing, and temporal scale	**Stage, Sequence, & Scale:** * Highlight accurate proportional relationship between stages and scale * Replace stage-related scientific vocabulary with color coding system to support visual comparison

In this second table, I describe each design's affordances, constraints, and possible solutions.

Table 17.2 Design affordances, constraints, and potential solutions

Design	Affordances	Constraints (and potential solutions)
Lifecycle Timeline	* Easier to visually compare total lifecycle duration between species * Easier to visually compare lifecycle stages duration within species * By moving the plastic dowel, child controls rate of time and time remains proportionally constant for all organisms in relation to one another	* Static visual representation seems less engaging (perhaps attach plastic rod to rollers?) * Linear design obscures the "cycle" aspect of the lifecycle (perhaps construct looping lifecycles in spiraling format)

(Continued)

Table 17.2 (Continued)

Design	Affordances	Constraints (and potential solutions)
Lifecycle Spinner	* Easier to visually compare lifecycle duration between species * By moving the spinner, child controls rate of time and time remains constant for all organisms in relation to one another	* Although a concentric design was used, the idea of a "cycle" was not clear * Developmental stage progression artificially static (perhaps blend colors into one another to represent fluid process?) * Possible interference from clock schema on design's interpretation (perhaps attend to starting and stopping points as well as spinner?)

Lifecycle Gears

moth

spider

* Materials intrinsically
  engaging and
  encourage active
  engagement
* "Cycle" part of
  lifecycle more visible
  both by turning cogs
  and by child's own
  turning of the central
  gear
* Fixed proportional
  relationship between
  species – regardless
  of rate

* Harder to visually
  compare total
  lifecycle duration
  between species
  because it is easy
  to lose count given
  all the movement
  (perhaps make sound
  emitted at each full
  turn of the circular
  cog to mitigate this
  constraint?)
* Visually complex
  (perhaps make only
  some features salient?)
* Possible interference
  from clock schema on
  design's interpretation
  (perhaps attend to
  starting and stopping
  points as well as
  spinner?)

(Continued)

Table 17.2 (Continued)

Design	Affordances	Constraints (and potential solutions)
Lifecycle Rolling Stamp	* Materials intrinsically engaging and encourage active engagement * Physical cycling of roller directly related to cyclic lifecycle * Child's physical rolling is time unfolding – space, distance, rate – all in one	* How will the linear product influence understanding of the cyclic process? * Will adding a sound effect with every rotation help children be mindful of a new lifecycle beginning or will it be too distracting?

References

Abrahamson, D. (2012). Discovery reconceived: Product before process. *For the Learning of Mathematics, 32*(1), 8–15.

Abrahamson, D., & Trninic, D. (2011). Toward an embodied-interaction design framework for mathematical concepts. In P. Blikstein & P. Marshall (Eds.), *Proceedings of the 10th Annual Interaction Design and Children Conference (IDC 2011)* (Vol. "Full papers," pp. 1–10). Ann Arbor, MI: IDC.

Bamberger, J. (2010). Noting time. *Min-Ad: Israel Studies in Musicology Online, 8*(1&2), 1–17. Retrieved from www.biu.ac.il/hu/mu/min-ad/

Bamberger, J., & Schön, D. (1983). Learning as reflective conversation with materials: Notes from work in progress. *Art Education, 36*(2), 68–73.

Brown, A., Campione, J., Metz, K., & Ash, D. (1997). The development of science learning abilities in children. In K. Härnqvist & A. Burgen (Eds.), *Growing up with science: Developing early understanding of science*. London, UK: Jessica Kingsley Publishers.

Clement, J. (1993). Using bridging analogies and anchoring intuitions to deal with students' preconceptions in physics. *Journal of Research in Science Teaching, 30*(10), 1241–1257.

Inagaki, K., & Hatano, G. (2002). *Young children's naive thinking about the biological world*. New York: Psychology Press.

Johnson-Glenberg, M. C., Birchfield, D., Megowan-Romanowicz, C., Tolentino, L., & Martinez, C. (2009). Embodied games, next gen interfaces, and assessment of high school physics. *International Journal of Learning and Media, 1*(2). Retrieved December 1, 2012 from http://ijlm.net/knowinganddoing/10.1162/ijlm.2009.0.

Lehrer, R., & Schauble, L. (2012). Seeding evolutionary thinking by engaging children in modeling its foundations. *Science Education, 96*(4), 701–724.

Chapter 18

Linking design and theory

Using conjecture maps to focus the design research process in art education

Nathalie Werner and Arthur Bakker

Summary

This chapter focuses on the process of orienting oneself within the early stage of a design research project. We show how using conjecture mapping helped to align educational theory and design in art education. In particular, conjecture mapping was used to construct a more focused line of theoretical reasoning and to improve the design.

This chapter presents the orientation process in the first eight months of a design research project with a focus on the alignment of design and theory. The insights provided here originate from working with Nathalie Werner, a student of the dual teaching PhD program at the University of Bremen, Germany. The program includes both a teacher training and writing a dissertation about the research done within the frame of the training. Nathalie is in the process of becoming a high school teacher of art and English and is interested in working with digital media in her classes. The aim of her research project is figuring out how to use tablets in art lessons for the exploration of spaces through aesthetic research in order to foster a change of perspective in Grade 8 students (ages 13–15).

We first discuss the rationale for the research and explain the setting. Next, we take a look at the research questions and the challenges Nathalie faced while developing the design. Last, we discuss how conjecture maps helped her to focus her project and what she learned by using them.

Rationale for the project

Current debates in education evolve around the increasing diversity in German schools in general, and the growing diversity in Bremen in particular, in respect to language as well as to cultural, transcultural, and motivational factors (cf. Peters & Roviró, 2017). The German Ministry of Education and Cultural Affairs states that the increasing level of diversity, especially with regard to educational inclusion, requires the development of individualized learning arrangements ("*individualisierte Lernarrangements*") (Kultusministerkonferenz 2016) and the fostering of transcultural competences (Kultusministerkonferenz, 2013). Despite this emphasis, still very little is known about how such arrangements could be realized.

Nathalie is teaching at a school in which about 80% of the students are first- or second-generation immigrants ("*Migrationshintergrund*"); in her Grade 8 art class only one child has grown up with German as his only mother tongue. Having grown up in two cultures herself, Nathalie's motivation in this research project is to find productive ways to use diversity in the classroom as an advantage rather than considering it a problem.

The aim of Nathalie's dissertation project in art education is to develop, trial, evaluate, and revise a theory-based and practice-approved lesson unit design for student groups with high levels of diversity. The research question is: To what extent can spatial experience through aesthetic research-based learning with a tablet computer contribute to students' change of perspectives? Furthermore, insights about conditions and requirements of cooperative learning with biographical and digital student artifacts will be gained. By working on these aims, Nathalie hopes to contribute to the development of individualized learning arrangements that foster transcultural learning to get closer to the long-term goal of not only seeing but really deploying diversity and different cultural backgrounds as an opportunity.

Challenges

Nathalie had many different design ideas throughout the process and went through several design changes. The main problem she faced in the development of the research project was to link design ideas with theoretical considerations. Current theories did not seem to express her design intuitions and what she read in the literature did not match or inform her design ideas. This quite common experience is one reason to use design research.

Nathalie used Kerrie Smith's books, especially *How to be an Explorer of the World* (2008), as a source of inspiration because they reminded her of the method of aesthetic research used in art education. She was also influenced by the tweets of a Syrian girl who depicted the terrors of the war in her hometown as well as everyday scenes of reading Harry Potter. Nathalie was very interested in the plurality of something so incomprehensible as life in a war zone and the relatable act of reading a book to younger siblings. It was clear from the beginning that Nathalie's general research direction would include using diversity and different points of view in the classroom as something productive, but it was not until she found the art piece *Alter Bahnhof Video*

Walk (Cardiff & Miller, 2012) that it finally "clicked": This artwork seemed to match her overall design idea.

Overall design idea

Spatial experience is one of the main topics within the field of art education that offers great opportunities to stimulate students in taking and making perspective. Research-based learning is used in this setting to initiate aesthetically motivated experiences with the tablet computer. Art education as a discipline with many visual impulses, in combination with the use of e-learning devices, allows students to create videos of their aesthetic experiences when exploring spaces. These videos with concrete instructions from the students who made them allow other learners to see the space from the film maker's point of view. The idea for this task is based on a piece by the artists Cardiff and Miller (2012), which they created for dOCUMENTA (13) in Kassel, Germany (Figure 18.1). Following the perspective and the instructions in the video on the digital device while actually walking through the same space allows for a multi-perspective view of the place. Students constantly switch between the real space and the digital captured space on the iPad. The differences between image and reality, the narrator's personal point of view, and the collective reflecting upon them are assumed to foster the ability to compare perspectives and, by doing such things more often, to foster the ability to take on others' perspectives.

Figure 18.1 Janet Cardiff and George Bures Miller, *Alter Bahnhof Video Walk* (2012). Video Walk, Duration: 26 minutes.

© Janet Cardiff and George Bures Miller; Courtesy of the artists and Luhring Augustine, New York.

Conjecture mapping in order to know what you do not know

To make her ideas researchable Nathalie wanted to further narrow down her design and connect it with the theory behind it. She used conjecture mapping to make explicit the things she thought intuitively, such as assuming that a comparison of perspectives also increases the ability to change perspectives. The construction of the conjecture maps then raised further questions about what perspective making and taking actually is (cf. Akkerman & Bakker 2011; Boland & Tenkasi, 1995) – a learning mechanism that also proved important in Konrad's research on music education (Chapter 20). Thinking and reading about this, she realized that having one's own perspective is crucial in order to be able to compare it with someone else's. In the design process, however, Nathalie was not aware of this assumption until she constructed a conjecture map and felt urged to break down the different stages of the design. Conjecture mapping thus helps to coordinate ideas from the literature, common sense, and experience.

Nathalie realized that using conjecture maps was more than making ideas explicit: The main effort was about making inferential connections that matter research- and design wise. The most important connection here is the relation of design characteristics, relevant mechanisms, and potential outcomes of the research design. Using theory to formulate these relations also helps to make them explicit for investigation in the form of testable conjectures.

Looking at the mediating process with the elements of perspective taking and making, Nathalie saw that she was missing a theoretical basis in her initial draft and could locate in which exact areas this was the case. The theoretical research here was necessary for her to build on theoretical and empirical work done by others in related areas and avoid reinventing the wheel as well as working with false assumptions.

One of the main problems Nathalie faced was how to address the developmental aspect of the design, because conjecture maps in themselves do not capture this progression dimension. In Nathalie's design idea, students first had to explore a certain space themselves before they video-recorded their experiences, while also giving clear instructions for their future viewers (Figure 18.2). In response to this potential limitation of conjecture maps, Nathalie added a vertical time dimension in relevant boxes of a conjecture map – an idea that Bill Sandoval considered an interesting solution (personal communication, November 7, 2017).

Apportioning the big design idea into the different small steps that had to happen made it possible for Nathalie to understand her own setting better and to transform it into a logical and realizable idea. The big structure with its smaller steps also raised its own questions. For example, the outcomes box directed the attention to the question of what exactly she wanted to be the outcomes: that the students change perspective once or twice or that they develop

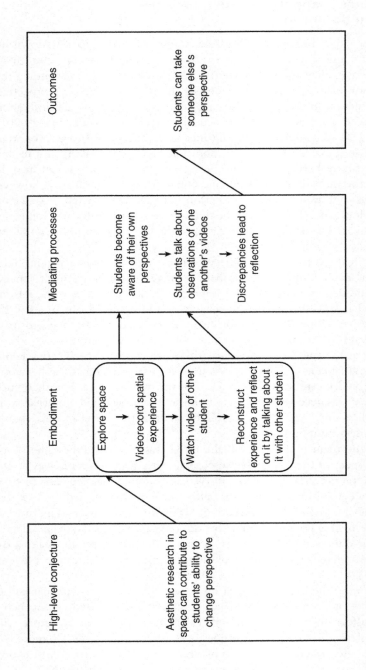

Figure 18.2 Conjecture map inspired by Sandoval (2014)

the ability to take on someone else's point of view in general? This question is different from the methodological question of how intended outcomes can be measured. Such methodological issues are not included in conjecture maps.

Reflection

Conjecture maps help to focus the efforts of understanding how design characteristics may be related to intended processes (or mechanisms) and outcomes. The theory and the design are inferentially intertwined in such a way that others will learn something they can repeat in new situations and know what to adjust in local settings. Moreover, the formulation of design and theoretical conjectures allows scientific verification and falsification. Conjecture mapping helped Nathalie to find the gaps in her design and figure out where theoretical backup was missing, and to organize the design in order to make it more coherent and comprehensible for others.

Explicating the high-level conjecture, the concrete embodiment, the mediating process, the anticipated outcomes, and formulating the connections between them also assisted her in the process of creating a design. Earlier versions of a design did not quite fit with her theoretical ideas but were important steps on the way to the design piloted in the classroom. Finding the artists's example mentioned above finally helped her to be able to properly link the theory with a concrete design approach.

References

Akkerman, S. F., & Bakker, A. (2011). Boundary crossing and boundary objects. *Review of Educational Research, 81*(2), 132–169.

Boland Jr, R. J., & Tenkasi, R. V. (1995). Perspective making and perspective taking in communities of knowing. *Organization Science, 6*(4), 350–372.

Cardiff, J., & Miller, G. B. (2012). Alter Bahnhof Video Walk [Old train station video walk] [Video file]. Produced for dOCUMENTA (13), Kassel Germany. Retrieved from www. youtube.com/watch?v=sOkQE7m31Pw.

Kultusministerkonferenz [Conference of the ministers of education and cultural affairs] (Ed.) (2013). Interkulturelle Bildung und Erziehung in der Schule. [Intercultural education in school]. Retrieved October 04, 2017 from www.kmk.org/fileadmin/Dateien/pdf/Themen/Kultur/1996_10_25-Interkulturelle-Bildung.pdf.

Kultusministerkonferenz [Conference of the ministers of education and cultural affairs] (Ed.). (2016). Bildung in der digitalen Welt. Strategie der Kultusministerkonferenz. [Education in the digital world: Strategies of the conference of the ministers of education and cultural affairs]. Retrieved October 04, 2017 from www.kmk.org/fileadmin/Dateien/pdf/PresseUndAktuelles/2016/Bildung_digitale_Welt_Webversion.pdf.

Peters, M., & Roviró, B. (2017). Fachdidaktischer Forschungsverbund FaBiT: Erforschung von Wandel im Fachunterricht mit dem Bremer Modell des Design Based Research [Subject didactics research association FaBiT: Research of change in subject teaching with the Bremen model of Design Based Research]. In S. Doff & R. Komoss (Eds.), *Making Change happen: Wandel im Fachunterricht analysieren und gestalten [Analyzing and shaping change in subject teaching]* (pp. 19–32). Wiesbaden, Germany: Springer.

Sandoval, W. (2014). Conjecture mapping: An approach to systematic educational design research. *The Journal of the Learning Sciences, 23*(1), 18–36.

Smith, K. (2008). *How to be an explorer of the world: Portable life museum.* London: Penguin Books.

Chapter 19

Literary education with narrative digital games

From formulating research questions to capturing the design rationale

Katharina Düerkop and Arthur Bakker

Summary

This chapter presents a case study of a design research project in its early phase. We discuss how the formulations of research questions developed and illustrate the exploratory design phase in which choices had to be made about how to capture design ideas as design principles, conjecture maps, or hypothetical learning trajectories.

This chapter presents a case study of the thinking done on the design research proposal and initial design, roughly covering the first eight months of a design research project. The thinking presented here stems from a student, Katharina Düerkop, who is simultaneously doing teacher training and PhD programs. Katharina's background is as a primary school teacher with an interest in literature. Her main goal is to figure out how one can use narrative video games, so-called ludonarratives, as part of literature teaching to primary school students. We first discuss the rationale for the research including the proposed research questions, after which we examine design principles and conjecture maps as well as ideas about sequencing learning activities. In doing so we try to show how many of the aforementioned theoretical points are at work in the puzzle of writing a research proposal and preparing a first design cycle.

Rationale for the project

The *problem and potential for improvement* that drives Katharina's interest is that literature teaching in primary schools is limited to printed media. This implies that literature teaching does not take advantage of students' life experiences with today's audio and visual media, including games, despite the fact that particular literature-related topics could be learned through these media. In fact, there is a societal call for taking narration in computer games seriously as a cultural phenomenon worth teaching about (e.g., Boelmann, 2015; Kepser, 2012). Promoting literary competencies in relation to computer games fits the standards of German primary education (e.g., dealing with text and media). Despite the popularity of games among primary school students, they are hardly used in German lessons. Apart from practical constraints, Boelmann points to teachers' hesitance and the lack of concepts regarding both theory about the educational use of narrative video games (Boelmann, 2015, p. 30) and concrete teaching materials (2015, p. 15).

The *solution direction* that Katharina wants to explore is to use a ludonarrative – a game world that offers a context for experiencing and playing stories. The example she chooses is *The Whispered World* (Special Edition, Daedalic Entertainment, 2014), in which Sadwick is the protagonist. Players first see a cut-scene of Sadwick as the main character of the story, after which they can explore Sadwick's world and influence how the story unfolds. The game experience is complemented with learning activities in which students reflect on the story and its characters, and practice taking characters' perspectives.

The *knowledge gap* is that hardly any research existed on such ludonarrative characters despite the need for good design and accompanying educational frameworks. Hence the *research aim* is to explore how these narrative video games and their ludonarrative characters can be used to teach literature in primary education.

If successful, the design and accompanying knowledge on how to use the design can be practically *relevant*, because teachers need inspiring and successful examples. The research can also contribute to much needed theory development for literary learning on ludonarrative characters and the use of narrative games in education more generally.

Research questions and methodological structure of the project

Both the idea of ludonarratives and the related educational opportunities are relatively new, so there were few materials that Katharina could use. In such a situation, educational design research can be an appropriate research approach to contribute to:

1   Theory on what ludonarrative and ludonarrative characters are, not only from a literature disciplinary perspective but also from a didactical one.
2   Design of an instructional sequence in which the idea of using a ludonarrative to promote literary learning is worked out (embodied).
3   Knowledge about learning processes as elicited by the design.

No theoretical framework that was ready for use in educational purposes existed at the start of Katharina's study. Instead, existing theories about narrative video games, transmedia narratology, literary characters, characters in video games, literary learning, and literary competencies needed to be combined into a new framework, with which the learning goals could be specified and used as a reference model to evaluate student learning – hence the need for a theoretical research question on ludonarratives. We number the research questions for easier reference but note that they are not necessarily to be answered in that particular order.

In many research projects, at least as presented, research questions are addressed one by one:

Figure 19.1 Series of research questions

Due to the cyclic nature of design research, such a linear order is not always possible. Subsequent design cycles are likely to provide better and more solid answers to each of these questions in relation to each other. So an initial answer to the third research question on elicited learning may feed back into a better answer to the first research question about the model to be used for specifying learning goals and evaluating to what extent these have been achieved. Katharina's idea is that together the answers form the basis for a local instruction theory on learning goals, learning processes, and how these are supported by the design (the sequence of learning activities and accompanying ways of teaching).

Design research works more like this, where darker colors represent a better empirical basis for more precise answers:

Figure 19.2 cyclic way of answering research questions

In the following subsections, we discuss how Katharina's research questions developed. To better understand each question in its relation to other questions as well as the changes being made, we use two visualizations. Figure 19.3 sums up the initial questions and structure of the project (first month of the project), and Figure 19.4 summarizes the project eight months later:

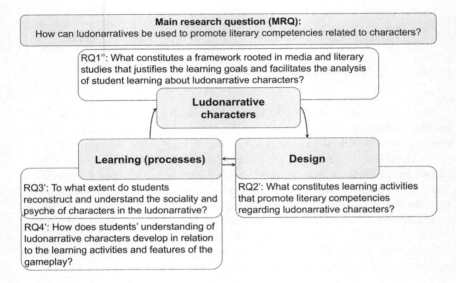

Ludonarratives	Design	Local theory
RQ1: How can ludonarratives be modeled from the perspective of media and literary studies?	RQ2: How can ludonarratives be used to promote literary competencies related to characters?	RQ3: How can the processes of learning and teaching regarding this teaching unit be described?

Figure 19.3 Overview (version from the first month)

Main research question (MRQ):
How can ludonarratives be used to promote literary competencies related to characters?

RQ1": What constitutes a framework rooted in media and literary studies that justifies the learning goals and facilitates the analysis of student learning about ludonarrative characters?

Ludonarrative characters

Learning (processes)

Design

RQ3': To what extent do students reconstruct and understand the sociality and psyche of characters in the ludonarrative?

RQ2': What constitutes learning activities that promote literary competencies regarding ludonarrative characters?

RQ4': How does students' understanding of ludonarrative characters develop in relation to the learning activities and features of the gameplay?

Figure 19.4 Overview (eight months later)

A research question to specify the learning goals

At the beginning of the project it was not clear yet on which aspects of the narrative video game the project could and would focus. So Katharina initially formulated this theoretical research question (RQ1):

> *RQ1: How can ludonarratives be modeled from the perspective of media and literary studies?*

Such a theoretical question was justified because no answer was readily available: hence it was a research question rather than just a researcher's question (see Chapter 5). However, one of the criteria that Oost (1999) formulates for research questions is that it must be clear in which discipline they are anchored. A possible disadvantage of RQ1 is that it may not be clear, apart from the surrounding text, whether the question is anchored in media–literary studies, in education, or both. Furthermore, Katharina decided to focus on ludonarrative characters. Characters (such as Sadwick, his brother, their grandpa, etc.) are important elements of narration. What students need to learn about them must be thought through. Katharina therefore considered more specific questions that made the purpose and home disciplines more explicit:

> RQ1': What are characters of narrative digital games from the perspective of media and literary studies?
> RQ1": What constitutes a framework rooted in media and literary studies that justifies the learning goals and facilitates the analysis of student learning about ludonarrative characters?

This series of research questions is typical. It is very common to start with a rather broad research question and realize along the way that specification is possible and a narrower focus is needed.

A research question about the design

One early formulation of the design question was

> RQ2: How can ludonarratives be used to promote literary competencies related to characters?

This is a proper research question, but instead of being a subquestion it serves well as the main question of the design research project. We thus need a formulation for RQ2 that ensures answers to subquestions together provide an answer to such a main question. An option may be:

> RQ2': What constitutes learning activities that (may) promote literary competencies regarding ludonarrative characters?

Research questions about learning processes

As a third question Katharina initially asked:

> RQ3: How can the processes of learning and teaching regarding this teaching unit be described?

She hoped an answer to this question would help her formulate a local theory around ludonarratives in teaching literature with grounding in practical testing and empirical research. Taken literally, this question is a methodological question (how can something be described?), but this is not the intention. Moreover, the question is phrased in a very general way. Given the function of the analysis, namely to evaluate if intended learning had taken place, it made more sense to ask a more specific and evaluative question with respect to the answer of RQ1':

> RQ3':To what extent do students reconstruct and understand the sociality and psyche of characters in the ludonarrative?

Note however that the formulation of this question, with reference to relevant aspects of characters (sociality and psyche), was only possible once Katharina had a partial answer to RQ1'. This illustrates how research questions can develop during a design research project.

The analysis is not only meant to evaluate to what extent intended learning had taken place, as information about the effectiveness of the design. It also has to feed forward and inform the design. Hence, Katharina was also interested in more developmental aspects of learning, so she asked in addition:

> RQ4: How does students' understanding of ludonarrative characters develop?

This question resembles the question addressed by Smit and Bakker in Chapter 21 on scaffolding mathematical language. That chapter illustrates that an answer to a purely descriptive or evaluative question is not as informative as a design researcher may hope, because what we need to know is not only how well students learned, but to which learning activities or mediating processes their learning can be attributed (cf. Sandoval's, 2014, inclusion of mediating processes in his conjecture mapping). At the same time, design researchers are careful not to suggest causality, which comes with its own methodological challenges. A reformulation of the question, more in line with the ambitions of design researchers, yet without suggesting strong claims on causality, could thus be:

> RQ4': How does students' understanding of ludonarrative characters develop in relation to the learning activities and features of the gameplay?

Furthermore, Katharina initially asked a question about obstacles and conditions for success (What are the conditions and obstacles for coming to understand ludonarrative characters?). It then became clear that – in the framework of her project – this was more like a researcher's question that she needed to answer during each cycle in order to improve the design (e.g., a conjecture map or HLT). Whether this requires a separate research question depends on the type of report. In a monograph reporting several design cycles it makes sense to ask explicitly for what needs to be improved in redesign. In a journal article reporting on the last cycle, advice for improvement could better be given in the discussion section and thus not require a separate research question.

Initial design principles

We now turn to an exploration of design principles, conjecture maps, and HLTs. We do not want to suggest that design researchers should use any or all of these. In Katharina's case we explored which of these functioned best to capture and test emerging design conjectures. We return to this issue at the end of this chapter.

Like many other PhD students doing design research, Katharina felt she should formulate design principles. Here are a few that she worked out two months into the project:

1   Respect students' *Lebenswelt* (the lived world), so take seriously their interest in and experience with games.
2   Make literature accessible to all students, including those with learning difficulties (e.g., reading).
3   Differentiate given the heterogeneity of the group in terms of ability, motivation, gender, etc. Offer adaptive support (scaffolds).
4   Promote self-regulated learning.

She then visualized reasons for these types of principles (in this case aspects of the students' heterogeneity) as well as how the initial design principles feed into more concrete action–guiding principles, which then lead to aspects that later become part of the conjecture map (see Figure 19.6 in Section 1.4), either as a learning goal or as specific tasks:

The first and second design principles were value-based choices, issues Katharina found important. The third was an intention to deal adaptively with the heterogeneity of the students. With respect to the fourth principle, it was not yet clear whether she conceptualized this as a desirable mediating process or as an important learning goal in itself. Given that her focus as illustrated in Figures 19.3 and 19.4 is on literary learning about characters, the former seems the better choice. However, she would then need to formulate how self-regulated learning could be promoted (a design conjecture) and how self-regulated learning would stimulate literary learning (a theoretical conjecture). It may turn out that such a topic drops out of the initial conjectures altogether, and that in the first design cycle other topics may turn out more important. As Collins (personal communication, June 28, 2017) noted: one of the key things that early career design researchers need to learn is to stay open to what matters. What turns out to be important is often different from what design researchers start with (unless they are very experienced).

At the same time this is one of the challenges of design research. Where some research groups specialize in a particular topic, such as self-regulated learning, and can ensure their studies are about this topic, the design researcher has to stay open to whatever comes up as salient. This may imply that during a study, design researchers need to become acquainted with bodies of literature that are new to them or, even better, involve experts on that topic.

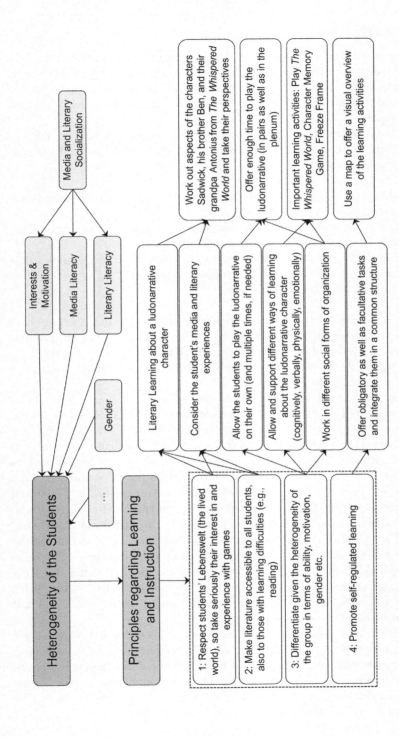

Figure 19.5 Initial design principles (two months into the project)

Initial conjecture map

The hunch that Katharina had when starting to write a proposal was that literary learning about characters can be promoted by working with ludonarratives and related instructional activities built on gameplay experiences. This high-level conjecture was embodied in a design as follows:

The choice fell on the adventure game *The Whispered World* for a few reasons. This game starts with a cut-scene that establishes the game itself as narrated: The students first see the hand of an unknown character that opens a book. They hear him say:

> It may make you sad to hear it. But this is the last story I'm going to tell you. [. . .] Well, my last story takes place in a land far away. A land that is about to die. It begins in the Autumn Forest. This is the story of Sadwick, the sorrowful clown. Sadwick is sleeping uneasily. Like every night.
> (*The Whispered World*, Level 1: The Autumn Forest)

After this, game players can see and hear the wagons of the circus of Sadwick's family and then notice Sadwick himself who is troubled by nightmares. After he wakes up, the player takes over and can decide where Sadwick moves and with whom or what he interacts. The students can either experience these actions as "helping Sadwick do something" or "being Sadwick, and doing something".

The gameplay of *The Whispered World* is not time constrained, which means the students can be in one room as long as they like as or with Sadwick, and click on objects or talk to other characters as much as they like. Most of the dialogue can be activated more than once, giving the students the possibility to re-hear it, if they want or need to. Furthermore, this game does not make use of the concept of "game-over." Instead, Sadwick will say something about an object not being the one that is needed right now or a specific kind of interaction not being possible without first doing something else. In this way the game establishes a narrated world with a timeline and does not break the immersion in forcing the player to start over when he or she makes a gameplay mistake.

With this information about the game, a first design conjecture would be:

> The game-design of *The Whispered World* promotes a narrative stance of reception and helps students experience the characters as fictional beings, situated in a narrated world.

One task that Katharina designed related to this gameplay experience is called "Character Memory Game." Embedded in the commonly known situation of a game of memory, the students map specific character-statements to their respective speakers. This, as a mediating process, presumably invites students to think about psychological features of characters and their social relations to others. Because the players decide for themselves what kind of dialogue to

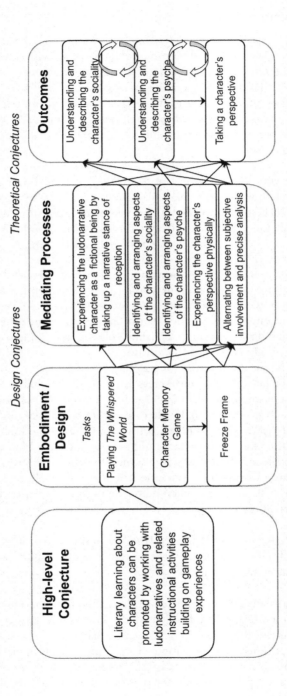

Figure 19.6 Conjecture map (eight months into the project)

choose while playing the game, it is possible that this task confronts the students with utterances they have not heard before. This promotes thinking about the character's perspective, because students have to think: could character Ben (Sadwick's brother) have said this? For example, who says: "Ah shoot! I'm just a terrible coward". or "Spot? Where could Spot be? He usually comes to see me in the morning" (*The Whispered World*, Level 1: The Autumn Forest). The first matching to Sadwick reveals his psychological self-perception; the second points to his relation to his pet Spot.

A corresponding theoretical conjecture would then be: The experience of watching, playing, and reflecting on characters and matching of utterances to characters stimulates students' awareness of the psyche and sociality of the characters in the ludonarrative.

One way to better understand such learning processes is by framing them theoretically. One option Katharina considers is by means of a semantic theory called inferentialism (Brandom, 2000), which assumes that people make small inferences all the time and that the content and use of concepts are rooted in reasoning practices in which these concepts are used. Grasping a concept, idea, or character implies the ability to draw relevant and correct inferences. To understand a character thus includes awareness of the reasons that characters have to do or say something. Katharina assumes that learning activities such as the memory game stimulate students to become explicit about possible inferences – not just relational statements such as "so Ben must be his brother" but also psychological ones (Sadwick has nightmares, so he is worried) and social ones (his relation to his grandpa). Understanding a character's psyche implies that one can take someone's perspective, empathize, and make many inferences about the character (he must feel lonely, he cares about his pet, he is angry with his brother, etc.).

Of course not every conjecture can be made explicit here, but to give an overview about more of the embodied tasks, the next section summarizes the instructional activities in relation to an initial hypothetical learning trajectory.

Initial hypothetical learning trajectory

A strength of conjecture maps is that they capture the hunch which drives the research and relates in general terms features of the design to intended processes and outcomes. However, conjecture maps do not spell out developmental stages. An advantage of HLTs is that they are explicit about how particular activities are assumed to lead to a next step in the intended learning progression. As Sandoval writes, conjecture maps can feed into HLTs.

Based on her conjecture map (see Figure 19.6) Katharina worked out in detail how the instructional activities build on one another. She then formulated conjectures about how these activities support processes that lead to the goals:

Learning goal

- The students can take a character's perspective and are able to describe aspects of the character's sociality and psyche.

Hypothesized starting points

- The students are in Grade 3 or 4 and are heterogeneous with regards to reading, media, and literary competency.
- The students know narratives in different media; if not in print media, then in audio-visual or interactive media. They therefore have a general idea of the concepts of "story" and "character."
- The students have experience in writing their own stories in school.
- The students are used to literature teaching that is focused on print media. Although their free time outside of school provides them with narratives presented by different media, they are not used to working with something like a digital game in German lessons.
- Most of the students know a few digital games, because they either play them themselves or they have friends or siblings who do and/or talk about it.
- Not all students are familiar with story-driven games like *The Whispered World* and instead play digital games like *Candy Crush Saga* (King, 2012) or *Clash of Clans* (Supercell, 2012). While the first is solely a puzzle game, the second only uses some ludonarrative aspects like embedding its strategic gameplay in a fictional world. Hence the students may need to get used to the idea that a game can tell them a story like a book or a movie does.

Instructional activities and assumptions about how the activities support processes that lead to the learning goal

- *1a: Playing The Whispered World:* The students play the beginning of the game up to 30 minutes. They move the protagonist Sadwick through his world. Before playing, the teacher tells the students to ask themselves: "Who is Sadwick? What is he thinking and feeling?"

In asking themselves who Sadwick is, and what he thinks or feels, the students focus on the narrative aspects of the game *The Whispered World*. In taking up this narrative stance whilst playing, they experience Sadwick and his family members as fictional beings (narrative mode of reception, see Fahlenbrach & Schröter, 2015, pp. 181–186) and not as game-pieces (ludic mode of reception, see Fahlenbrach & Schröter, 2015, pp. 176–180). This forms the basis for ascribing a sociality as well as a psyche to them.

- *1b: Retelling the story with pictures:* The students put screenshots of the game in a right order and retell the beginning of the story.

  In retelling the storyline, the students isolate the narrative level of the game and contextualize the ludonarrative characters and their actions. It gives the students the possibility to recall what happened in the story and to ask questions. This puts the students in a position in which they study the game rather than play it, which constitutes the basis for later analysis and reflection (tasks 2 and 3). This activity also helps the teacher to get an idea of what the students took from the playing-experience, and with what kind of understanding of the fictional world and its characters they might get into the following learning activities.

- *2: Character Memory Game*: Embedded in the commonly known situation of a game of memory, the students relate specific character-statements to their respective speakers (Sadwick, Ben, or their grandpa). The students work in pairs; they can choose to play against each other or work as a team.

  The game of memory consists of character-statements that include (and/or allow to infer) important aspects of the character's sociality and psyche. In matching these statements to their respective speakers, the students deal with these aspects and make their previous observations of the characters explicit. It is possible that the students are confronted with utterances that they do not know yet (because they focused on other in-game conversations whilst playing the ludonarrative). In this case, the students think about and maybe even discuss what character matches best to the given statement. Therefore, they not only reflect on the characters, but also have the possibility to learn from each other.

This instructional activity is based on working with written utterances and therefore focuses on a cognitive and verbal way of learning. As was stated previously in this chapter as a theoretical conjecture, the reflecting on characters and matching of utterances to characters is supposed to stimulate students' awareness of the psyche and sociality of the characters in the ludonarrative. The task therefore prepares the students (indirectly) to take the perspective of one or more ludonarrative characters, by supporting them to infer aspects of their sociality and psyche. In the following learning activity (3: Freeze Frame), they will enrich their understanding of the characters by getting emotionally involved, by identifying themselves with a character and/or by developing empathy for a character. While all this may be possible by playing the ludonarrative and the memory game, the following task builds on the inferences that students draw by working on tasks 1a, 1b, and 2, and promotes important aspects of perception-taking like emotional involvement, empathy, and identification more directly.

- *3: Freeze Frame*: The students re-enact a situation from the game in the form of a freeze frame. They make decisions regarding the character's positions, postures, and facial expressions.

The process of building a freeze frame is considered a productive activity ("produktives Verfahren," Spinner, 1999, p. 39). These kinds of activities allow the learners to work with the literary medium in different ways, to get involved with it and construct meaning (Spinner, 1999, p. 34) instead of only talking about it.

In re-enacting a situation from the ludonarrative in the form of a freeze frame, the students experience aspects of the character's sociality and psyche physically and emotionally. The students make decisions regarding the character's positions, postures, and facial expressions (these are the essential aspects according to Krump, 2005, p. 33) and therefore need to ask themselves how the characters are feeling and how their constellation works. In creating this freeze frame, the students alternate between subjective involvement and precise analysis regarding these characters. Bringing both (subjective involvement and precise analysis) into action is assumed to deepen literary understanding (Spinner, 2006, p. 8–9). It helps to understand and to fill so-called "Leerstellen" (Iser, 1970); elements of the literary medium which need to be related to each other and which stimulate the recipient to hypothesize about the narrative. This also stresses that the recipient is actively involved in the process of meaning-making. McCloud describes this process as "observing the parts but perceiving the whole" (McCloud, 1993, p. 63) and calls it "closure."

Reflection

Design researchers typically formulate conjectures that they subsequently test and refine. Many do so in the form of design principles, conjecture maps, or HLTs, but rarely use combinations of these approaches. While the approaches needed may differ for every research project, Katharina found that each approach helped her to focus on different key aspects and on different levels of abstraction for important questions of her project.

Katharina's case shows that design principles, conjecture maps, and HLTs can be used in combination, as they seem to serve different purposes. In her example, design principles were starting points of things she valued or wanted to achieve. Conjecture maps served well to capture succinctly what the structure of her instructional unit using ludonarratives is about in terms of how design features are assumed to relate to mediating processes and learning outcomes. However, as mentioned before, conjecture maps do not specify how learning activities build upon prior activities. To this end an HLT was more useful.

We predict that conjecture maps are useful for publication in journal articles that require concise summaries of a design idea. Yet we think that HLTs can also serve valuable functions. First they may make the designer's thinking more and more explicit and thus open to scrutiny from colleagues and teachers. Second they may guide the implementation of design ideas, and last they may allow for detailed analysis (comparison of hypothesized and observed learning). Where HLTs are typically too long and detailed for publication in journal articles, it may be possible to present relevant parts in monographs (see Chapter 21).

References

Boelmann, J. M. (2015). *Literarisches Verstehen mit narrativen Computerspielen. Eine empirische Studie zu den Potenzialen der Vermittlung von literarischer Bildung und literarischer Kompetenz mit einem schüleraffinen Medium [Literary understanding with narrative video games: An empirical study about the potentials of teaching literature with a student-affine medium]* (Doctoral dissertation, PhD thesis). München: Kopaed (Medien im Deutschunterricht, 13).

Brandom, R. (2000). *Articulating reasons: An introduction to inferentialism.* Cambridge, MA: Harvard University Press.

Fahlenbrach, K., & Schröter, F. (2015). Game Studies und Rezeptionsästhetik [Game Studies and the aesthetics of reception]. In K. Sachs-Hombach & J.-N. Thon (Eds.), *Game Studies. Aktuelle Ansätze der Computerspielforschung [Game studies: Current approaches of researching video games]* (pp. 165–208). Köln: Herbert von Halem Verlag.

Iser, W. (1970). *Die Appellstruktur der Texte. Unbestimmtheit als Wirkungsbedingung literarischer Prosa [The act of reading: A theory of aesthetic response].* Konstanz. Universitätsverlag (Konstanzer Universitätsreden, 28).

Kepser, M. (2012). Computerspielbildung. Auf dem Weg zu einer kompetenzorientierten Didaktik des Computerspiels [Video game education. Heading for competence-oriented didactics of the video game]. In J. M. Boelmann & A. Seidler (Eds.), *Computerspiele als Gegenstand des Deutschunterrichts [Video games as subjects of German education]* (pp. 13–48). Frankfurt am Main: Lang (Beiträge zur Literatur- und Mediendidaktik, 24).

Krump, S. (2005). Krabat. Zentrale Momente des Romans durch Standbilder erschließen [Krabat. Access central moments of the novel through freeze frames]. *Deutschmagazin* (2), 33–38.

McCloud, S. (1993). *Understanding comics: The invisible art.* New York, NY: Harper Perennial.

Oost, H. (1999). *The quality of research problems in dissertations* (Doctoral dissertation, PhD thesis). Utrecht: Utrecht University.

Sandoval, W. (2014): Conjecture mapping: An approach to systematic educational design research. *Journal of the Learning Sciences, 23* (1), 18–36.

Spinner, K. H. (1999). Produktive Verfahren im Literaturunterricht [Productive activities in literature education]. In K. H. Spinner (Ed.), *Neue Wege im Literaturunterricht* (pp. 33–41). Hannover: Schroedel.

Spinner, K. H. (2006). Literarisches Lernen [Literary learning]. *Praxis Deutsch* (200), 6–16.

Video Games

Candy Crush Saga (King 2012).
Clash of Clans (Supercell 2012).
The Whispered World (Special Edition, Daedalic Entertainment 2014).

Chapter 20

From implementer to co-designer
A teacher's changing role in a design research project

Ute Konrad and Arthur Bakker

Summary

This chapter highlights the roles that teachers can take within a design research project. The example provided here, by Ute Konrad who is one of the students in a Bremen research group, concerns music education at secondary school. She initially approached the teacher as an implementer of her design ideas, but increasingly felt the need to involve the teacher as a co-designer, both to ensure a design that would work in that context and to engage him. As a result, the teacher also changed his own teaching approach.

Within the research group Creative Unit: Fachbezogene Bildungsprozesse in Transformation [subject-specific formation processes in transformation] at the University of Bremen (Germany), Ute Konrad was one of the PhD students. The initial problem leading to Ute's study was the gap between the aims of educational policies and their realization in band lessons. The major aims of the curriculum, to foster cultural learning and aesthetic experiences in music lessons (Die Senatorin für Bildung, Wissenschaft und Gesundheit, 2012), are not achieved in practical music lessons such as band classes if students practice music by playing instruments without reflecting on their practice (cf. Bradler, 2014; Wallbaum, 2005). Aesthetic experiences are subjective, so it is difficult to think of a pedagogy as eliciting such experiences.[1] What would a design look like that creates opportunities for the aesthetic reflection that is aimed for?

The direction in which Ute sought a solution was to promote meaning making. The German terms are *Bedeutungskonstruktion* (Krause, 2008) and *Bedeutungszuweisung* (Weber-Krüger, 2014). These concepts constituted the focus in Ute's research project (Konrad, 2017), because the literature suggests that music-based meaning-making and negotiation of meanings are conditional for communication about aesthetic experiences (Geuen & Orgass, 2007).

Such mechanisms are very general, so what was unknown at the beginning of the study was how to ascend from the abstract to the concrete, in this particular case of fostering meaning-making and negotiations of meaning in the context of band lessons – this was the design problem (cf. Chapter 9). The initial research goal was to contribute knowledge of how to create opportunities for negotiation of meanings during band lessons. Furthermore, it was unknown how wide or narrow the design had to be: a series of learning activities to be implemented by a teacher, or something broader? It was thus unclear at the start of the study what the design would entail. In our experience it is common in design projects that early career design researchers initially focus their design work on learning activities and/or tools, leaving the question of the teacher's role for a later stage. The topic of this chapter is, in our view, quite general: The teacher is often of crucial importance as the implementer of a design, as part of the design, or as a co-designer. This chapter summarizes the search for the appropriate role of the teacher involved in Ute's project's various design stages. Other aspects of the project inevitably have to stay in the background (see Konrad, 2017, 2019).

Design 0: inventory of the situation before the design's implementation

At the start of her design research project, Ute envisioned the teacher as someone who would implement her new design (learning activities) and validate her analysis of student learning afterwards. As a first step, Ute decided to make an inventory of the current situation of the teacher's band lessons (design 0) and to pilot the data collection through videotaping in band lessons. This combined baseline and pilot study involved video observation of this teacher and his students. Table 20.1 summarizes the various design stages.

Ute conducted a pre-interview with the teacher and a group interview with the students to introduce the study and acquire basic information about the band class. When Ute started her project, it seemed obvious to promote and analyze the students' learning processes, so she focused on the students via multi-angled videography of typical lessons and used the teacher's expertise in stimulated recall interviews (Messmer, 2015) to gain more information about the processes in lessons and to get a communicative validation of the analysis.

However, it turned out that there were hardly any interactions between students, only interactions directed by the teacher. Ute then realized she had implicitly assumed that negotiation of meaning would occur between students, with the teacher's role that of a facilitator. But the nature of the interaction between teacher and students seemed to be rather unidirectional and directive, which is presumably not suitable to create space for aesthetic experiences to be shared. This had implications for both future data collection and the design.

Table 20.1 Overview of design versions to illustrate the teacher's changing role

Design	Design made by	Design informed by	Discussed with	Design addresses
0	Teacher (regular lessons)		Researcher	Students
I	Researcher	Inventory study (0), SRI*	Teacher	
Ia	Researcher	Discussion with teacher	Teacher	Students
II	Researcher	Study I	Teacher	Teacher
IIa	Researcher and during implementation the teacher finished it	Discussion with teacher	Teacher	Teacher and in the second step of implementation students
III	Researcher and teacher together	Study II and discussions with the teacher	Mutual between teacher and researcher	Students

*Note: SRI = stimulated recall interview

To gain useful data about communication processes, it was necessary to adjust the methods of data collection. In the first lesson, the cameras were oriented toward the students and the teacher was only filmed from the back. But in the second lesson of design phase 0, Ute also used a camera to film the teacher's face. In addition, Ute took audio recordings of every student and the teacher using lavalier microphones, which led to a better recording of the complex communication and interaction processes at different levels.

The analysis of the data collected in the second lesson showed that the teacher considered communication in the class as disturbance. Discussion among students about the music only happened backstage – something Ute was only able to infer because students were audio-recorded individually. She realized that she should create a platform for such discussion to take place – not as illegitimate disturbance, but as targeted negotiation of meaning, for example about the volume or registers of instruments being used.

The initial challenge of how to pedagogize aesthetic experiences was confirmed: The negotiation processes that from a theoretical perspective were most important were unpredictable, and in this case took place despite the teacher's efforts to control talk in the classroom. One design challenge was becoming more concrete though: how to get the teacher to centralize rather than marginalize productive talk. Contrary to Ute's observation, when she asked the teacher during the video-stimulated recall interview about his own role, he claimed:

> This is an interesting question, which I've never thought about. But I perceive myself as a band member. Actually I feel myself belonging to the

band. Maybe with an aspect of being a coach. I don't perceive myself as a teacher in a classic role.

(teacher in an interview, translation UK)

Design I: teacher as implementer

In her first design, Ute made a work plan for the teacher, including a phase structure of the lesson, tasks for the students that the teacher had to introduce verbally, and instructions for the teacher on when to lead the students and when to promote student-led interaction and practice. The teacher's role in this design (I) was to implement Ute's ideas.

Before the teacher would do so, however, Ute checked in an intervention interview with him whether the design was viable and practical in the context of his band class. On the basis of this interview, she revised the design (to Ia) by giving the teacher a bit more scope of action and authority to decide depending on the situation. This was the first step of involving the teacher in the design process.

Design Ia still focused on the students, with the teacher as an implementer of the design. But while implementing this design, the teacher's behavior did not come across as very genuine. He just seemed to carry out the given instructions without reflecting on them or seizing opportunities to promote relevant communicative processes during the lesson. In the video analysis and in the interviews it became clear that for design II the concept of "direct ownership of design" (Design Based Research Collective, 2003, p. 8) should become an additional aim.

Design II

For design II it was thus necessary to generate new ways to involve the teacher in the design process. On the basis of the implementation data and the retrospective interviews with video stimuli, Ute developed a new form of design that should give the teacher much more scope of action and authority, aimed at flexibility to formulate emergent tasks. The new design should give a structure which is not rigid, but can be modified whenever teaching-learning processes in lessons do require it (cf. Konrad, 2019). Ute created a pilot design (II) of a planning tool with rudimentary contents as an example for a possible design, and interviewed the teacher to see if he would like to use it. The teacher also suggested emendations, which Ute incorporated in her redesign (IIa). Ute provided the teacher with a redesigned planning tool which entailed a repertoire of strategies he could use, all written on cards. These strategies included a warm–up activity, a phase of differentiation and practicing, examples, tips, and elaborations on the teacher's role in that phase. With this tool, the teacher planned his own lesson structure while using the educational contents provided by Ute. For example, when he planned the "warm up" as teaching phase, he was expected to fill the table with cards such as *tasks for the students, position of the teacher, what does the teacher have to do?, reflection tasks for the students,* etc. Ute thus gave him freedom as a teacher, but hardly as a designer.

The implementation was not as easy as Ute expected. For example, one of the cards was on changing sound, because in analyzing the data, Ute had found that changing sound elicited negotiation of meaning. Ute had also reported this to the teacher, who seemed to understand its importance, but there was still a gap between understanding and realization in the lesson. He tried to formulate tasks to use other sounds, but in the next step, when it was his task to create spaces for negotiation, it proved difficult for him to give the students space to communicate, which Ute considered relevant for negotiation. So there was no reflection about the students' experiences and a redesign again proved necessary.

Gradual shift to co-design

In design II the teacher was no longer just the person who implements the design. Instead the planning tool gave him the opportunity to create his own version of lesson, based on the researcher's ideas. It also gave him the possibility to make changes during lessons, if some unexpected processes took place, and to reflect on his changes using the planning tool by switching the cards. The expectation was that the planning tool would let the teacher find his "direct ownership of design" (Design Based Research Collective, 2003, p. 8). The idea of involving him in this way in the design process was, among other things, for the teacher to become more authentic during the implementation of design in lessons. But this problem was not completely solved. After the implementation in the lessons, Ute conducted a retrospective interview in which the teacher reflected on his experiences with the use of the tool and the implementation in his lessons. In this retrospective interview, however, the role of the teacher as a person which is "just" involved, organically evolved into that of a co-designer (cf. McKenney & Reeves, 2012). Given his knowledge of the setting, the teacher brought in ideas, which led to a joint discussion of solutions and possibilities, as we discuss in the next section.

Design III: teacher as co-designer/building a design team

When reflecting on the handling and implementation of design II in stimulated recall interviews with the teacher it became clear that merely involving the teacher in the design process was not sufficient. The teacher had the opportunity to only fine-tune the contents of the planning tool in an interview (see above). It was necessary to give him more voice in the whole design process. So Ute facilitated the teacher's ideas from the beginning of the redesign process (development of design III).

The transformation of their collaboration was rather implicit, but the teacher became a co-designer. So Ute and the teacher put their ideas together to design tasks for the students. Design III included two levels: (1) based on the commonly developed ideas, Ute made the student tasks, which should support their independent work; (2) the second outcome of the meeting with the teacher was the teacher's tasks, which should help to regulate his part in the lessons. Ute then structured the teacher's tasks in a plan.

More generally, we think such teams can be very fruitful for the design process, because of the different professions of the members. In the present case, teacher and researcher were complementary due to their different perspectives. The teacher looked from inside the system – as an expert on his school, his students, and their backgrounds, and hence what is possible in the lessons. Ute took an outsider's perspective with the possibility to bring in ideas from the literature and her own experience as a music teacher, but also to share findings from collecting and analyzing data. She had time to study what eluded the teacher's attention, for example that some of the student talk was productive.

Video-stimulated recall interviews have been very useful, because they opened up the possibility to take the outsider's perspective. To promote this making and taking perspectives (Akkerman & Bakker, 2011; Boland & Tenkasi, 1995), Ute used types of stimuli. One prompt was to show only parts of lessons, as a way to get the teacher's interpretation of parts that Ute found important. Then again, Ute tried to get the teacher's own interpretation which was not forced by her. Therefore Ute showed the teacher videos of whole lessons and let him talk about the things he saw without using leading questions or preselected stimuli. In this way Ute aimed for an (inter)action which was more led by the teacher than the interests of the interviewer.

Reflections

In the beginning of the design research project, Ute envisioned the teacher as the person who would implement her design. When he did not quite do what she hoped he would do, she was initially in despair. From a typical perspective on interventionist research, this is fully understandable: If the implementation of an intervention has poor fidelity, then no conclusions about the design can be drawn from the resulting learning effects. However, some design researchers consider implementation to be a dependent rather than an independent variable – if they want to think in terms of variables at all within a learning ecology. So rather than conceptualizing the teacher as an obstacle that needed to be overcome, Ute shifted her object of research from tasks and students to the whole setting including the teacher and broadened the unit of what needed to be designed. Where she initially thought of the design as the learning activities, she realized that the teacher could become part of the design, so that his role would change from implementer of her plans to someone who was part of the design, to that of a co-designer (cf. McKenney & Reeves, 2012).

Ute started her project with a broad idea of promoting negotiation of meaning during the band classes. How this could be realized, however, was initially unknown. By observing what interaction took place concerning the music in the background, outside the teacher's control, and trying out different ways of creating more space for productive talk, Ute found out that changing the sound was a key mechanism to elicit aesthetic experiences. Students responded fiercely whenever someone changed the volume or when in the designed warm-up activity the composition of those who play varied, when the keyboard player used the "wrong" adjustment, or when the guitar player unexpectedly used the distortion pedal – the next step was to allow for such discussion about these experiences.

In the band classes, the student conversations in the earlier phases of the research were much controlled by the teacher, but he gradually created more space for the students to talk about their experiences. So while he initially thought their talking was disturbing the lesson, he came to appreciate their emotional responses to changes of sound as productive in negotiating meaning and communicating about aesthetic experiences.

The teacher played a big role in the design process and was a key person for the design to function well. But how should one frame the leading role of the teacher in a conjecture map? Initially, Ute envisioned what the teacher did as mediating processes. What she had designed was handed over to the teacher, which should lead to the intended teaching-learning processes, and subsequently to intended learning outcomes. However, as the teacher became a co-designer, it became less clear how his role could be captured in a conjecture map. Involving a teacher in design suggests a feedback loop into the embodiment box of a conjecture map (Chapters 3, 18, or 19), which is not obviously captured by Sandoval's initial formulation. The linearity of conjecture maps turned out to be a limitation when trying to formulate testable conjectures. Of course one could formulate a conjecture on the importance of involving a teacher in the design, but that would lead to knowledge of limited practical value: The one-researcher/one-teacher proportion is far too expensive to be sustainable as a model to be adopted more widely.

The way to involve the teacher as a co-designer in a design team opened different opportunities in the design and research process. Co-design was necessary to arrive at a proper design, because the teacher's expertise gave Ute insights, which she could not infer from the videos nor stimulated recall interviews. The teacher's conception of giving tasks and the reason for doing it this way and not another made it possible for Ute to reconsider her conception and to develop a new format based on both conceptions.

We started this chapter with the challenge of how to develop a pedagogy or didactical approach to evoke aesthetic experiences in music education. From a deterministic perspective on education, this does indeed sound paradoxical: One cannot cause students to have particular experiences. Was Wenger (1998, p. 225) right after all, that "learning cannot be designed?" As a designer one might indeed feel empty-handed. Yet, as Ute's project shows, through the iterative quest with help from the teacher as a co-designer and changing his position during band lessons, it turned out to be possible to find mechanisms (though not deterministic ones) to lead students to express their meaning makings and negotiate those meanings with each other. This indicates that it may help in evoking aesthetic experiences to change sound and allow for discussion about the resulting experiences. The teacher's role is then to sustain those negotiations and involve every student. One may be tempted to think that lack of control is typical for music or art education in general. However, as Bakker and Gravemeijer (2003) observed in the context of statistics education, the more autonomy one wants to give students in learning, the better one has to plan. In Bakker and Gravemeijer's research the plan was not a fixed blueprint, but a flexible hypothetical learning trajectory that could be adjusted to local circumstances.

One might worry about the statistical generalization of the principle on changing sound, and argue it is based on one research project with one teacher and a limited number of students. However, if it is true that the mechanism identified here is really what matters, then it is through theoretical generalization that the insights gained may turn out to be productive. As pointed out in Chapter 3, generalization is eventually up to those who use existing findings in new situations, not a characteristic of the original research project (cf. Gutiérrez & Penuel, 2014).

What we have tried to do in this chapter is what Freudenthal considered the essence of development research: "Experiencing the cyclic process of development and research so consciously, and reporting on it so candidly that it justifies itself, and that this experience can be transmitted to others to become like their own experience" (Freudenthal, 1991, p. 161).

Note

1 See the debate about aesthetic experiences in educational contexts in the late 20th century (e.g., Jank et al., 1986).

References

Akkerman, S. F., & Bakker, A. (2011). Boundary crossing and boundary objects. *Review of Educational Research*, 81(2), 132–169.

Bakker, A., & Gravemeijer, K. P. E. (2003). Planning for teaching statistics through problem solving. In R. Charles & H. R. Schoen (Eds.), *Teaching mathematics through problem solving: Grades 6–12* (pp. 105–117). Reston, VA: NCTM.

Boland, R. J., & Tenkasi, R. V. (1995). Perspective making and perspective taking in communities of knowing. *Organization Science*, 6(4), 350–372.

Bradler, K. (2014). *Streicherklassenunterricht: Geschichte – Gegenwart – Perspektiven [Practical music lessons with string instruments: History – present – perspectives]*. Augsburg: Wissner (Forum Musikpädagogik, Bd. 127).

Die Senatorin für Bildung, Wissenschaft und Gesundheit (2012). *Die Oberschule im Land Bremen: Musik: Bildungsplan für die Oberschule: Bremen [The Oberschule in the state of Bremen: Music: Education plan for the Oberschule: Bremen]*. Retrieved from www.lis.bremen.de/six cms/detail.php?gsid=bremen56.c.21948.de.

Freudenthal, H. (1991). *Revisiting mathematics education*. Dordrecht, the Netherlands: Wolters Kluwer.

Geuen, H., & Orgass, S. (2007). *Partizipation – Relevanz – Kontinuität: Musikalische Bildung und Kompetenzentwicklung in musikdidaktischer Perspektive [Participation – relevance – continuity: Music education and development of concepts in a music didactic perspective]*. Aachen: Shaker Verl. (Berichte aus der Pädagogik) [Reports from Education].

Gutiérrez, K. D., & Penuel, W. R. (2014). Relevance to practice as a criterion for rigor. *Educational Researcher, 43*(1), 19–23.

Jank, W., Meyer, H., & Ott, T. (1986). Zur Person des Lehrers im Musikunterricht: Methodische Probleme und Perspektiven zu einem Konzept offenen Musikunterrichts [About the person of the teacher in music lessons: Methodological problems and perspectives about a concept of open teaching methods]. In H.-J. Kaiser (Ed.), *Unterrichtsforschung* [Educational research] (pp. 87–131). Laaber: Laaber (Musikpädagogische Forschung, 7).

Konrad, U. (2019) (in preparation). "Flexibilisierung der Lehrkraft" – Entwicklung eines Designprinzips zwischen starren Strukturen und individuellen Bedürfnissen im Bandklassenunterricht ["Flexibilisation of the teacher" – development of a design principle between rigid structures and individual needs in band classes]. In A. Bikner-Ahsbahs & M. Peters (Eds.), *Unterrichtsentwicklung macht Schule: Forschung und Innovation im Fachunterricht [Development of teaching: Research and innovation in subject teaching]*. Wiesbaden: Springer VS.

Konrad, U. (2017). Kulturelle Bildung im Instrumentalklassenunterricht [Cultural learning in practical music lessons]. In S. Doff & R. Komoss (Eds.), *Making change happen: Wandel im Fachunterricht analysieren und gestalten [Making change happen: Analyzing and designing changes in subject teaching]* (pp. 51–56). Wiesbaden: Springer VS.

Krause, M. (2008). Bedeutung und Bedeutsamkeit. In *Interpretation von Musik in musikpädagogischer Dimensionierung [Meaning and significance: Interpretation of music in music education dimensions]*. Hildesheim: Olms (FolkwangStudien, 7).

McKenney, S., Reeves, E., & Thomas, C. (2012). *Conducting educational design research*. London: Routledge.

Messmer, R. (2015). Stimulated Recall als fokussierter Zugang zu Handlungs- und Denkprozessen von Lehrpersonen [Stimulated recall as a focused approach to action and thought processes of teachers]. *Forum qualitative Sozialforschung, 16*(1). Retrieved from http://nbn-resolving.de/urn:nbn:de:0114-fqs150130.

Wallbaum, Ch. (2005). Klassenmusizieren als einzige musikalische Praxis im Zentrum von Musikunterricht? [Musical practice as class as the only practice in the centrum of music lessons?]. In H.-U. Schäfer-Lembeck (Ed.), *Klassenmusizieren als Musikunterricht? Theoretische Dimensionen unterrichtlicher Praxen: Beiträge des Münchner Symposiums 2005 [Musical practice as class as music lessons? Theoretical dimensions for practice in lessons: Contributions of the Munich symposium]* (pp. 71–94). Assisted by K. Mohr. München: Allitera Verlag.

Weber-Krüger, A. (2014). *Bedeutungszuweisungen in der Musikalischen Früherziehung. Integration der kindlichen Perspektive in musikalische Bildungsprozesse [Meaning making in elementary music education: Integrations of the childlike perspective in processes of musical learning]*. 1. Aufl. Münster: Waxmann Verlag GmbH (Perspektiven musikpädagogischer Forschung, 1) [Perspectives of research in music education].

Wenger, E. (1998). *Communities of practice: Learning, meaning, and identity*. Cambridge, MA: Cambridge University Press.

Chapter 21

Using hypothetical learning trajectories in design research

Arthur Bakker and Jantien Smit

Summary

This chapter provides an example of a design research project to substantiate the idea of a hypothetical learning trajectory as discussed in Chapter 3, and to illustrate the type of results that can be expected from analyzing the differences between hypothesized and observed learning. Because hypothetical learning trajectories are often too elaborate to publish in journal articles, we also illustrate how summaries of our findings could be formulated in the form of design principles and conjecture maps.

Background and research question

The key problem addressed by Smit (2013) was that so many multilingual students in mathematics classrooms do not have sufficient linguistic proficiency to participate. An important goal was to give all students, including native speakers with low proficiency in Dutch, access to the language required for mathematical learning. From descriptive research much is known about the problems second-language learners experience in learning subject-specific language. Much less is known, however, about how to remedy the situation, so interventionist research in this domain (Moschkovich, 2010) leading to actionable knowledge is needed. Smit argued that genre-based pedagogy (Gibbons, 2002) and the idea of scaffolding would be useful sources of inspiration, but these ideas had not yet been worked out for mathematics education. The main research question was: *How can teachers in multilingual primary classrooms scaffold students' language required for mathematical learning?*

The mathematical domain that was central in the intervention was the domain of line graphs – a mathematically and linguistically challenging domain.

It is, for example, known that students may be good at pointwise reading of graphs but typically much less so at interpreting segments of graphs that represent periods in time (Leinhardt, Zaslavsky, & Stein, 1990). As explained later in this chapter, the learning goals were summarized in terms of an "interpretative description of line graphs" specified in terms of linguistic and structural features of this text-type (a domain-specific genre). Answering the main question required many stages, including an underpinning of the learning goals, iterative cycles of design, testing, and evaluation (Chapters 1 and 4). Within this design research process we considered it important to address several questions including the following evaluative one: *How did students' proficiency in a genre for interpreting line graphs develop?*

An answer to this question was necessary to check whether students indeed developed the language skills required for interpreting line graphs as planned. Without an at least partially affirmative answer it would be impossible to answer the main question.

In this chapter we focus on using hypothetical learning trajectories (HLTs, see Chapter 3), in particular how they can be compared with the observed learning of four case study students. Simon (1995) defined these as follows:

> I use the term "hypothetical learning trajectory" to refer to the teacher's prediction as to the path by which learning might proceed. It is hypothetical because the actual learning trajectory is not knowable in advance. It characterizes an expected tendency. Individual students' learning proceeds along idiosyncratic, although often similar, paths.
>
> (p. 135)

> The hypothetical learning trajectory is made up of three components: the learning goal that defines the direction, the learning activities, and the hypothetical learning process – a prediction of how the students' thinking and understanding will evolve in the context of the learning activities.
>
> (p. 136)

Elsewhere we have addressed the question of proficiency development by means of pre- and posttest results of the whole group and a single case study (Smit, Bakker, Van Eerde, & Kuijpers, 2016). The purpose of presenting the analysis is to show how HLTs can be used to gain insight into the process of supporting students to get from A to B.

This emphasis on process rather than just two points of measurements (pre- and posttest) may sound laudable, because this emphasis on students' learning processes is not often seen in experimental studies such as randomized controlled trials. However, we hasten to add that this process analysis did not end up in a journal article because the analysis procedure and results were rather tedious and wordy. This consideration is the reason why we also explore in this chapter what summaries of our findings in terms of a design principle or a

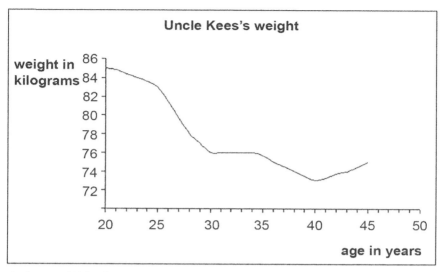

At the age of 20 Uncle Kees weighs 85 kilograms. Between his 20th and his 25th birthday, he slowly loses weight. The graph descends gradually. Between his 25th and his 30th birthday his weight decreases quickly. You can tell as the graph shows a steep fall. From his 30th to his 35th birthday his weight remains more or less the same. The graph is constant. Between his 35th and his 40th birthday he slowly loses weight; the graph gradually descends. When Uncle Kees is 40 his weight reaches its minimum: about 74 kilograms. From the age of 40 on his weight increases slightly. In this part, the graph gradually rises.

Figure 21.1 Line graph and exemplary text from a genre for interpreting line graphs

conjecture map look like. This chapter thus also tries to address the question of how insights from design research can be presented in a succinct form.

Summary of the design

To answer the main question, Smit (2013) conducted three cycles of design research in schools with a high percentage of multilingual students, mostly first- and second-generation immigrants. After two cycles of co-design with an experienced teacher (Smit & Van Eerde, 2011), the design consisted of nine lessons accompanied by:

1   A specification of the *learning goals*: mathematical understanding of line graphs but also awareness of the features of the genre in which Smit and the teacher wanted students to talk about line graphs. For an exemplary text in the genre, see Figure 21.1. The structure and linguistic features of

Table 21.1 Structure and linguistic features of the genre

	Structure features	Examples
	A student proficient in this genre . . .	
S1	describes each segment in terms of what happens in reality	*Between his 25th and his 30th birthday his weight quickly diminishes*
S2	describes each segment in terms of the course of the graph	*The graph descends gradually*
S3	describes the starting point of the line graph	*At the age of 20 Uncle Kees weighs 85 kilograms*
S4	describes peaks and troughs when present in the graph	*When Uncle Kees is 40, his weight reaches its minimum: about 74 kilograms*
	Linguistic features	**Examples**
	A student proficient in this genre . . .	
L1	includes general academic language in the interpretation of reality	*. . . his weight decreases quickly*
L2	includes topic-specific mathematical language in the description of the course of the graph	*descends gradually*
L3	distinguishes between gradations (e.g., of steepness) to express mathematical precision	*The graph shows a steep fall* *The graph descends gradually* *He slowly loses weight*
L4	uses words such as *as, at, in,* and *when* to refer to moments in time (i.e., points in the graphs)	*At the age of 20* *In 2010*
L5	uses word combinations such as *from . . . to, between . . . and,* and *from . . . onward* to refer to periods in time (i.e., segments of the graph)	*Between his 20th and his 25th birthday* *From 2010 to 2012*

the genre were based on the literature (Table 21.1) and informed by inter-views with mathematics educators on what ways of talking they would find desirable at this level of education (Grades 5–6, when students are about 9–11 years old).

2   A series of lessons including instructional activities. The overall series was informed by the idea of scaffolding: temporary adaptive support, which we characterized in terms of diagnosis, responsiveness, and handing over independence (Smit, Van Eerde, & Bakker, 2013). The idea of scaffolding in turn informed the structure of the genre-based lesson series in four phases: building the field, modeling the genre, joint construction, and independent writing (the teaching and learning cycle as Gibbons, 2002, calls it).

3 HLTs for each lesson (see Table 21.3 for an example). These HLTs were adaptations of HLTs used in earlier design cycles, which in turn were informed by information gathered on students' starting points (pretest), specifications of the learning goals, and progressive insight from the design cycles along with continuing to read the relevant literature and discussing intermediate findings with researchers and the co-designing teacher. Furthermore, the HLTs functioned as the teacher's guidelines for what to focus on in her teaching and what to look out for in student contributions so she could be responsive to diagnoses she made of student linguistic proficiency levels.

4 A repertoire of *scaffolding strategies* that the teacher was asked to use during the lessons, in particular during whole-class discussion (Table 21.2). This list was the result of reading the literature on scaffolding but also filtering out the most effective ones in earlier design cycles. This repertoire (along with the design of the instructional sequence of nine lessons) is an important element in the answer to the research question, namely how teachers can scaffold students' language required for mathematical learning.

Table 21.2 Strategies for scaffolding language and examples for each strategy

	Strategies	Examples
1	Reformulating or extending students' spoken or written utterances	[In response to *the graph goes higher and higher up*:] *Yes, the graph does rise steeply.*
2	Explicitly referring to or reminding of linguistic features (e.g., topic-specific words or temporal prepositions), or doing so implicitly by referring to or pointing at the word list, or by referring explicitly to supportive gestures	*Look, the word you are looking for is written down here.*
3	Explicitly referring to or reminding of structure features (e.g., the use of a specific type of language such as topic-specific language)	*Into how many segments can we split the graph?*
4	Asking students to improve language (e.g., asking for more precise language) or to elaborate their utterance	*How can we rewrite this in more mathematical language?*
5	Repeating correct student utterances	*Yes, the graph does descend slowly.*
6	Asking for or explicitly encouraging students to independently produce spoken or written language	*And now try to formulate a sentence yourself.*

Table 21.3 HLT as formulated for lesson seven

Mathematical and linguistic goals

- Students view a line graph as a representation involving different segments (stages) and can determine these segments (stages) independently.
- Students develop a richer understanding of what points and segments of a line graph represent.
- Students describe each segment in terms of reality and in terms of the course of the graph, using previously made agreements written on the whiteboard.
- Students describe reality by deploying general academic language (e.g., his *weight decreases slowly*) and they describe the graph's course by deploying topic-specific language (e.g., the *graph descends gradually*); in both cases they make use of the growing word list on the classroom wall.
- Students can relate words belonging to general academic language to words belonging to topic-specific language in terms of meaning (e.g., the relation between *decrease* and *descend*).
- Students can correctly use temporal prepositions (*from ... to*; *between ... and*; *at*; *in*) for referring to points of the graph (moments in time) or segments of the graph (periods in time).

Starting points

- Students have been introduced to topic-specific words (constant, axis, etc.).
- Students are familiar with reading off information from line graphs and tables.
- Students have collaboratively constructed graphs themselves.
- Students have difficulty interpreting changing direction in a graph.
- Students have been introduced to the idea that a graph can be divided into segments and that each segment can be described in terms of reality and in terms of its direction.
- In most cases, students include the description of important points (peaks, troughs, starting point) when describing and interpreting line graphs.
- Some students still have difficulty using temporal prepositions to refer to periods or moments in time: *from ... to, between ... and, at, in*, etc.

Instructional activities

---

1 Teachers and students collectively divide a line graph representing Uncle Kees's weight into segments.
2 Students match sentences about Uncle Kees's weight (reality) and about the course of the graph with the different segments of the graph, followed by a whole-class discussion.
3 Teacher explains temporal prepositions to the whole class, visually supported by using timelines; whole-class discussion of examples.
4 Students conduct a writing activity in which they fill in temporal prepositions in a writing frame containing a text about Uncle Kees's weight in the targeted genre.

Table 21.3 (Continued)

Assumptions about how the instructional activities support mental activities that lead to the mathematical goals

(Ad 1) In discussing how to divide a line graph in different segments, students realize that changes in the course of the graph (direction) represent changes in reality.

(Ad 2) In matching sentences with segments of the graph, students' understanding of gradations of steepness in the graph is promoted.

(Ad 3) By using a timeline in visualizing the use of temporal prepositions, which is related to the horizontal axis in the representation, students' mathematical understanding of moments and periods in time is promoted.

(Ad 4) In consciously employing temporal prepositions in the activity of interpreting and describing a line graph, students develop conceptual understanding of points versus segments of the graph as well as of changes in the course of the graph.

Assumptions about how the instructional activities support mental activities that lead to the linguistic goals

(Ad 1) In discussing how to divide a line graph in different segments, students prepare the activity of interpreting and describing a line graph.

(Ad 2) In matching pre-formulated sentences with segments of a line graph, students are provided with genre sentences that will foster their genre proficiency. Furthermore, by providing students with given formulations, they can focus on and develop their understanding of attributing *both* an interpretation *and* a description to each segment of the graph.

(Ad 3) Students reinforce their knowledge and use of temporal prepositions.

(Ad 4) By actively using temporal prepositions in a meaningful context, students' (second) language development concerning this aspect of the genre is promoted.

Data analysis: comparison of hypothetical and observed learning

Here we only address the aforementioned research question about the development of student proficiency in the genre of interpreting line graphs. Data collection consisted of audio recordings of interviews held with four case-study students of mixed ability after each lesson, as well as before and after the teaching experiment. Their pseudonyms were Abdul, Moad, Rabia, and Youness (for selection criteria see Smit, 2013). Each interview lasted 10 to 15 minutes and was carried out by two members of the research team following an interview scheme that was aligned with the HLT of that lesson. In line with the overall phasing of the lessons, the students increasingly were asked to write about graphs. All interviews were transcribed verbatim.

For each lesson, Smit (2013) compared hypothesized learning with observed learning. Table 21.4 provides an example of how she approached this for students that she interviewed right after every lesson. The first column summarizes the activity conducted in class, with hypothesized learning in the second column. Then the third column shows relevant quotes from the interviews and the fourth column the conclusion of the comparison. Again, this is not necessarily how the analysis would be presented in a journal article, but it shows how it was conducted.

We focused the cross-case analysis of students' genre proficiency as evidenced in the interviews on the following three topics – each including two particular features of the genre in which we intended students to interpret line graphs (see Table 21.1):

1   The organization of the graph in segments and the description of each segment both in terms of reality and in terms of the course of the graph (structure features 1 and 2: S1 and S2).
2   The use of general academic language for describing reality and topic-specific language for describing the course of the graph (linguistic features L1 and L2).
3   The use of temporal prepositions to refer to either moments or periods in time (L4 and L5).

Table 21.4 Example of the comparison of hypothesized learning and students' utterances during interviews (Lesson 7)

Activity	Hypothesized learning	Quotes from interviews	Conclusion
Whole-class explanation of temporal prepositions, visually supported by using timelines; whole-class discussion of examples. Writing activity in which students fill in temporal prepositions in a writing frame containing a text about Uncle Kees's weight in the targeted genre.	Students reinforce their knowledge and use of temporal prepositions and gain a better conceptual understanding of points versus segments in the line graph. By actively using temporal prepositions in a given meaningful context, students' (second) language development concerning this aspect of the genre is promoted.	His weight? His weight was first 85 kilograms. Then, yes then he descended very much. Then it was, from his, from his 20th to his 25th he was, he went descending little. Descended gradually. And then from his 25th to his 30th he descended quickly. Then he stays from 30 up and to including 35 he stays gradually, then he stays 76 kilograms. [. . .]	Youness has started to actively use temporal prepositions. When he does, it is mostly done correctly (confirming hypothesized learning). However, it also occurs incorrectly (up and to including), and mixed with his previous style of "then . . ." (rejecting hypothesized learning).

To trace the four case-study students' progress concerning these three topics, we carried out one analysis for each topic. Table 21.4 provides an example, concerning the interview held after lesson 7, of how the HLT was employed (see also Table 21.3 for the HLT for lesson 7 and Figure 21.1 for the line graph discussed). From the interviews we identified all students' quotes in which genre features were used in a correct, partly correct, or incorrect way. As we conducted separate analyses for the three aforementioned topics, all transcripts of interviews were analyzed through three different lenses (structure features, linguistic features, and temporal propositions). In the conclusions based on students' quotes, one researcher summarized the extent to which hypothesized learning was confirmed. The same researcher formulated a few key aspects of each case-study student's development in the particular topic that seemed most typical. These key aspects can be seen as a summary of a student's learning process that is based on all separate conclusions drawn for one student for each topic. As a cross-case analysis (Borman, Clarke, Cotner, & Lee, 2006; Miles & Huberman, 1994) conclusions across students were summarized. Another researcher from the team judged both the conclusions and the summaries. The rare instances of disagreement were discussed until agreement was reached.

Summary of results of the cross-case analysis

In this section, we present the development of case-study students' proficiency in the genre throughout the lesson series. As mentioned before, it may be part of a dissertation (monograph), but it may not be the form of analysis presented in a journal article because journals typically prefer more concise and general results.

Students increasingly included all segments of the line graph in their graph descriptions. In early lessons, as anticipated in the HLTs, students showed difficulty with inclusion of all segments in their interpretative description of a line graph. This particularly held for Rabia (who described no segments after lesson 3, so she only gave a description in general terms) and for Abdul (two out of four segments included after lesson 3). Over time, however, the case-study students provided increasingly complete interpretative descriptions. An exception is Moad: He did not show a clear improvement over time in terms of segments included in his interpretative descriptions.

Concerning the genre features of describing each segment in terms of reality (structure feature one, abbreviated as S1) and in terms of the course of the graph (S2) we conclude that hypothesized learning corresponded with observed learning only to a limited extent: Youness only once, and Abdul as well as Rabia only twice (out of eight interviews) included interpretation of reality *and* description of the course of the graph for a segment of the graph. Moad did not describe graph segments in a dual sense during the interviews. The median lesson number from which onward the other three students included descriptions of reality was eight (S1). The median lesson number from which onward all four students included a description of all segments was six (S2).

Concerning students' use of general academic language, we concluded that both Rabia and Youness included little general academic language in line graph descriptions. This can be related to their tendency to focus on the course of the graph rather than on interpreting reality. Furthermore, the fact that general academic language was context-dependent for each activity (e.g., *losing weight*), whereas topic-specific language (*rise, descend, constant*, and *gradually*) was used for each of these contexts cannot be ignored. Observed development thus did not fully correspond to anticipated development.

When interpreting reality, students tended to draw unjustified causal conclusions (e.g., "here he does sports"), a phenomenon also observed by Leinhardt et al. (1990). Confirmations of hypothesized learning were found in occasional (adequate) use of general academic language in later interviews, for instance Abdul's use of *increase*, as well as students' capability to provide correct word meanings for *increase* and *decrease* in later interviews (both Abdul and Moad). In brief (L1), Rabia did not include much general academic language in her line graph descriptions. The other three did so toward the end of the series. For example, words such as *increase* and *decrease* were correctly used and defined later on.

Students increasingly used topic-specific language to describe the course of the line graph. This corresponded with hypothesized learning. They did this in increasingly differentiated and adequate ways. However, all case-study students occasionally used topic-specific language to interpret reality in unconventional ways (as in "Uncle Kees descends with his weight") as well as occasionally used topic-specific language informally or ungrammatically.

When developing proficiency in a new genre, students need time and space to explore such new ways of using language. Imperfections in deploying the genre should in our view be interpreted as manifesting language development rather than as deficient employment of the genre. We further remark that topic-specific language, although increasingly used by case-study students, proved conceptually difficult in several instances in interviews: for example, the difference between *constant* and *gradually* (cf. analysis of Abdul's learning). Despite the repeated attention to these words and underlying mathematical conceptions, all students kept struggling with their meanings. In brief, all four students increasingly used words such as *descend, rise, constant*, and *gradually*; and they did so with increasing correctness (L2).

Corresponding with hypothesized learning, students began using temporal prepositions more to describe points (L4) or segments (L5) on the graph. This implies that they improved their ability to distinguish between moments (represented by points) and periods (represented by segments) in time. Thus, by adequately using temporal prepositions, students improved in mathematical precision concerning line graph interpretation. Occasional self-corrections related to the use of temporal prepositions indicate in our view that students developed a heightened awareness of the need to interpret and describe line graphs more precisely, implying that students became more independent.

Despite all case-study students' progress concerning their use of temporal prepositions, they showed differences in the way they developed proficiency. Abdul and Rabia predominantly used moment-related temporal prepositions (e.g., *at*) for interpreting both points and segments in early interviews. Only in later interviews did they start to adequately use temporal prepositions for describing periods in time. Although Youness initially focused on periods (across-time reading) more than on moments (pointwise reading), he continued to use moment-related temporal prepositions for describing periods until interview six. Remarkably, it is only in the last interview (nine) that he correctly referred to a moment in time. Moad stuck to the use of moment-related words, even when referring to periods in time (i.e., when conducting across-time reading). In brief, in the first interviews, all students predominantly use a limited repertoire of temporal prepositions (e.g., *first, then*). They all expand their repertoire over time, for example with *from . . . to, after, at*. Their capability to distinguish between moments and periods increases throughout interviews. There are some instances of relapses but also of correcting initially incorrect usage. In the beginning they make many mistakes (e.g., *from* without *to*) but in the later interviews they mostly use these temporal prepositions correctly.

In summary, the cross-case analysis of the variability between the four students showed gradual progress with some minor falling back over the course of the lessons. By and large their development was in line with what we had intended or predicted in the HLTs. For instance, they all showed progressive capability of using topic-specific language (*rise, descend, gradually, constant*) to describe the course of the line graph. For none of the four case-study students did it become a habit to provide graph descriptions in terms of reality (e.g., "slowly loses weight") and in terms of the course of the graph (e.g., "descends gradually"). In such cases, where hypothetical and observed learning differed, the differences indicate that even more attention and time is needed to support multilingual and language-weak students' learning processes in the required genre.

Dear reader, did you manage to get through this section? We doubt it. Reviewers of our manuscripts found such writing to be tedious and, indeed, the link to broader, more interesting theory is not easy to make. In our own view, only sharing the results in this way stays "too close to the data," as many researchers would call it.

Reflection on the analysis and results

As mentioned previously, results of such evaluative analysis can be boring to some readers unless they are very experienced in this subject. Yet such evaluation is necessary to check whether the intervention led to increased proficiency in what was defined as the learning goals. Without some evidence of this it would not make sense to make claims about how teachers could scaffold their students in the intended genre for interpreting line graphs.

But an answer to our evaluative research question is not enough. As one of the reviewers commented, in the results from the analysis the relation between teaching and learning was out of sight. In the end we decided to focus a new analysis on one case-study student's development (Abdul) over the nine lessons in relation to the main learning activities of each lesson. This allowed us to embed one student's learning in a story about the design of the instructional activities and the teacher's employment of scaffolding strategies (Smit et al., 2016). Thus we lost detailed information about the variation among students' progress but gained the opportunity to give the reader insight into the question of how teachers can scaffold students' mathematical language – the type of actionable knowledge that we were after in the first place.

So what is worth sharing with which audience? In our experience, most readers prefer brief results that are easy to digest and remember. Perhaps this is why numbers are so popular as ways to report aspects of interventions. To explore how our findings could be shared more concisely we now turn to conjecture maps (Sandoval, 2014) for a research-oriented audience, and design principles (Van den Akker, 1999) for a more practice-oriented audience (see Chapter 3).

Conjecture map of the scaffolding case

To present analysis and results in a concise form, we now explore whether a conjecture map would be useful for communicating the main insights from Smit's (2013) design research project. In the next section we do the same for design principles.

The *high-level conjecture* that we formulated in retrospect is: Using instructional materials inspired by genre pedagogy and idea of scaffolding, teachers can scaffold strategies to help their students develop proficiency in the language needed for interpreting line graphs. This conjecture was *embodied* in a design that consisted of different elements:

1   Following heuristics from genre pedagogy, the instructional materials aimed to support students' long-term build-up and progress toward learning goals. Hence we designed a series of nine lessons consisting of learning activities that were modeled after the teaching and learning cycle, inspired by the idea of scaffolding (high support in the beginning, handing over independence toward the end). This cycle consists of a series of four stages in which a particular text-type needed at school is introduced, modeled, jointly practiced, and eventually individually performed by the students. It is to be used in content classrooms (e.g., history, science, or mathematics). Underlying this cycle is the idea that students need to gradually develop language skills along a mode continuum (Gibbons, 2002) from spoken-like everyday language into written-like academic language, bridged by literate spoken language, also referred to as "bridging discourses" (as in

Gibbons's book title, 2006). The written-like academic language includes those aspects of the second language that are most relevant to curriculum learning.

2   Accompanying HLTs that functioned as guidelines for the teacher of what to focus on (here to co-design and be used as teacher guidelines rather than research instruments).

3   An overview of the domain-specific genre features for interpreting line graphs that captured key aspects of what the teacher could focus on (Table 21.1).

4   A repertoire of scaffolding strategies that the teacher could use whenever she thought suitable during class or group discussion (Table 21.2).

Design conjectures that specify how design characteristics are expected to lead to mediating processes or mechanisms might be summarized as follows:

1   The tasks and teacher elicit mediating processes: student reasoning about graphs, contributions to small-group and whole-class discussion, language production, and classroom interaction. The opportunity to produce language, to highlight one example, is considered a key mechanism or mediating process in second-language learning (Gibbons, 2002).

2   If teachers know on the basis of HLTs the detailed learning goals and hypotheses about how students will reason, and what language they will use, they will better diagnose mathematical and linguistic levels of student reasoning and respond adaptively (where diagnosing and responding adaptively are examples of intended scaffolding processes).

3   If teachers are aware of features of the genre, it helps them and their students focus on what matters most in developing student proficiency in this genre. The mediating process here is teachers' and students' increasing awareness of linguistic and structure genre features.

4   The scaffolding strategies will make students aware of what are correct or desired ways of talking and writing about line graphs, and invite them to start reasoning about line graphs in the intended genre. For example, asking students to say something more precisely is also a push toward independence, so another mediating process here is handing over independence, one of the key characteristics of scaffolding.

Theoretical conjectures restricted to some of the scaffolding strategies (Table 21.2) might be formulated as follows:

1   If teachers repeat correct linguistic expressions from students, the rest will hear them better and implicitly learn that these are approved.

2   If teachers make explicit which student utterances are considered linguistically correct and mathematically adequate, their peers will hear what are considered better ways of talking in the genre. The establishment and

internalization of relevant mathematical and linguistic norms is assumed to contribute to proficiency development.

3   Through producing language within the genre and receiving responsive feedback from the teacher, students become more independent users of the genre of interpreting line graphs.

Outcomes: the learning goal was that students would become much more proficient in the predefined genre of interpreting line graphs. Our analysis shows to what extent this was the case for four case-study students. A single case study and a pre-posttest comparison with an effect size estimate can be found in Smit et al. (2016).

Note that much of what is presented here as a conjecture map could also be part of an overall HLT for the whole intervention. Note that HLTs per lesson functioned as more detailed guidelines.

We think that Sandoval's idea of conjecture mapping is very useful in various stages of a design research project. In retrospect, however, one limitation that we face when using it for this particular design study is that conjecture maps are rather linear: As formulated by Sandoval, conjecture maps assume a one-way influence of design characteristics via mediating processes to outcomes. Yet when embodying the ideas of genre pedagogy and scaffolding in a design, we inevitably need feedback loops. For example, if teachers or design researchers observe during or in between lessons that adjustments in the design are needed, they make adjustments. Their on-the-fly inferences then form the basis for redesign (arrow back from mediating processes or intermediate outcomes into the embodiment of design characteristics). The concept of scaffolding being enacted here even requires a continuous adaptivity to what happens in the classroom. Some of these adaptive responses are purely how a teacher interacts with students, but some may lead to changes in the instructional activities. More generally, conjecture maps are useful for macro-cycles rather than for micro-cycles of design research.

Another limitation of conjecture maps is they have no time dimension that captures how particular processes are expected to follow each other. To some extent this limitation can be overcome, as illustrated in Chapters 18 and 19, in the vertical dimension of the various boxes of conjecture maps. If hypothesized development over time is important in a design study, HLTs seem better geared to explicate how intermediate activities assist in getting closer to the learning goals.

Reformulation as a design principle

As a second way of presenting Smit's (2013) findings more succinctly, we now make an attempt to summarize them in the format of a design principle. We then explore to what extent conjecture maps and design principles are equivalent. When we rework the conjecture map of the previous section to be a design principle, following Van den Akker's (1999) format, we get something like this:

If you want to scaffold the language that students in multilingual mathematics classrooms (context) need to participate in learning about a mathematical topic (purpose), you are advised to use instructional materials inspired by genre pedagogy and the general idea of scaffolding (see appendices of Smit, 2013) and ask the teacher to use scaffolding strategies from the repertoire in Table 21.2 (procedures) because

- The teaching and learning cycle from genre pedagogy has already been deployed successfully in several domains such as science (Gibbons, 2002);
- Using scaffolding strategies and employing them responsively to students' linguistic levels invites mediating processes that are known to support (second-)language development (Gibbons, 2002);
- Students in Smit's (2013) research indeed made considerable progress in the genre of interpreting a mathematical topic (line graphs).

Note that we have used ideas from the conjecture map to strengthen the arguments that are called for in Van den Akker's (1999) format (Chapter 3):

1 Arguments about design experiences and prior success with similar designs
2 Arguments about what is known from the literature about mediating process or mechanisms in relation to outcomes
3 Arguments based on evaluation from the underlying research.

This exercise shows a few things: Design principles and conjecture maps are different things but can capture similar ideas. A major difference is that design principles in Van den Akker's format do not specify mediating processes (unless incorporated via arguments as we have done above), whereas they are explicit in conjecture maps. Furthermore, while design principles are formulated in practical advisory terms (do this, do that), conjecture maps are more research oriented (conjectures about relations between design, mechanism, and outcomes that can be empirically tested). The choice for one or the other therefore depends on the focus (design or research) and hence the audience one is addressing.

Reflections on HLTs, conjecture maps, and design principles

Last, we reflect on the strengths of each of these research instruments. All three together function as an interface between theory and practice. They are informed by both theoretical insights and practical experience. They can all be useful at different phases in design cycles. For example, in the preparation and design phase, they can help to make explicit what matters theoretically and help to specify what the design is supposed to accomplish (see Chapters 18 and 19). All three instruments can also assist in the communication with other stakeholders such as teachers. For example, Bakker (2004) and Smit and Van Eerde (2011) shared their HLTs with the collaborating teachers who implemented the designs.

HLTs and conjecture maps are more research oriented than design principles (in the Van den Akker, 1999 or 2013, format), because they are configurations of testable conjectures. In the data analysis phase we therefore see a clearer role for HLTs and conjecture maps than for design principles (also see Chapter 3). Yet in the communication phase to potential users, design principles sound easier to digest for nonresearchers. For example, in his work on school development, Mintrop (2016) formulates design principles to summarize the advice coming from the research he does in collaboration with schools.

One strength of HLTs is that they incorporate a developmental dimension that hypothesizes students' progression through learning activities. They are about how to get learners from A to B. The starting point, for example students' prior knowledge or attitudes, is explicitly in the picture – in contrast to conjecture maps or design principles. Yet, conjecture maps may be enhanced with a time dimension (as indicated earlier in Chapters 18 and 19). One could also use multiple conjecture maps to show progression. Sometimes people who read about HLTs initially consider them to be linear, but they are neither meant to be (Simon, 1995), nor need to be (see Bakker, 2004, on the branching of trajectories).

All three instruments are intended to stay hypothetical: It is acknowledged that each new setting may require local adjustment. Table 21.5 summarizes the advantages and disadvantages of the three instruments. We do not want to suggest that design researchers have to choose between these three research

Table 21.5 Overview of the nature and advantages as well as disadvantages of HLTs, conjecture maps, and design principles

	General nature	Advantages	Disadvantages
HLT	Research oriented, but more local than conjecture maps	Time dimension Developmental Testable conjectures Explicit attention to prior knowledge or expertise	Tedious to report Difficult to summarize Trajectory sounds linear but need not be
Conjecture map	Research oriented but more general than HLTs	Compact graphical representation Mediating processes in focus Testable conjectures	Linear No time dimension No feedback loops
Design principle	Advice directed to users	Formulated as actionable knowledge or advice	Mediating processes not necessarily in focus

instruments. First of all, other options may also work: Some design researchers use none of these three. Second, as this chapter shows, it is often possible to formulate a conjecture map or design principle on the basis of HLTs, or transform a conjecture map into a design principle. Whether this makes sense depends on the audience to which one wants to communicate as well as the time and space one has available to do so.

References

Bakker, A. (2004). *Design research in statistics education: On symbolizing and computer tools*. Utrecht, the Netherlands: CD-β Press.

Borman, K. M., Clarke, C., Cotner, B., & Lee, R. (2006). Cross-case analysis. In J. L. Green, G. Camilli, & P. B. Elmore (Eds.), *Handbook of complementary methods in education research* (pp. 123–139). New York, NY: Routledge.

Gibbons, P. (2002). *Scaffolding language, scaffolding learning: Teaching second language learners in the mainstream classroom*. Portsmouth, NH: Heinemann.

Gibbons, P. (2006). *Bridging discourses in the ESL classroom: Students, teachers and researchers*. London, UK: A&C Black.

Leinhardt, G., Zaslavsky, O., & Stein, M. K. (1990). Functions, graphs, and graphing: Tasks, learning, and teaching. *Review of Educational Research, 60*(1), 1–64.

Miles, M. B., & Huberman, A. M. (1994). *Qualitative data analysis: A sourcebook*. Beverly Hills, CA: Sage.

Mintrop, R. (2016). *Design based school improvement: A practical guide for education leaders*. Cambridge, MA: Harvard Education Press.

Moschkovich, J. N. (2010). *Language and mathematics education: Multiple perspectives and directions for research*. Charlotte, NC: IAP.

Sandoval, W. A. (2014). Conjecture mapping: An approach to systematic educational design research. *Journal of the Learning Sciences, 23*(1), 18–36.

Simon, M. A. (1995). Reconstructing mathematics pedagogy from a constructivist perspective. *Journal for Research in Mathematics Education, 26*(2), 114–145.

Smit, J. (2013). *Scaffolding language in multilingual mathematics classrooms*. Utrecht, the Netherlands: FISME library Utrecht University.

Smit, J., Bakker, A., Van Eerde, D., & Kuijpers, M. (2016). Using genre pedagogy to promote student proficiency in the language required for interpreting line graphs. *Mathematics Education Research Journal, 28*(3), 457–478.

Smit, J., & Van Eerde, H. A. A. (2011). A teacher's learning process in dual design research: Learning to scaffold language in a multilingual mathematics classroom. *ZDM The International Journal on Mathematics Education, 43*(6–7), 889–900.

Smit, J., van Eerde, H. A. A., & Bakker, A. (2013). A conceptualisation of whole-class scaffolding. *British Educational Research Journal, 39*(5), 817–834. doi:10.1002/berj.3007

Van den Akker, J. (1999). Principles and methods of development research. In J. van den Akker, R. M. Branch, K. Gustafson, N. Nieveen, & T. Plomp (Eds.), *Design approaches and tools in education and training* (pp. 1–14). Dordrecht, Netherlands: Springer.

Van den Akker, J. (2013). Curricular development research as specimen of educational design research. In T. Plomp & N. Nieveen (Eds.), *Educational design research. Part A: An introduction* (pp. 53–70). Enschede, the Netherlands: SLO.

Chapter 22

Reflection and wish list

Arthur Bakker

Summary

In this last chapter I reflect on the mission of this book to contribute to a pedagogy of design research. I briefly mention how experienced researchers came to develop a version of design research and how they supervised a first generation of PhD students doing design research. What is still relatively unexplored territory, however, is how to teach master's students about design studies, or how to supervise design studies if one is experienced in educational research but not in design research. This chapter ends with a wish list to help new generations of educational researchers focus on worthwhile themes.

Reflection on my mission to make design research teachable and learnable

As mentioned in the preface, my mission for this book is to make the relatively new methodological genre of design research in education more teachable and learnable. One could call this endeavor a step toward a pedagogy or didactics (in continental European terms) of design research.

Why would such a pedagogy or didactics be important? The history of science shows that education and training are crucial to the development of a discipline. For example, the rigorous undergraduate training in mathematics that took place in Cambridge since the eighteenth century was a key to the success of generations of physicists (Warwick, 2003). One obvious reason is that a solid knowledge base allows scientists to make progress. However, Warwick also points to the importance of communication to a wider audience of which one can expect a particular expertise—not just mathematical, but also the embodied experimental expertise of handling instruments. The fact that so many eminent earlier scientists such as Christiaan Huygens found Newton's *Principia Mathematica* from 1687 so hard to follow indicates that they did not share the necessary common background.

In design research we face a somewhat similar situation: Design researchers have to make a judgment about what their reviewers and readers know about design research, and typically have to explain much more than researchers conducting a well-known type of study, such as an experiment or a case study. A broader community of educational researchers who know what design research is, and how it can be judged and reported, will help a next generation not only conduct such research, but also judge its quality on its own merits (see also Chapter 8). As Nathan, Rummel, and Hay (2016) write: "The future capacity of LS [the learning sciences] to carry out its research and development mission relies heavily on the effectiveness of its associated graduate education programs" (p. 191). My hope is that standard works of research methodology will increasingly include a chapter on design research to facilitate these processes of building on the giants' shoulders and communicating findings to a wider audience.

In the early years of design research, very experienced and highly respected educational researchers set the first steps. Among these researchers were Collins (1990), Brown (1992), and Cobb, Confrey, diSessa, Lehrer, and Schauble (2003) in the US; the group around Freudenthal (Goffree, 1979; Gravemeijer & Koster, 1988) at Utrecht University; and the group at the University of Twente in the Netherlands (van den Akker & Plomp, 1993). As Schoenfeld (1992) described in his introduction to a special issue in the *Journal of the Learning Sciences* on design experiments, all contributors felt inadequately prepared for the educational research they were conducting. Because educational research methodology did not offer them what they needed to change educational practice and study it at the same time, they felt the need to work out a new research approach. As described in Chapter 2, a genre of approaches emerged, called *design experiments* (Brown, 1992; Collins, 1992) or *design studies* (Confrey, 2006; Linn, 2000) in the US. The Dutch used the terms *development research* (van den Akker, 1999) or *developmental research* (Gravemeijer, 1994).

Next came a generation of educational researchers who were raised in this tradition. For some of them, such as Chris Hoadley (personal communication, October 25, 2017), this felt as if it were the way that educational research was done until they discovered that they were the odd ones compared with those practicing standard educational research. In 2002, Hoadley (2002) first used the term *design based research* in published work, a term also preferred by a young group calling themselves the Design Based Research Collective (2003). In the Netherlands, examples of the first generation of PhD students raised in this new tradition were Nieveen (1997) and McKenney (2001) at Twente, and several of De Lange and Gravemeijer's PhD students (Bakker, 2004; Doorman, 2005; Drijvers, 2003; van Amerom, 2002). These students learned to do design research under the supervision of experienced design researchers, but what about future generations? How can design research move from solely PhD research to be included in master's programs and perhaps even bachelor's programs?

Herrington, McKenney, Reeves, and Oliver (2007) argue that design based research is feasible for doctoral students, but I am not aware of literature about the teaching of design research to master's students. I know of a few people who offer design research courses, such as Bill Penuel, Bill Sandoval, and Dor Abrahamson (Chapter 9). More people probably addressed design research in their research methods courses (this is what Dolly van Eerde and I did in our courses at least). However, in the interviews I conducted with design researchers, some interviewees expressed hesitance in response to the question of whether design research can be taught in a one-semester course. The best way to learn design research, in their view, is still to become a master's or PhD student in a bigger team that does a long-term design research project.

Even though such apprenticeship in a larger project may perhaps be the royal road to design research, I see more and more teachers and early career researchers wanting to do design studies, and they often have supervisors without a background in design research. Moreover, their design studies are often solo PhD projects with a limited time span of 3 or 4 years. In my own institute, there has been regular discussion about whether we should allow master's students do small design studies. Some of my colleagues thought we should not expect master's students to be able to design and research a series of tasks in several iterations within one semester. However, others helped their students do it. They supported their students by keeping the study small enough in terms of tasks, number of participants, or otherwise. My primary aim to include examples from a bachelor's student (Bilici, Chapter 15) and master's students (Chapters 10–14, 16, 17) was to show that design research is teachable and learnable. I also hope that these examples give a sense of the ways in which such a design study can be made manageable.

Another aspect that has so far received no attention in the educational literature (as far as I know) is how PhD students learn to do design research. To give a sense of what beginning PhD students struggled with, I asked Nathalie Werner (Chapter 18, art education) and Katharina Düerkop (Chapter 19, literary teaching) to reflect on the first eight months of their respective design studies. Nathalie tells how she used conjecture maps to tie her design ideas to theoretical ideas. Katharina discusses various versions of research questions as well as initial versions of a conjecture map and hypothetical learning trajectories. These chapters allow others to see the early and fluid stages of research that researchers normally do not write about. Yet I think sharing such stories can help early career researchers get a sense of the start of their journeys in educational research.

Chapter 20 summarizes a different learning process: Ute Konrad summarizes her journey that started with seeing the teacher she worked with as the executor of her design and ended with the same teacher being co-designer.

Although the idea of co-design is by no means new, Ute's story shows the stepwise inevitable development toward working differently with the teacher. This story hopefully helps future generations of design researchers decide how to collaborate with teachers, trainers, or other stakeholders in their projects.

Like the previous chapters, Chapter 21 provides what the Dutch call a peek into the kitchen (*kijkje in de keuken*) of design researchers. As Kali (2016) said during her keynote at the International Conference of the Learning Sciences, very little of the design work conducted by design research teams is visible to outsiders. Yet this messy process can still be very informative for other designers and researchers. With Jantien Smit, I try to show how working with hypothetical learning trajectories (HLTs) could be done, but we also point out the pitfall of staying too close to the data as well as the challenge of publishing findings in a concise form. We suggest conjecture maps and design principles as compact summaries of the wealth of information that is derived from comparing HLTs and actual learning as observed.

A wish list

In this section I reflect on themes that kept recurring when writing this book. These themes led to a wish list of how I hope design researchers will strengthen the genre of design research.

A pedagogy or didactics of design research

The previous section points to the need of a pedagogy or didactics of design research. Many colleagues offer sessions in courses or workshops on design research, but I am not aware of any systematic research on what master's or PhD students do learn and should learn from such courses or workshops. Yet I think more insight into how to teach and learn how to conduct design studies will improve the quality of empirical studies and help to communicate such studies to a wider audience. This wish aligns well with the following view:

> If design research is to become accepted as a serious scholarly endeavor, the learning-sciences community needs to take responsibility for creating standards that make design experiments recognizable and accessible to other researchers.
>
> (Collins, Joseph, & Bielaczyc, 2004, p. 16)

In particular, I think what would be helpful are the following steps:

- Evaluations of existing theses and dissertations to formulate guidelines on how to improve both the quality of the research and the writing about it. A source of inspiration could be Oost (1999, 2003), who formulated criteria for the quality of problem statements. However, these criteria need to be complemented with criteria for the quality of the design (Plomp, 2013).

- Design research to develop and improve courses on this research orientation. Such courses should in my view also pay explicit attention to how to define smaller studies within a larger design research project and to how one can report on design studies succinctly.
- Multiple case studies of what and how students learn when doing a design study.
- Journal article formats that are suitable for publishing findings from design research. Design researchers often grapple with the question of where and how they should weave in the rationale for and description of their design within the standard format of empirical papers. One could argue that the rationale belongs to the theoretical background and the description in the methods section, but sometimes the (improved) design itself is also a result. Reporting on different cycles or iterations does not fit the standard format very well either.

A more elaborate history and philosophy of design research

Chapter 2 is a brief overview of many streams that came to be known under different names (*developmental research, design experiments, design research, design based research*). Various groups in the world had different primary concerns to develop new approaches, such as ecological validity, the need to improve curricula, or the lack of practical usage of most educational research (Nathan & Wagner Alibali, 2010; Pea, 2016).

Yet I would welcome a more thorough historical analysis, complemented with a philosophy of science analysis, because the history of design research is interesting from a more general perspective too. For example, Flis and Van Eck (2017) showed that the disunity of psychology (correlational vs. experimental psychology) identified by Cronbach in 1957 and 1975 is still there today. For decades, educational researchers have complained about the gap between research and practice (Kolodner, 1991). Design research still seems to be a promising but also a "hazy" approach (Ormel, Roblin, McKenney, Voogt, & Pieters, 2012). I assume that other disciplines can learn from the development of design research, but also that design researchers can learn from the historical development of other disciplines dealing with similar theory-practice challenges (e.g., veterinary and agricultural research).

I also think that it helps design researchers to have historical and philosophical awareness of how science works more generally, so they can underpin their own approach. After all, several interviewees emphasized that design researchers struggle with similar issues of validity and reliability that scholars in most sciences face. For example, reading about Faraday's experiments in physics (e.g., the Faraday cage) made me more aware of the multifaceted expertise and many phases of research that are necessary before an experiment works and can be brought to the public domain (Gooding, 1985). The expertise is not only mathematical and physicist, but also includes embodied skills of handling physicist instruments. The phases include discrimination on what matters: What is an artifact of measurement, and what is the phenomenon under investigation? If one would stack Faraday's diaries on his experiments (lab journals), the pile would be many times higher than the stack of his publications: 18 inches versus an eighth of an inch is the estimate by Gooding (1985). The route from private discovery to public demonstration of his experiments involved many iterations of perfecting the instrumentation and procedures. Why would educational research not require such exploratory experimentation? After all, educational science is far more complex than physics (Berliner, 2002; Wieman, 2014) in the sense that nature behaves similarly across the globe, whereas teaching and learning are highly situated, culture-dependent, and involve humans who have agency and freedom.

Causality, change, or constitution?

One of the phenomena I became more aware of when working on this book is that educational researchers have an uneasy relationship with causality. On the one hand, many scholars consider educational research to be a design science about how to improve teaching and learning (Glaser, 1976; Simon, 1967; Wittmann, 1995). This requires insight into how educational practice can be influenced. This view seems to underlie Cobb's position that

> The golden rule to me is to always assume that it is a design failure rather than a person failure [when teachers or students do something undesirable].
> (Paul Cobb, interviewed in Qvortrup, Wiberg, Christensen, & Hansbøl, 2016, p. 264)

On the other hand, educational researchers hardly ever make causal claims and often assume that randomized controlled trials are the most rigorous approach to identify causality (Nathan & Wagner Alibali, 2010). One reason that may explain the hesitance to make causal claims is the view that educators and designers have no direct influence on learning. In Wenger's (1998) words:

> Learning cannot be designed. Ultimately, it belongs to the realm of experience and practice. It follows the negotiation of meaning; it moves on its own terms. It slips through the cracks; it creates its own cracks. Learning happens, design or no design.
>
> (p. 225)

It was my former supervisor, Koeno Gravemeijer, who alerted me to the fact that I did not mention causality in a conference paper on argumentative grammars of design research (Bakker, 2017). Design research is all about causality:

changing something in practice to understand how teaching and learning work, and trying to understand educational processes so as to be able to improve them. This would suggest that argumentative grammars of design research need to be able to provide insight into how educators can support others in learning something or solving education problems. So why did my interviewees avoid the topic of causality when talking about argumentative grammars?

I think it may help design researchers to know about the history and philosophy of causality in order to have an underpinned view on causality when suggesting that their interventions had particular consequences. In particular, it would be worth developing a common-sense notion of influence or change that captures what teachers and educators do on a daily basis: help students learning something and solve educational problems. They may not have a direct, immediate effect on learners or educational settings that can be explained in a physical way, yet they have an influence, though perhaps indirect and mediated by design.

It turns out that the concept of causality has a very interesting history with many contested views on what it is. Aristotle (384–322 BC) already wrote about different types of causes. Many historical accounts address David Hume (1711–1776), Immanuel Kant (1724–1804), and John Stuart Mill (1806–1873), because their ideas are still very influential on today's science (Biesta, 2015; Cartwright, 2004; Packer, 2017). Cartwright and Munro (2010) explain, for example, how the basic idea behind experiments is based on Mill's method of difference:

> If an instance in which the phenomenon under investigation occurs, and an instance in which it does not occur, have every circumstance save one in common, that one occurring only in the former; the circumstance in which alone the two instances differ, is the effect, or cause, or a necessary part of the cause, of the phenomenon.
>
> (Mill, 1843, p. 455)

This way of thinking is the reason why comparison of pre- and posttests, and of learning gains in experimental and control groups is so common in educational research. Mill's focus on difference does not only apply to quantitative research; also qualitative research rests on identifying differences, for example when using multiple case studies (Miles & Huberman, 1994) or the constant comparative method (Boeije, 2002). The easiest way to infer if someone has learned is still by comparing what this person was able to do from one moment to another. However, as Cartwright and Munro (2010) write, the focus on differences does not tell practitioners what they really need to know: the tendencies or capacities of interventions to change something.

In the social sciences, Hammersley (2014) provides a useful historical overview of causality. Interestingly, contradictory views have been dominant over the past centuries. Today, the general opinion seems to be that experiments are the strongest methodological approach to show causal relations, and many qualitative researchers deny that causal analysis in the social sciences is possible. However, there have been times where qualitative case studies were the preferred research approach to provide causal explanations (see also Hammersley, 2008). For Karl Pearson, famous in the history of statistics (Stigler, 2002), scientific laws were just patterns that do not tell us anything about underlying forces—an idea that can be traced back to Hume's skepticism about understanding causality beyond regularities and that is still popular today (Maxwell, 2004).

The route suggested by Packer (2017) is to speak of constitutive rather than causal relations. He observes that a community constitutes people who live in it, and citizens constitute the community in which they live. "Constitution, then, is this relationship of mutual formation between people and their forms of life" (p. 10). This type of thinking is common in cultural-historical lines of research (Roth & Lee, 2006). For example, Cole and his colleagues from the Laboratory of Comparative Human Cognition observed that "the cultural becomes individual and individuals create their culture (LCHC, 1983, p. 349). Although I admire Packer's project, there still seems to be a long way to provide educators with knowledge about how to influence such constitutional processes, which brings us back to causality.

I agree with Hammersley's (2008) statement "that social scientists cannot avoid assuming some notion of causality, but that this concept involves deep problems that are as yet unresolved, and which may have significant implications for how we do research" (p. 1). This tension may explain a few challenges that design researchers encounter. Design research in education is about how to get things done and how to resolve educational problems by means of design. As Collins, Joseph, and Bielaczyc (2004) observe, design research tries to combine the strengths of experiments (intervention) and ethnography (sensitivity to the uniqueness of specific situations and the ecology of systems). However, when making claims about how design researchers managed to support learners or teachers in achieving some educational goal, they often encounter the critical voices of both experimentalists and non-intervening qualitative researchers: How do you know this is due to your design? This is why design researchers often avoid causal claims but present their research as descriptive or evaluative, and thus leave any assumptions on causality to the reader. This is at least a trick I have used myself (Ben-Zvi, Aridor, Makar, & Bakker, 2012; Dierdorp, Bakker, Ben-Zvi, & Makar, 2017) and often recommend to students and colleagues for pragmatic reasons of getting design studies published.

Hammersley's (2008) argument cited in the previous paragraph may even explain why the gap between educational research and practice is so hard to close. The fear about making causal claims stands in sharp contrast to the actionable and useful knowledge that educational practice is waiting for. I think this leads to researchers doing either experiments in which they have some control or giving up every control by becoming observers rather than tackling the hard question of how to change practice. If Hammersley's analysis is correct, we need a "therapeutic" philosophy on causality or constitution: Much of philosophy is called therapeutic in the sense that philosophers try to cure people from thinking in the wrong way (Wittgenstein, 1953/2009), for example about the dualism between mind and world (McDowell, 1996). What is needed, in my view, is a common-sense notion of causality that reflects how educators operate in teaching.

A database of design studies conducted by students

One powerful way to learn about design research is by studying good examples of a similar size and scope as what you intend to do yourself. The International Association for Statistical Education (IASE) has an archive of dissertations in statistics education.[1] Such an archive for master's theses and PhD dissertations using design research would also be very useful for early career researchers. An existing helpful resource is the online set of 51 illustrative cases in Plomp and Nieveen (2013).

More high-quality reports of design studies

Compared to what is written *about* design research, there are still relatively few good examples of primary reports of design studies. Yet such reports can inspire new design researchers on what to do and how to present their findings in a sufficiently complete yet concise way. Apart from reports about the whole project (how design researchers managed to support students or teachers to learn something in a design with particular characteristics), what would also be useful are publications about studies within such a larger project. As mentioned at the end of Chapter 4 and Table 6.1, options for studies within the larger project can be: problem analysis, needs analysis, underpinning of a design, implementation processes, and co-design with other stakeholders (see also Table 8.1 in McKenney, 2016). Although evaluations are often easier to publish, design researchers also often stumble upon phenomena that are worth investigating in their own right—often to better understand why something did not quite work or why something special happened that was unanticipated (Bakker & Hoffmann, 2005). See Chapter 8 for more examples.

One possible future direction may be the publication of papers with the design, possibly complemented with video. The journal *Educational Designer*[2] already offers a web structure rather than only linear papers, for example with links to educational materials. Some journals publish video and other multimedia files as electronic supplementary materials (e.g., *International Journal of Technology and Design Education*). I think that so-called *video papers* might also get across impressions better than purely verbal reports about design studies.

A tool for keeping track of conjectures

In a design study, conjectures evolve. They are multiple, sometimes temporary, emergent, and they are often refined along the way. In my interview with David deLiema (personal communication, June 21, 2017) he suggested the option of making a tool that would help design researchers keep track of their evolving conjectures and design rationale. This sounds especially welcome in larger teams where reasons for all the smaller and bigger choices might get lost. Such a tool could be more than an archive, because establishing a culture of recording conjectures and design rationales in such a tool could also have the effect that much more of everyone's thinking is expressed rather than staying implicit in oral communication.

- The conjecture map could be pulled up on a phone so that teachers could easily reference it in the classroom
- The conjecture map could be collaboratively constructed by multiple parties
- Each party working on the conjecture map could perhaps have their own way of selecting connections between design aspects and mediating outcomes, et cetera. Perhaps there would be conjecture maps designed by individuals and then an agreed-upon collective conjecture map that represents the team's hypotheses
- Similarly, each party could add and remove aspects of the conjecture map, such as adding or deleting a mediating outcome
- The tool would offer a way for the team to collect data tied to specific aspects of the map (e.g., offer a place to record notes about which specific outcomes are panning out as expected and which are not, how design decisions were actually enacted, etc.)
- The tool would have a built-in record of the changes made to the map, including a way to represent graphically which parts of the conjecture map have evolved and which have stayed the same.

Using Bayesian statistics

In my interview with David Reinking (personal communication, October 25, 2016), he suggested using Bayesian statistics to quantify the strength of evidence for particular conjectures. His suggestion is in line with Chris Hoadley's (personal communication, October 25, 2017) wish for researchers to indicate their confidence in particular claims. Where classical statistical inference techniques only work to provide evidence for a difference between situations (say against a null hypothesis), Bayesian techniques work with degrees of belief. Such degrees can be updated based on new evidence pro or contra the conjecture at stake. Evidence can come from multiple sources, including expert judgment. These temporal and inclusive features make Bayesian thinking in principle suitable for design research, but I am not aware of serious attempts to incorporate it.

Terminology

I think design research would benefit from a more consistent terminology. One could argue against my concern that the language for experiments is also very diverse. Randomized controlled trials are also called randomized trials, randomized field trials, true experiments, and there are more variations. However, this methodological approach is so widely known that little confusion seems to result from the variability in terminology. Design research, however, does not have this advantage.

I propose to avoid terms that cause confusion or have become obsolete such as *design experiments*; *development research*, and *developmental research*. In this book and in line with the views of most authors in this field, I have used the term *design research* as the umbrella term for a genre of research that includes design. In communicating outside the discipline of education, a useful term is *educational design research* (McKenney & Reeves, 2012) to distinguish it from design research in other disciplines (Laurel, 2003). When integrating design and research, the emphasis can be on *research-based design* or *design based research*. These terms are useful to distinguish design that is informed by research from research that is based on new designs. For example, there is a lot of research-based design that produces wonderful designs but does not count as research. In line with Cobb, Jackson, and Dunlap (2017), I use the term *design study* for a particular project or research project that uses the more general approach of design research.

As mentioned in Chapter 8, I hope that early career researchers feel encouraged to make progress in bridging educational practice and research. The wonderful thing about using an emergent methodological approach such as design research is that there is still a lot to be learned and much to contribute to the field.

Notes

1 https://iase-web.org/Publications.php?p=Dissertations
2 www.educationaldesigner.org

References

Bakker, A. (2004). *Design research in statistics education: On symbolizing and computer tools*. Utrecht: CD-β Press.
Bakker, A. (2017). Towards argumentative grammars of design research. In T. Dooley & G. Gueudet (Eds.), *Proceedings of the Tenth Congress of the European Society for Research in Mathematics Education (CERME10, February 1–5, 2017)* (pp. 2730–2737). Dublin, Ireland: DCU Institute of Education and ERME.
Bakker, A., & Hoffmann, M. H. G. (2005). Diagrammatic reasoning as the basis for developing concepts: A semiotic analysis of students' learning about statistical distribution. *Educational Studies in Mathematics, 60*(3), 333–358.
Ben-Zvi, D., Aridor, K., Makar, K., & Bakker, A. (2012). Students' emergent articulations of uncertainty while making informal statistical inferences. *ZDM Mathematics Education, 44*(7), 913–925.
Berliner, D. C. (2002). Comment: Educational research: The hardest science of all. *Educational Researcher, 31*(8), 18–20.

Biesta, G. (2015). Freeing teaching from learning: Opening up existential possibilities in edu-cational relationships. *Studies in Philosophy and Education*, *34*(3), 229–243.

Boeije, H. (2002). A purposeful approach to the constant comparative method in the analysis of qualitative interviews. *Quality & Quantity*, *36*(4), 391–409.

Brown, A. (1992). Design experiments: Theoretical and methodological challenges in cre-ating complex interventions in classroom settings. *Journal of the Learning Sciences*, *2*(2), 141–178.

Cartwright, N. (2004). Causation: One word, many things. *Philosophy of Science*, *71*(5), 805–819.

Cartwright, N., & Munro, E. (2010). The limitations of randomized controlled trials in pre-dicting effectiveness. *Journal of Evaluation in Clinical Practice*, *16*(2), 260–266.

Cobb, P., Confrey, J., diSessa, A., Lehrer, R., & Schauble, L. (2003). Design experiments in educational research. *Educational Researcher*, *32*(1), 9–13.

Cobb, P., Jackson, K., & Dunlap, C. (2017). Conducting design studies to investigate and support mathematics students' and teachers' learning. In J. Cai (Ed.), *First compendium for research in mathematics education* (pp. 208–233). Reston, VA: National Council of Teachers of Mathematics.

Collins, A. (1990). *Toward a design science of education. Technical report*. New York, NY: Center for Technology in Education.

Collins, A. (1992). Towards a design science of education. In E. Scanlon & T. O'Shea (Eds.), *New directions in educational technology* (pp. 15–22). Berlin: Springer.

Collins, A., Joseph, D., & Bielaczyc, K. (2004). Design research: Theoretical and methodologi-cal issues. *Journal of the Learning Sciences*, *13*(1), 15–42.

Confrey, J. (2006). The evolution of design studies as methodology. In R. K. Sawyer (Ed.), *The Cambridge handbook of the learning sciences* (pp. 137–143). New York, NY: Cambridge University Press.

Design Based Research Collective. (2003). Design based research: An emerging paradigm for educational inquiry. *Educational Researcher*, *32*(1), 5–8.

Dierdorp, A., Bakker, A., Ben-Zvi, D., & Makar, K. (2017). Secondary students' consideration of variability in measurement activities based on authentic practices. *Statistics Education Research Journal*, *16*(2).

Doorman, L. M. (2005). *Modelling motion: From trace graphs to instantaneous change*. Utrecht, The Netherlands: CD-β Press.

Drijvers, P. H. M. (2003). *Learning algebra in a computer algebra environment: Design research on the understanding of the concept of parameter*. Universiteit Utrecht, Utrecht, The Netherlands: CD-Beta Press Database.

Flis, I., & Van Eck, N. J. (2017). Framing psychology as a discipline (1950–1999): A large-scale term co-occurrence analysis of scientific literature in psychology. *History of Psychology*. Retrieved from http://psycnet.apa.org/search/results?id=27152c1e-c725-ca0e-f219-888b5878e408.

Glaser, R. (1976). Components of a psychology of instruction: Toward a science of design. *Review of Educational Research*, *46*(1), 1–24.

Goffree, F. (1979). *Leren onderwijzen met Wiskobas: Onderwijsontwikkelingsonderzoek "wiskunde en didaktiek" op de pedagogische akademie [Learning to teach Wiskobas. Educational development research.]*. Utrecht, The Netherlands: Rijksuniversiteit Utrecht.

Gooding, D. (1985). "In nature's school": Faraday as an experimentalist. In D. Gooding & F. A. James (Eds.), *Faraday rediscovered: Essays on the life and work of Michael Faraday, 1791–1867* (pp. 105–136). New York: Springer.

Gravemeijer, K. P. E. (1994). Educational development and developmental research in mathematics education. *Journal for Research in Mathematics Education*, 443–471.

Gravemeijer, K. P. E., & Koster, K. (1988). *Onderzoek, ontwikkeling en ontwikkelingsonderzoek. [Research, development, and developmental research]*. Utrecht, The Netherlands: OW&OC.

Hammersley, M. (2008). Causality as conundrum: The case of qualitative inquiry. *Methodological Innovations Online*, 2(3), 1–5.

Hammersley, M. (2014). *The limits of social science: Causal explanation and value relevance.* London, UK: Sage.

Herrington, J., McKenney, S., Reeves, T., & Oliver, R. (2007). Design based research and doctoral students: Guidelines for preparing a dissertation proposal. *Paper Presented at the Proceedings of World Conference on Educational Multimedia, Hypermedia and Telecommunications 2007*, Chesapeake, VA.

Hoadley, C. P. (2002). Creating context: Design based research in creating and understanding CSCL. In G. Stahl (Ed.), *Proceedings of the conference on computer support for collaborative learning: Foundations for a CSCL community* (pp. 453–462). Boulder, CO: ISLS.

Kali, Y. (2016). *Transformative learning in design research: The story behind the scenes*. Keynote Presentation at ICLS 2016, Singapore. Retrieved from https://www.isls.org/icls/2016/docs/Keynote2-Yael_Kali-ICLS2016-keynote-FINAL(condenced).pdf

Kolodner, J. L. (1991). The Journal of the Learning Sciences: Effecting changes in education. *Journal of the Learning Sciences*, 1(1), 1–6.

Laurel, B. (2003). *Design research: Methods and perspectives*. Cambridge, MA: MIT Press.

LCHC. (1983). Culture and cognitive development. In P. H. Mussen & W. Kessen (Eds.), *Handbook of child psychology* (pp. 295–356). New York, NY: Wiley.

Linn, M. C. (2000). Designing the knowledge integration environment. *International Journal of Science Education*, 22(8), 781–796. doi:10.1080/095006900412275

Maxwell, J. A. (2004). Causal explanation, qualitative research, and scientific inquiry in education. *Educational Researcher*, 33(2), 3–11.

McDowell, J. (1996). *Mind and world (with a new introduction)*. Cambridge, MA: Harvard University Press.

McKenney, S. (2016). Researcher–practitioner collaboration in educational design research: Processes, roles, values, and expectations. In M. A. Evans, M. J. Packer, & R. K. Sawyer (Eds.), *Reflections on the learning sciences* (pp. 155–188). Cambridge, UK: Cambridge University Press.

McKenney, S., & Reeves, T. C. (2012). *Conducting educational design research*. London: Routledge.

McKenney, S. E. (2001). *Computer-based support for science education materials developers in Africa: Exploring potentials*. Twente, the The Netherlands: University of Twente.

Miles, M. B., & Huberman, A. M. (1994). *Qualitative data analysis: A sourcebook*. Beverly Hills, CA: Sage.

Mill, J. S. (1843). *A system of logic, ratiocinative and inductive: Being a connected view of the principles of evidence and the methods of scientific investigation*. London, UK: John W. Parker.

Nathan, M. J., Rummel, N., & Hay, K. E. (2016). Growing the learning sciences: Brand or big tent? Implications for graduate education. In M. J. Packer, M. A. Evans, & R. K. Sawyer (Eds.), *Reflections on the learning sciences* (pp. 191–209). Cambridge, UK: Cambridge University Press.

Nathan, M. J., & Wagner Alibali, M. (2010). Learning sciences. *Cognitive Science*, 1(3), 329–-345.

Nieveen, N. M. (1997). *Computer support for curriculum developers: A study on the potential of computer support in the domain of formative curriculum evaluation*. Twente, The Netherlands: University of Twente.

Oost, H. (1999). The quality of problem statements in dissertations: An evaluation of the ways in which technical aspects of problem statements are realized. [*De kwaliteit van probleemstellingen in dissertaties: Een evaluatie van de wijze waarop vormtechnische aspecten van probleemstellingen worden uitgewerkt*]. Utrecht, The Netherlands: WCC.

Oost, H. (2003). *Circling around a question. Defining your research problem*. Utrecht, The Netherlands: Utrecht University.

Ormel, B. J. B., Roblin, N. N. P., McKenney, S. E., Voogt, J. M., & Pieters, J. M. (2012). Research–practice interactions as reported in recent design studies: Still promising, still hazy. *Educational Technology Research and Development, 60*(6), 967–986.

Packer, M. J. (2017). *The science of qualitative research* (2nd ed.). Cambridge, UK: Cambridge University Press.

Pea, R. D. (2016). The prehistory of the learning sciences. In M. J. Packer, M. A. Evans, & R. K. Sawyer (Eds.), *Reflections on the learning sciences* (pp. 32–58). Cambridge, UK: Cambridge University Press.

Plomp, T. (2013). Educational design research: An introduction. In T. Plomp & N. Nieveen (Eds.), *Educational design research. Part A: An introduction* (pp. 10–51). Enschede, The Netherlands: SLO.

Plomp, T., & Nieveen, N. (Eds.). (2013). *Educational design research. Part B: Illustrative cases*. Enschede, The Netherlands: SLO.

Qvortrup, A., Wiberg, M., Christensen, G., & Hansbøl, M. (Eds.). (2016). *On the definition of learning*. Odense: University Press of Southern Denmark.

Roth, W.-M., & Lee, Y.-J. (2006). Contradictions in theorizing and implementing communities in education. *Educational Research Review, 1*(1), 27–40.

Schoenfeld, A. H. (1992). Research methods in and for the learning sciences. *Journal of the Learning Sciences, 2*(2), 137–139.

Simon, H. A. (1967). *The sciences of the artificial*. Cambridge, MA: MIT Press.

Stigler, S. M. (2002). *Statistics on the table: The history of statistical concepts and methods*. Cambridge, MA: Harvard University Press.

van Amerom, B. A. (2002). *Reinvention of early algebra: Developmental research on the transition from arithmetic to algebra*. Utrecht, The Netherlands: Utrecht University.

van den Akker, J. (1999). Principles and methods of development research. In *Design approaches and tools in education and training* (pp. 1–14). New York: Springer.

van den Akker, J., & Plomp, T. (1993). *Development research in curriculum: Propositions and experiences*. Paper Presented at the AERA annual meeting in Atlanta, GA.

Warwick, A. (2003). *Masters of theory: Cambridge and the rise of mathematical physics*. Chicago, IL: University of Chicago Press.

Wenger, E. (1998). *Communities of practice: Learning, meaning, and identity*. Cambridge, MA: Cambridge University Press.

Wieman, C. E. (2014). The similarities between research in education and research in the hard sciences. *Educational Researcher, 43*(1), 12–14.

Wittgenstein, L. (1953/2009). *Philosophical investigations* (G. E. M. Anscombe, P. M. S. Hacker, & J. Schulte, Trans.). Chisester, UK: Wiley Blackwell.

Wittmann, E. C. (1995). Mathematics education as a "design science". *Educational Studies in Mathematics, 29*(4), 355–374.

Appendix: Further resources

Some useful methodology books

Bikner-Ahsbahs, A., Knipping, C., & Presmeg, N. (2015). *Approaches to qualitative research in mathematics education*. Berlin, Germany: Springer.

Boeije, H. (2010). *Analysis in qualitative research*. London, UK: Sage.

Creswell, J. W. (2013). *Qualitative inquiry and research design: Choosing among five approaches*. London, UK: Sage.

Denscombe, M. (2014). *The good research guide: For small-scale social research projects*. New York, NY: McGraw-Hill Education.

Erickson, F. (2012). Qualitative research methods for science education. In B. J. Fraser, K. Tobin, & C. J. McRobbie (Eds.), *Second international handbook of science education* (pp. 1451–1469). Dordrecht, The Netherlands: Springer.

Ericsson, K. A., & Simon, H. A. (1993). *Protocol analysis*. Cambridge, MA: MIT Press.

Green, J. L., Camilli, G., & Elmore, P. B. (Eds.). (2012). *Handbook of complementary methods in education research*. New York, NY: Routledge.

Hammersley, M., & Atkinson, P. (2007). *Ethnography: Principles in practice*. London, UK: Routledge.

Kazdin, A. E. (1982). *Single-case research designs: Methods for clinical and applied settings*. Oxford, UK: Oxford University Press.

Kelly, A. E., & Lesh, R. A. (Eds.). (2000). *Handbook of research design in mathematics and science education*. New York, NY: Routledge.

Krathwohl, D. R. (1998). *Methods of educational and social science research: An integrated approach* (2nd ed.). New York, NY: Longman.

Miles, M. B., & Huberman, A. M. (1994). *Qualitative data analysis: A sourcebook*. Beverly Hills, CA: Sage.

Neuman, L. W. (2002). Social research methods: Qualitative and quantitative approaches. London, UK: Pearson.

Packer, M. (2017). *The science of qualitative research* (2nd ed.). Cambridge, UK: Cambridge University Press.

Ragin, C. (2014). *The comparative method: Moving beyond qualitative and quantitative strategies*. Berkeley, CA: University of California Press.

Strauss, A., & Corbin, J. (2008). *Basics of qualitative research: Techniques and procedures for developing grounded theory* (3rd ed.). London, UK: Sage.

Thomas, G. (2013). *How to do your research project: A guide for students in education and applied social sciences*. London, UK: Sage.

Yin, R. (1994). *Case study research: Design and methods*. Thousand Oaks, CA: Sage.

Some websites

Interviews with design research experts: http://dbr.coe.uga.edu/expertinterview.htm

Plomp and Nieveen (2013) collected 51 illustrative cases of education design research online: http://www.international.slo.nl/edr/

Webinar on design based research: http://isls-naples.psy.lmu.de/intro/all-webinars/puntambekar/index.html

Design based implementation research: http://learndbir.org/

I keep a blog at: https://designresearcheducation.wordpress.com/

Index

Made in the USA
Las Vegas, NV
18 April 2022

47664750R00175